MW01069998

DAL CHAWAL

85 VEGETARIAN INDIAN RECIPES COMBINING THE POWER OF DAL AND RICE

SAPNA PUNJABI

Hardie Grant

PUBLISHING

To my dad, for giving me my name, Sapna (meaning "a dream"), and always believing in and supporting my dreams. I cherish your zest for life and our food and shopping adventures together. I miss you and love you.

To my mom, who taught me how to cook with intention rather than measurements, and for feeding me and my kids pure love in the form of freshly cooked meals. Your joy for cooking and immense strength inspire me every day. I love you.

To my kids, Aditya and Mihika, who are my biggest fans and eager taste testers, and who made sure all their favorite recipes from Mom (Ma) and Grandma (Nani ma) were included in this book. I love you both more than you can imagine.

CONTENTS

RECIPE LIST

INTRODUCTION
Cooking My Way from Mumbai to Dallas

I WAS BORN AND RAISED in Mumbai (formerly called Bombay), India, and came to the United States more than two decades ago buckling under the load of two suitcases bursting at their seams, a backpack, and a carry-on filled to the maximum weight permitted by the airlines. I was raised as a vegetarian, and my parents were worried about how life in a foreign country might impact my daily nourishment. Lovingly tucked among my clothes were a bag of basmati *chawal* (rice), a few varieties of *dals* (pulses and legumes), and a brand-new *masala dabba* (spice box) with an assortment of spices. My mom even found room for a pressure cooker and a wooden rolling pin! She was more worried about what I would eat than my coursework or grades, which was a bit ironic because, although I was surrounded by my mom's joy of cooking growing up, she fervently pushed me out of the kitchen and into the classroom. It was because of her encouragement and determination that I was the first female in our family to pursue graduate studies in a foreign country, though my chosen major in nutrition and dietetics would eventually lead me back to the kitchen, focusing on culinary wellness.

After arriving in Cleveland in the midst of a snowstorm, the first meal I prepared on American soil was dal and chawal. Despite burning my inaugural pot of rice, my dad—who had accompanied me on my trip—and I still enjoyed a warm meal, which provided both comfort and a healthy dose of homesickness. My dad left after a week, and I began to immerse myself in my course load at Case Western Reserve University, slowly embracing certain aspects of my new Western lifestyle while staying true to my Indian roots. I vividly remember my first trip to an American grocery store, where I was mesmerized by the sheer size of the store and the endless options in every aisle. I spent hours reading food labels, a privilege I didn't have in India, as most store-bought foods there provided little nutritional information at the time. It is both a powerful and terrifying feeling to know the details of the food we eat, and I was overwhelmed by the abundance of processed and packaged options. While initially tempted to grab these convenience foods, I instead began honing my own cooking skills, relying on the memories of my mother's kitchen, the aromas, sights, and sounds all gently reminding me of the way.

Cooking is a form of divine love, one that my mom dished out generously in her freshly cooked daily meals. My first memories of food started in an 8-by-10-foot kitchen in our modest flat in Mumbai as I watched her lovingly prepare different dals during the week. She always had a stash of homemade fermented batter for idlis and dosas for a quick meal or snack, could magically transform leftover cooked rice into delicious lemon rice, or have my favorite tamarind rice ready for my school lunch the next day. Although she never provided me with a scientific explanation, after years of studying Ayurveda, the world's oldest practicing holistic medicine, I now know she had a clear understanding of Ayurvedic principles. A huge part of staying healthy in Ayurveda lies in proper digestion and one's gut health. We often hear "You are what you eat," but Ayurveda teaches us "You are what you can digest" and encourages us to pay attention to how and when we eat with mindfulness and awareness of our digestive capacity. Our food and how we choose to nourish ourselves ultimately shapes our body, mind, and consciousness.

Food is deeply personal for each of us. My food choices, cravings, and dislikes reflect my unique history, the foundation of which was laid during my childhood as well as through my work as a registered dietitian and Ayurvedic practitioner. My reliance on home-cooked meals when I moved to the United States was initially due to the lack of true vegetarian choices at the time, but it also connected me back to my culture. While my peers were eating salads and frozen ready-to-eat meals, I felt at ease with enjoying warm dal chawal, idlis, and sambhar for my lunches at work in a busy hospital in Dallas. The food I brought from home often created genuine curiosity, and I was constantly answering questions about ingredients, spices, or cooking techniques, and it was a perfect way to share not only my food but also my culture.

My true love for cooking began with preparing my first child's earliest meals. My son's pure, unadulterated love for food provided fresh motivation to cook and experiment with new recipes each day, even after working long hours as a neonatal dietitian caring for extremely fragile children in the intensive care unit, where it was a struggle to help them eat and maintain their daily nutrition. Seeing my son finish his bowl of plain dal or *khichdi* was immensely gratifying, and when my daughter came along a few years later, she would want to eat whatever her big brother ate, loving her meals with an extra dash of spice, even as an infant. By the time she was a year old, she had been introduced to over a dozen seasonings, with salt and sugar being the last ones on the list. It was this combination of my years of professional nutrition focus at the hospital, counseling my patients and their families to eat healthy, and practicing the same principles at home for my own young family that helped me nurture a passion for culinary wellness.

It has been just over a decade now since I took a leap of faith and carved a new career path for myself, moving from clinical practice to opening my home kitchen to strangers who were interested in plant-focused meals and vegetarianism, weary of tofu dishes and heavily processed veggie burgers as their main protein choices, curious about Indian spices, and open to cooking—no matter their skill level. From a handful of encouraging friends in my first class to rapidly growing monthly cooking classes at home and

Our food and how we choose to nourish ourselves ultimately shapes our body, mind, and consciousness.

beyond, my dad's entrepreneurial gene (more on that later) was blossoming within me. Immersing myself in deep study and formal training in Ayurveda, I found the missing link that connected my path of Western nutritional expertise with my Eastern roots, giving me a clear vision by enriching my life's purpose to share this knowledge with others. I found myself writing articles for magazines and newspapers, getting invited to speak at public events and professional conferences, and launching my line of heirloom spice blends and wellness products within a year. The organic reach of my brand beSPICED created through word of mouth soon became a close-knit community around me that pushed me to create content online, helping me reach an audience beyond the local Dallas metroplex.

My name, Sapna, means "a dream," and this exciting journey, from my childhood in Mumbai to my American life today, has been about following my dreams. Sharing my culture, my passion, in the form of a cookbook honors my entrepreneurial dad, who started his own thriving independent book business from our tiny living room in Mumbai; growing up, I was literally surrounded by piles of books in every corner of our 500-square-foot flat. While my dad is no longer around to hold this book in person, I feel his *sapna* is being fulfilled through every single copy reaching around the world!

This cookbook also honors Indian cuisine the best way I was taught by my mom, several aunties, friends, and through my travels and my own lessons in the kitchen. While my mom was my first cooking teacher, my kids have continued to inspire me over the years, from being my number-one fans at the dinner table with their empty plates at the end of every meal to pushing me to hold my ground during my recent transition as a single parent. They have never complained about dal chawal in their lunch boxes and eagerly look forward to *kadhi chawal* for a midweek dinner just as much as their favorite pasta and Tex-Mex dishes. They have also been my eager taste testers and approved each and every single recipe in this cookbook—including many they would like to make someday for themselves and their own children.

The recipes in this cookbook are my favorite home-cooked meals, reminiscent of what I ate while growing up in Mumbai and still in regular rotation on my family table in Dallas. These are not modernized or fusion recipes; rather, I have provided practical suggestions on how these traditional dishes can fit seamlessly on any modern table: for example, the traditional *sukhi moong dal* (page 48) makes a perfect plant-based filling for tacos, *Amritsari chole* (page 84) can be served in lettuce cups, and even the versatile *besan ka chila* (page 89) can be used as a burger filling. These flavor-packed recipes check off my dietitian-focused, science-based nutritional benchmarks, balancing the traditional Eastern Ayurvedic perspective with anyone's busy lifestyle. And while I don't expect our kitchens to be similar, I hope this cookbook becomes an integral part of your kitchen: a trusted friend providing encouragement, support, and plant-focused inspiration, from quick weeknight meals to festive special occasions.

With love and gratitude, from my kitchen to yours!

—Sapna

WHY DAL CHAWAL?

Dal Chawal celebrates Indian comfort food—simply put, pulses and rice. More than that, the term *dal chawal* invokes a deep emotional response for every Indian, a taste of home. When traveling for days, after a busy workday, or when under the weather, every Indian home, no matter where it is in the world, leans on its own special combination of dal chawal, providing ultimate solace for the family.

Dal (also spelled daal, dhal, and dahl) is a Hindi word commonly used to describe all forms of pulses, including dried beans, lentils, peas, and whole and split legumes. The term *dal* is also used to refer to a dish made of these pulses. *Chawal*, the Hindi word for rice, is the perfect soulmate for dal. While almost every Indian cookbook includes dal and rice recipes in some form, I wanted to primarily focus on the endless plant-powered, sustainable, and affordable potential of pulses and rice (dal chawal) dishes that are an integral part of every Indian pantry.

The recipes in *Dal Chawal* highlight the two food categories—dal and chawal—that form the foundation of a traditional, homestyle Indian vegetarian diet.

Pulses have been part of India's rich culinary tradition for centuries, served at just about every meal. The variation in regional dal dishes is so vast that you can make a different dal for every day and still not repeat for months. Pulses are ground into flour, cooked as soups and hearty stews, transformed into chutneys, desserts, salad, side dishes, breads, and more. Every jar of dal in my pantry holds unimaginable potential.

Pulses are inexpensive sources of protein, vitamins, complex carbohydrates, and fiber. One cup of cooked pulses provides more than half the amount of dietary fiber (soluble and insoluble) needed for the day, and ½ cup of a cooked pulse provides 6 to 9 grams of protein. Pulses also contain resistant starch, a type of carbohydrate that behaves like dietary fiber in the body and has been shown to reduce circulating cholesterol and blood sugar levels as well as improve gut health. Regular consumption of pulses has been linked with several health benefits, including lower rates of heart disease, hypertension, and some types of cancer.

As a nutrient-dense complex carbohydrate, chawal (rice) provides increased satiety when combined with plant proteins and vegetables. It is gluten-free, highly digestible, and the least allergenic of all grains, which makes it an ideal choice for those with celiac disease, gluten intolerance, or other food sensitivities. Rice protein is deficient in the essential amino acid lysine, which is abundantly present in pulses. On the other hand, pulse proteins are deficient in the essential amino acids methionine and tryptophan, which rice contains in good quantities. When rice and dal are eaten throughout the course of the day or together in a meal, they complement each other's incomplete amino acids and create a complete protein through a process of mutual supplementation. In traditional Indian cuisine, rice and dal have enjoyed each other's company for centuries, creating a harmonious and nutritionally balanced combination.

Both pulses and rice can also help minimize food waste since they can be dried and stored for relatively long periods of time without losing their nutritional value.

My hope is that when you open your pantry and grab a jar of dal, you can easily flip to the section in this book on that variety and discover all the potential recipe possibilities. Or you can invest in one new variety of dal at a time and master it before moving on to the next and, therefore, slowly and sustainably build your pantry and recipe repertoire.

From busy weekdays to lazy weekends, from special holidays to elaborate festivals, dal chawal is the quintessential meal that highlights the diversity and vibrancy of India's varied cuisines.

My goal is for this book to introduce you to authentic homestyle Indian cooking and the endless possibilities of dal chawal for making plant-based meals practical and accessible for modern living.

AYURVEDA AND KEY CONCEPTS

While I've been surrounded by traditional Indian cooking—with its foundation in Ayurveda—my whole life, it was only when I began to study Ayurveda formally with revered teachers that I came to understand the impact of the energy that every food carries and how it affects our body, mood, and spirit. As you cook my recipes, you will come across several Ayurvedic terms. This section reviews simple definitions and Ayurvedic concepts so it creates enough curiosity within you to plan your meals and appreciate the qualitative impact of what we eat.

Dating back more than five thousand years, with its roots in the Vedic Indian traditions, the term Ayurveda combines the Sanskrit words *ayur* (life) and *veda* (knowledge) and is also known as the "science of life."

> Ayurveda is the oldest practiced indigenous medicine in the world; it teaches respect for nature, instills appreciation of life, and provides practical means to empower every individual.

Ayurveda is the oldest practiced indigenous medicine in the world; it teaches respect for nature, instills appreciation of life, and provides practical means to empower every individual. You don't have to be born in India or eat Indian food to practice Ayurveda. It deals with health in all its aspects: physical, mental, emotional, spiritual well-being, social and environmental considerations, dietary and lifestyle habits with seasonal variations, as well as treating and managing specific diseases. Unlike most Western medicine applications, which focus on symptom management and cure, Ayurveda emphasizes prevention of disease by understanding the root cause of imbalance. Ayurveda is a highly personalized health care—the opposite of a "one size fits all" prescription. In India, you will find traditional Ayurvedic physicians (*vaidyas*) with community-based clinics and full-fledged Ayurvedic hospitals that work together with Western medicine to provide holistic care. Every Indian home that follows traditional practices in any form, be it in cooking, food choices, lifestyle, or spiritual rituals, embraces Ayurveda even if they don't realize it.

Ayurveda's Definition of Health

According to the classic texts of Ayurveda, health is defined as a state of equilibrium and harmony within the body, mind, and spirit. It is not merely the absence of disease but a dynamic balance of the three doshas—*vata*, *pitta*, and *kapha*—along with proper functioning of bodily tissues, optimal digestion and metabolism (*agni*), proper elimination of wastes, and a peaceful, contented mental state in which one is *svastha* or "situated in the self."

समदोषाः समाग्निश्च
समधातुमलक्रियाः ।
प्रसन्नात्मेन्द्रियमनाः स्वस्थ
इत्यभिधीयते ॥ ३८ ॥

"The one who is established in Self,
who has balanced doshas, balanced
agni, properly formed tissues, proper
elimination of wastes, properly
functioning bodily processes, and whose
mind, soul, and senses are quiet and
content is called a healthy person."

SUSHRUTA SAMHITA, CH 15 V 38

The Elements

According to Ayurveda, there are *panchamahabhutas*, or five great elements—the building blocks of nature and all creation—that are constantly engaged in sustaining life's processes. These five elements are space, air, fire, water, and earth. Every single being in the universe, from flowers to food to humans to animals and all life matter, is composed of these five elements in varying proportions. The unique composition and proportions of these elements are what makes each of us unique and different. Ayurveda teaches us we are a microcosm of the macrocosm. The elements and qualities in our environment affect the elements and qualities within us. When it is cold outside, we are cold inside. Just as we need external layers to warm our bodies, we crave naturally warming soups and teas to warm us internally. The predominance of elements is ever-changing, and our intelligence or lack thereof can either create or disrupt balance.

Akasha
space/ether

The first element, **space/ether (*akasha*)**, is the most subtle of all the elements. It is universal, nonmoving, and a container in which everything exists. Its qualities are clear, light, subtle, soft, and immeasurable. Foods predominant in the ether element include green leafy vegetables, bitter melon, and healing herbs like fenugreek and turmeric. These foods are bitter in taste. Eating such foods helps detoxify the body and cleanse and improve all bodily tissues.

Vayu
air

From ether/space comes **air (*vayu*)**, the energy of movement that accounts for oxygen and wind around our planet. It initiates and directs motion. Its qualities are mobile, dry, light, cold, rough, and subtle. Vayu is the principle of movement necessary for keeping the body and its myriad functions in constant motion. *Prana* is the principle of the air element, the vital force that is primarily taken in through breath and without which life cannot exist. Some foods predominant in the air element include beans, lentils, dals, and green leafy vegetables. These foods have bitter and astringent tastes. Eating such foods creates lightness and movement in the body and clarity in the mind.

Agni
fire

The third element created from the friction of air is **fire (*agni*)**. It governs all metabolic processes, including digestion, absorption, regulation of body temperature, and even the transformation of experiences into thoughts, feelings, and emotions. If our digestive fire is low, it makes us sluggish, low in energy, and tired. If it is too high, it can lead to anger and irritability. The qualities of fire are hot, sharp, light, dry, and subtle. Some of the foods with predominant fire elements include ginger, black pepper, chile peppers, garlic, and all salts. These foods are pungent in taste. Foods made up of the fire element help with digestion, give radiance to the skin, and provide clarity in our thoughts.

Apas
water

When fire cools, it forms condensation or steam and becomes **water (*apas*)**. The main action of water is cohesion and adhesion. Plants and animals can't live without the lubricating flow of water and neither can human bodies. The element of water helps us experience taste (*rasa*) through the sense organ of the tongue. The qualities of water are cool, liquid, dull, soft, oily, and slimy. Foods with water dominance include fruit juices, water, buttermilk, cucumber, coconut, and watermelon. These foods have sweet and salty tastes. Eating these foods helps to maintain fluid balance in the body, moisten the joints and internal passages, and create a sense of contentment in the mind.

Prithvi
earth

The element of **earth (*prithvi*)** is solid, hard, and the densest of all. It is responsible for giving shape and structure to all things. Its qualities are heavy, dull, dense, gross, and immobile. The earth element shapes all the body's solid structures and tissues, including the bones, cartilage, nails, teeth, hair, and skin. Foods with a predominant earth element include all grains (such as rice, wheat, oats), root vegetables (like potatoes, carrots, sweet potatoes, beets), nuts, and seeds. These foods are sweet and astringent in taste. Eating them provides stability and strength and rebuilds the tissues in the body.

Ayurveda Gunas

Qualities that promote **strength, growth, and building** (brahmana)	Qualities that promote **cleansing and lightening** (langhana)
HEAVY (GURU): Dairy, meat, cheese, sugar, processed food, brown rice, beans, wheat	**LIGHT (LAGHU):** Leafy greens, berries, white rice, popcorn, cilantro, celery
SLOW OR DULL (MANDA): Dairy, meat, nutmeg, fried and fatty foods	**SHARP (TIKSNA):** Chile pepper, pungent spices, salt, onion, garlic
COLD (SHITA): Ice cream, chilled milk, mint, wheat	**HOT (USHNA):** Ginger, garlic, alcohol, chiles, tobacco
OILY OR UNCTUOUS (SNIGDHA): Oils, nuts, avocado, coconut, butter, fried foods	**DRY (RUKHSHA):** Millet, rye, dry cereal, honey, dry fruits, toast
SMOOTH OR SLIMY (SLAKSHA): Ghee, sesame oil, avocado, rice flour	**ROUGH (KHARA):** Raw vegetables, beans, dals, chips, popcorn
DENSE (SANDRA): Meat, cheese, root vegetables, grains	**LIQUID (DRAVA):** Water, juices, broth, milk
SOFT (MRUDU): Oat porridge, butter, ghee, avocado, ripe bananas	**HARD (KATHINA):** Nuts, coconut, seeds, beans, crackers
STATIC OR STABLE (STHIRA): Sweets, yogurt, ghee, yams, wheat	**MOBILE (CHALA):** Sprouts, alcohol, popcorn, spices, coffee, tea
GROSS (STHULA): Meats, mushrooms	**SUBTLE (SUKSHMA):** Ghee, honey, alcohol
CLOUDY OR STICKY (PICCHILA): Oils, oat porridge, milk and dairy products, molasses, gum resins	**CLEAR (VISHADA):** Sprouted beans, turmeric, neem

Mind Our Gunas:
The Twenty Qualities of Nature

As a dietitian, I am used to counting calories, macronutrients, and micronutrients in food. But as an Ayurvedic practitioner, I pay equal attention to the qualities inherent in food. The twenty qualities of Ayurveda, known as *gunas*, are fundamental attributes that describe the characteristics of all matter and energy in the universe. Quantified thousands of years ago by the ancient *rishi*, or seers, these qualities encompass opposites such as heavy/light, hot/cold, oily/dry, dense/liquid, rough/smooth, sharp/dull, hard/soft, stable/mobile, subtle/gross, and cloudy/clear. The twenty qualities form the basis for understanding the composition and behavior of all substances and energies according to Ayurvedic principles.

My Ayurvedic teacher, Dr. Vasant Lad, introduced me to the profound underlying premise of all Ayurvedic practice: "Like increases like, opposites balance each other." In this way, Ayurvedic medicine effectively uses the inherent qualities in food, herbs, exercise, and daily routines to counter and heal specific imbalances in the body and mind. The table on page 22 lists some practical examples to describe foods we eat from the qualitative perspective of gunas.

Understanding the gunas can offer us a new dimension through which we can plan our meals, shop for groceries, and look at foods in general. For example, if it's a hot summer day and we eat spicy foods and go for a run in the middle of day, we may find ourselves complaining about hyperacidity and heat rashes based on the principle of "like increases like." We could instead choose activities and foods that balance the day's heat with the opposite quality of cold: gentle yoga or a more cooling food like fresh coconut water or cucumber salad, which would bring balance and better support our health.

The Doshas

The entire cosmos is an interplay of the five elements—space, air, fire, water, and earth. Ayurveda further groups the five elements into three energies known as doshas—vata, pitta, and kapha. Doshas can be thought of as the fundamental energies that govern the physiological and psychological functions in the body. While each of the three doshas contains aspects of all the five elements, two elements are predominant in each. All of us have a different balance of doshas that make us unique individuals, but most often one of the three doshas makes up our predominant constitution, manifesting as our physical attributes and psychological tendencies.

Doshas can also be observed in our environment—foods, seasonal shifts, times of day, and even stages of life can be categorized by their predominant dosha, along with its inherent elements and their qualities.

Vata
(air + space) =

dry, light, cold, rough, subtle, mobile, clear

Vata is the air element that is held within the confines of space/ether. It is the most mobile of the three doshas and governs the energy of movement, including circulation, elimination, creativity, and intelligence. When out of balance, it can cause disruption of other doshas. In fact, without vata, the other two doshas are inert.

Pitta
(fire + water) =

hot, sharp, light, mobile, liquid, oily

Pitta expresses itself as the metabolic system of the body and functions as the energy of transformation. It is associated with the endocrine function, hormone levels, temperature regulation, visual perception, hunger, thirst, digestion of food, and sensory input.

Kapha
(water + earth) =

heavy, slow, cold, oily, liquid, smooth, dense, soft, static, sticky, hard, gross

Kapha gives shape, aids growth, and functions as the energy of stability, structure, and lubrication. It provides moisture to skin, maintains immunity, and helps in smelling and tasting of our food.

When we begin to observe ourselves and the world around us through the lens of Ayurveda, we discover the five elements, twenty qualities, and three doshas everywhere. The dry, clear, subtle, and mobile qualities of vata can be observed daily during early morning and evening, seasonally in autumn, and biologically in the characteristics of old age. Likewise, the fiery, sharp qualities of pitta are especially present at midday, when the sun is at its highest, as well as during the hot, humid summer season. Biologically, the predominance of pitta from puberty to middle age helps one to focus on the demands of school, career, and family. Finally, heavy and slow kapha rules morning and early evening, helping us ease into sleep at night. Its liquid, cold qualities can be observed in the thaw and snowmelt of early spring, and its softness and tendency toward growth govern human development from birth until puberty.

Open the refrigerator or walk through the grocery store or farmers' market—the elements, qualities, and doshas are present there too, in the physical attributes and tastes of our food.

Ayurvedic Six Tastes (Shad Rasas)

Ayurveda classifies six primary tastes (*rasas*) in our food—sweet, sour, salty, pungent, bitter, astringent. The word *rasa* in Ayurveda is deeper than just the taste of food. It can mean essence, juice, sap, plasma secretion, comprehension, interest, emotion, and zest for life. The sense of taste offers more than sensory pleasure and satiation. Every substance has a predominant taste, and each taste has its own physical and emotional effects on our overall well-being. Each of the six tastes is made up of combinations of the five elements, which influence the doshas—body and mind. According to Ayurveda, a balanced meal is one that incorporates all the six tastes in accordance with one's dosha and seasonal mindfulness. The six tastes not only influence the doshas but have a direct effect on our consciousness.

Taste	Elements	Quality	Effect on Doshas	Foods
SWEET (MADHURA)	Earth + water	Heavy, oily, cooling	↓V, ↓P, ↑K	Whole grains (such as wheat, rice), sweeteners (including honey, maple, jaggery), milk, cream, ghee, fish, meat, fats, most ripe fruits and their juices, dried fruits, root vegetables, cardamom, cinnamon
SOUR (AMLA)	Fire + earth	Liquid, light, heating	↓V, ↑P, ↑K	Yogurt, sour cream, cheese, vinegar, fermented foods, citrus fruits, tomato, tamarind, unripe mango, wine, alcohol, sourdough breads
SALTY (LAVANA)	Fire + earth	Heavy, oily, heating	↓V, ↑P, ↑K	Sea salts, rock salts, sea vegetables
PUNGENT (KATU)	Fire + air	Light, dry, heating	↑V, ↑P, ↓K	Onions, garlic, ginger, mustard, horseradish, wasabi, raw radishes, turnips, chiles, cloves, asafoetida, mustard seeds, black pepper
BITTER (TIKTA)	Air + ether	Light, dry, cooling	↑V, ↓P, ↓K	Leafy green vegetables, dandelion, bitter melon, aloe vera, coffee, fenugreek, turmeric, neem, dark chocolate
ASTRINGENT (KASHAYA)	Air + earth	Heavy, dry, cooling	↑V, ↓P, ↓K	Pulses (dals, beans, lentils), raw cruciferous vegetables, fruits (pomegranates, unripe bananas, cranberries), mushrooms, basil, bay leaves, caraway seeds, nutmeg, oregano, poppy seeds, saffron, turmeric, coffee, tea, and wine

*the ↑ and ↓ in the chart above indicate how the tastes affect the doshas (aggravating [↑] or pacifying [↓])

The standard American diet (SAD) is predominantly rich in sweet, sour, and salty tastes and lacks pungent, bitter, and astringent flavors, which can cause the tendency for excess kapha qualities such as weight gain, sluggishness, and poor digestion over a period of time. Taking a peek in our refrigerators and grocery carts and observing our food cravings conveys information about our present state of imbalance and can guide our health road map.

The predominant taste of rice is sweet, whereas dals, including beans and lentils, are mostly astringent in taste. Incorporating dals cooked with bitter/pungent spices as a part of our regular meals is an easy, practical, and affordable way to add the missing astringent, bitter, and pungent tastes often missing in Western diets.

Virya: The Energetic Thermal Action of Food

Our tongue is the first to experience the taste of food. Once the food is ingested, the stomach and small intestine experience either heating or cooling energy from the food. This potent energy is called *virya*. For example, eating chile peppers creates heat in the body, and eating a bowl of cucumbers or watermelon is extremely cooling. Sweet taste has a cooling energy owing to the qualities of its predominant elements: water and earth. There are some exceptions to this rule. Honey and molasses are sweet but have heating energy. Similarly, sour taste is usually heating, but limes have a cooling potency, while lemons have a heating effect in our bodies.

Pulses and rice can either be heating or cooling. Kidney beans, brown lentils, toor dal, urad dal, and brown rice are heating in nature, whereas moong, chana, masoor dal (split red lentils), and white rice are cooling. Understanding the potency of food is helpful in menu planning for specific body constitutions and seasonal balance.

Vipaka: The Post-Digestive Effect of Food

Food not only gives us nutrition but nourishes us too! The subtle concept of digestion and absorption and how food is transformed in the body is unique to Ayurveda. I am referring to the deep transformational effect of food on both body and mind. There are three post-digestive effects (*vipaka*): sweet, sour, and pungent. Generally, sweet and salty tastes (*rasa*) of food have a sweet vipaka, promote tissue growth and elimination, and increase kapha. Sour rasa has sour vipaka, promotes metabolic functions, and increases pitta. Pungent, bitter, and astringent tastes have pungent vipaka, enhance catabolic activity, and increase vata dosha. Western biochemistry explains that food, after digestion by acidic and alkaline juices in the gastro-intestinal tract, assumes one of the three types of pH—neutral, acidic, or alkaline. Ayurvedic vipaka is similar: sweet vipaka can be equated to neutral, sour to acidic, and pungent to alkaline.

Digestive Fire in Ayurveda

Agni, or digestive fire, is a fundamental concept in Ayurveda. Agni is the body's ability to metabolize and assimilate food, thoughts, and experiences. Since proper digestion is essential for our overall well-being, agni is a cornerstone of health, which is why paying careful attention to what, when, and how we eat is so important. Ayurveda categorizes four main types of agni:

SAMA agni is the ideal digestive fire, operating smoothly and consistently and efficiently transforming food into nutrients.

VISHAMA (irregular) agni is associated with vata dosha and is characterized by digestion that fluctuates in strength and efficiency, leading to inconsistent appetite, energy levels, and elimination.

TIKSHNA (sharp) agni is associated with pitta dosha and is very intense, quickly burning calories, and often resulting in hyperacidity, inflammation, excessive hunger, and irritability.

MANDA (dull) agni is associated with kapha dosha and characterized by a digestive fire that's weak or sluggish, leading to incomplete digestion and a buildup of toxins (*ama*) in the body.

Vishama, tikshna, and manda agni can follow the vata, pitta, and kapha Ayurvedic recipe suggestions, respectively.

Ayurvedic Properties of Common Indian Pulses and Rice

Dal/Chawal	Rasa and Guna	Virya	Action on Dosha
MOONG: Whole, green split, and yellow split varieties	Sweet, astringent, light, dry	Cooling	↓V, ↓P, ↓/↑K tridoshic, easy to digest
MASOOR: Split red masoor dal variety	Sweet, astringent, light, soft	Cooling	↓/↑V, ↓P, ↓K tridoshic, easy to digest
MASOOR: Brown whole masoor	Astringent, rough, heavy	Heating	↑V, ↓/↑P, ↓K
URAD: Whole black gram, split black gram, and deskinned split variety	Sweet, heavy, soft, unctuous	Heating	↓V, ↑P, ↑K strengthening, grounding
TOOR: Yellow toor dal	Sweet, astringent, dry, light, rough	Heating	↑V, ↑P, ↓K
CHANA: White kabuli garbanzo bean variety	Sweet, astringent, dry, rough, heavy	Cooling	↑V, ↓P, ↓K
CHANA: Brown kala chana, chana dal, besan (chickpea flour)	Sweet, astringent, dry, light	Cooling	↑V, ↓P, ↓K
CHAWAL: Long-grain basmati	Sweet, light, soft	Cooling	↓V, ↓P, ↓K tridoshic
CHAWAL: White rice	Sweet, soft	Cooling	↓V, ↓P, ↑K
CHAWAL: Brown rice	Sweet, heavy	Heating	↓V, ↑P, ↑K

THE COSMIC INFLUENCES OF DAL AND RICE

In the tradition of Vedic astrology called Jyotish, *Navagraha*, or the nine celestial bodies and deities, are believed to influence human life on earth. The term comes from the Sanskrit words *nava* (nine) and *graha* (planet), and each planet is an archetype representing different aspects of nature and cosmic forces. The ancient classical texts of Jyotish describe the characteristics of each planet and associate them with certain colors, foods, body parts, articles of clothing, days of the week, et cetera.

Since the planets are believed to influence human lives according to their positions at the time of birth, a common practice based on traditional Jyotish involves offering different types of dal and rice to them. In the list that follows, the dal and rice linked to each planet frequently reflects the planet's color. Traditionally, this practice is believed to either pacify or strengthen the influence of a planet in one's life while hopefully assimilating some of the planet's positive characteristics.

Interpretations and associations in astrology, as in Ayurveda, can vary across different traditions and lineages.

Here's a general outline of the grains associated with each planet:

SUN (SURYA): According to the Vedic tradition, wheat is sacred to the sun, who is considered the king of the planets. Preparing dishes made from wheat is believed to appease the sun and enhance vitality, health, and leadership abilities. The sun's day is, unsurprisingly, Sunday. Ayurvedically, the fiery sun is associated with the energy of pitta dosha.

MOON (CHANDRA): Rice—particularly white rice—is associated with the moon. Offering cooked or raw rice is believed to bring emotional stability, fertility, and nourishment. Other foods associated with the moon are milk, almonds, and tapioca. The moon's day is Monday. Ayurvedically, the moon's cooling energy is associated with vata and kapha doshas.

MARS (MANGAL): Red lentils (split masoor dal), toor dal, and whole masoor beans are associated with Mars. Offering dishes made from red lentils is believed to mitigate the malefic effects of Mars and promote courage, strength, and energy. Tuesday is the day associated with Mars. Ayurvedically, the "red planet" is associated with both pitta and kapha doshas.

MERCURY (BUDHA): Since green is the color associated with Mercury, green gram (whole moong and moong dal) is its associated legume. Offering green gram is believed to enhance communication skills, intellect, and financial prosperity. Wednesday is the day of Mercury. Ayurvedically, Mercury is a tridoshic planet, associated with the energy of vata, pitta, and kapha.

JUPITER (GURU): Jupiter's color is yellow. Offering yellow split gram (chana dal) is thought to bring wisdom, prosperity, and spiritual growth. Other foods associated with Jupiter are ghee, coconut, and rye. This planet's day is Thursday. Ayurvedically, the planet Jupiter is associated with both kapha and vata.

VENUS (SHUKRA): The "whitish" color of Venus means that offerings of white beans, barley, and oats are believed to enhance love, romance, creativity, and artistic abilities. The day of Venus is Friday. Venus is another planet with both vata and kapha energetics.

SATURN (SHANI): Saturn's colors are black and dark blue, so dishes made with dark urad dal are thought to mitigate the malefic effects of Saturn and promote discipline, perseverance, and stability. Black sesame seeds and blue corn can also be thought of as Saturn-appeasing foods. Saturn's day is Saturday, and it is associated with vata dosha.

RAHU AND KETU: Unlike the other planets, Rahu and Ketu are not physical celestial bodies, but mathematical points in space known as lunar nodes, where the paths of the sun and moon intersect. In Vedic astrology, they are often referred to as "shadow planets." This term conveys their unique nature and role in astrological interpretation. While they don't have associated legumes, sesame seeds and rice are considered appropriate offerings.

Pictured opposite: During traditional Vedic Navagraha puja rituals, grains and pulses are placed on cloths in their associated planet color as an offering to the nine celestial bodies.

A Note About Rice

Rice holds significant astrological and cosmic importance in Vedic texts, particularly in the realms of Jyotish and Ayurveda. The components of a grain of rice—the husk, bran/germ, and endosperm—symbolize the cosmic gunas (qualities) of sattva, rajas, and tamas, respectively the harmony or protection, dynamism, and inertia of the living universe. Rice is used as both an offering and a remedy. In traditional Vedic ceremonies like *puja* and *havana* (fire ceremony), rice is offered to invoke the blessings of the deities as it symbolizes abundance, fertility, and prosperity.

THE MAGIC OF MASALAS (SPICES)

One clear example of how modern science supports ancient concepts of Ayurveda is in the use of spices. Spices support the traditional Indian and Ayurvedic diet to improve digestion, enhance the sensory experience, and contribute to overall health. The main benefit of culinary herbs and spices is primarily due to their antioxidant properties. And with a growing body of evidence-based research, the medicinal properties and pharmacological activity of many spices continue to confirm what has been practiced in indigenous medical systems like Ayurveda for centuries.

> For me, spices are nature's edible gemstones. They hold the power to elevate, mesmerize, and heal when added to food in the right amount at the right time in the right way.

India is one of the largest exporters of spices in the world. A spice is defined as a dried seed, fruit, root, bark, or vegetative substance used in nutritionally insignificant amounts as a food additive for flavor or color, or as a preservative that kills harmful bacteria or prevents their growth. But for me, spices are nature's edible gemstones. They hold the power to elevate, mesmerize, and heal when added to food in the right amount at the right time in the right way. You can even identify which region of India a dish is from based on the spices used: For example, in North India, a simple moong dal features cumin seeds, and the same dal will be tempered with black mustard seeds in the South. In the East, that moong dal is dressed with a special five-spice blend called *panch phoran* (see recipe, page 119), while fenugreek seeds are added in the western state of Gujarat.

Except for *amchur* (dried mango powder), turmeric, and chile powder, try to buy spices whole when possible. Check for color and aroma. Intense aroma assures freshness and good quality. Store spices in airtight glass or metal containers in a dark space. Whole spices can keep for up to five years or longer when stored properly. For larger quantities, double bag and store in the freezer for longer storage.

Essential Spices in My Pantry

Spices play a key role in promoting digestive enzyme function, a foundation of good health in Ayurveda. Spices should never be used in therapeutic doses or for medicinal purposes without consulting your medical doctor. I am sharing the seven essential spices that are part of my masala dabba that I cook with almost every day before moving on to other important spices in my pantry.

TURMERIC (HALDI): An Indian spice box is incomplete without turmeric, considered the star of all spices and one of the best and safest spices for all ages. It is used not only for cooking but also therapeutically in Ayurvedic medicine, as a beauty aid, and in the textile industry as a natural dye. There are more than one thousand research studies that have demonstrated the protective effect of the active compound, curcumin, for its anti-inflammatory, antifungal, and anti-microbial properties. It is regarded in Ayurveda to be one of nature's best medicines. Fresh turmeric is available as rhizomes and used in certain teas and pickles, while the ground form of turmeric is used most often in daily cooking.

CUMIN (JEERA): An essential spice in Indian cooking. I keep **WHOLE CUMIN SEEDS** and **GROUND TOASTED CUMIN (BHUNA JEERA)** in my masala dabba, making my own ground cumin at home by dry-roasting the whole seeds in a skillet and grinding to a powder once cooled. I refer to cumin as a gut buddy as it is one of the best medicines for digestive sluggishness in Ayurveda, also helping to relieve gas and kindle gastric fire.

CORIANDER (DHANIYA): One of the world's oldest spices, the strong scented leaves of the coriander plant are also known as cilantro—an excellent summer herb. Its digestive properties clear flatulence and bloating, and it is also a diuretic. Buy whole seeds and grind in small batches as needed, because the volatile compounds dissipate fairly quickly once ground. Its favorite companion is cumin seeds.

MUSTARD SEEDS (RAI): In India, mustard is used as an oil, seed, and ground spice, with black or brown mustard seeds most commonly used for their strong flavor and aroma. Mustard seeds are always popped in hot oil

Tadka

Indian cooking often begins or ends with the sizzling sound and aroma of a tadka. *Tadka* translates as "tempering," a crucial step in Indian cuisine. The term *tempering* here simply refers to the introduction of heat to any form of spices, whole or ground, combined with oil or ghee.

Tadka is also called chhonk, baghar, vaghar, oggarane, or phodni depending on the region of India—all are similar in technique but may differ in the type of oil and spices used. For example, there are more cumin seeds in a North Indian tadka and more black mustard seeds and fresh curry leaves in a South Indian tadka. While tadka is the quickest and most aromatic way of enhancing flavor in Indian dishes, it also has nutritional benefits. Exposing spices to heat and/or oil releases some of their volatile medicinal compounds. Usually, a small skillet or a tadka pan is used to heat oil or ghee before the other ingredients are added in rapid succession. If you are new to Indian cooking, have all the ingredients ready as it may take only a few seconds once the tempering process has started. Tadka preparation is an immersive sensory experience that can turn any mundane dish magical in just a few seconds and, once mastered, will become an integral part of your everyday cooking, I promise. Happy tadka!

and never consumed raw. I keep two forms in my pantry: black mustard seeds for cooking and *rai kuria*, crushed hulled mustard seeds, generally used in Indian pickles.

RED CHILES AND CHILE POWDER (LAAL MIRCH): There are so many different varieties of chile peppers grown in India with varying heat levels and many varieties of chile powders available. The two I use in my everyday cooking are Kashmiri, for mild heat but vibrant red color, and *deggi mirch*, which is slightly hotter than paprika. I also keep a couple of varieties of whole dried chiles on hand: the North Indian Kashmiri red chiles and the South Indian Guntur Sannam red chiles. If the recipe doesn't call for a specific variety of red chile powder, you may use any variety of your choice, including cayenne or paprika (non-smoky variety).

DRIED MANGO POWDER (AMCHUR): Made by drying green (unripe) mango slices in the sun and pulverizing the dried slices to powder, amchur has a tart, tangy taste that is an excellent souring agent and salt substitute. Amchur gives the characteristic flavor to the popular spice blend chaat masala. It can be used in a similar way as lime and lemon. It is best to buy this spice already powdered.

ASAFOETIDA (HING): The dried sap or resin obtained from the gum of a perennial *Ferula* plant, asafoetida has a strong piercing aroma and flavor and is beloved for its digestive properties. It is ground into a powder either with wheat flour, rice flour, or fenugreek powder to keep it from clumping. I often joke in my cooking classes that India doesn't have Beano (the popular over-the-counter tablet that helps relieve gas), we have asafoetida. I use this spice almost every day when I cook dals and beans to aid digestion, but adding too much can cause more harm than good—a pinch is all it takes. Due to its strong aroma, I store it separately in the container it comes in and avoid keeping it open or near other spices.

What's in My Masala Dabba?!

The Indian spice box—*masala dabba*—is an intrinsic part of every Indian kitchen and my trusted companion in my daily cooking. It is commonly a circular metal (often stainless steel but sometimes brass), wooden, or plastic box with seven small cups filled with spices that represent each family's story, their lineage, the community they live in, and their personal preferences. The seven spices in my masala dabba are similar to my mom's box and what I use in my daily cooking. I also have spices in individual spice jars in my pantry. My masala dabba contains ground turmeric, whole cumin seeds, ground toasted cumin (always homemade), Kashmiri red chili powder, ground coriander, dried mango powder, and black mustard seeds.

FENNEL (SAUNF): One of the few plants that has it all—vegetable, herb, and spice. Fennel seed is a key ingredient in many Indian spice blends. It is an excellent appetite stimulant and digestive aid: calming digestion while also working as a mild laxative and diuretic. Its strong flavor works well in both savory and sweet recipes.

GREEN CARDAMOM PODS (ELACHI): Referred to as the queen of spices, cardamom has a cooling effect in our body. It contains the antioxidant cineole, which stimulates weak digestion, treats bad breath, and, according to Ayurveda, helps clear coughs and sore throats. It is best to buy whole cardamom in pods. Cardamom pairs well with many other spices, such as clove, coriander, cumin, fennel seed, and ginger, and is a great addition to desserts, summer drinks, fruit salads, and rice dishes.

FRESH GINGER (ADRAK): The ginger root is the edible rhizome of the ginger plant. It is regarded as Vishwabheshaja, or a universal medicine, in Ayurveda. Every home should have a knob of ginger for its healing properties: aiding digestion, supporting upper-respiratory health, and soothing sore throats, cough, and cold. I use fresh ginger every day in my daily cooking and tea.

DRIED GROUND GINGER (SUNTH): This is typically added to spice blends and desserts. Ground ginger is excellent to stimulate appetite and kindle digestive fire and digestive enzymes. It is very potent and a little bit goes a long way.

CLOVES (LAVANG): Cloves add warmth, depth, and sweetness when used in small quantities. I use them in spice blends, rice dishes, and certain desserts. I always buy whole cloves and crush them in a mortar and pestle as needed.

BLACK PEPPERCORNS (KALI MIRCH): Warming, drying, and stimulating to the circulatory, digestive, and respiratory systems. I use them both whole and ground.

FENUGREEK SEEDS (METHI DHANA): Fenugreek seeds are used for their extreme aroma and bitter flavor in various Indian curries and should always be tempered in hot oil and never consumed raw. The seeds can also be soaked and sprouted to add to salads.

DRIED FENUGREEK LEAVES (KASURI METHI): I love adding dried fenugreek leaves to a variety of dal dishes for their captivating aroma, adding a mild bitterness to balance tomato- and cream-based gravies.

Pictured opposite (left to right, top to bottom): Ground ginger, Guntur Sannam red chiles, fenugreek seeds, dried fenugreek leaves, whole nutmeg, nigella seeds, carom seeds, saffron, Indian bay leaf

Easy Garam Masala

Garam means "hot" but not necessarily hot and spicy, while *masala* means "blend of spices." Garam masala is a blend of warm and earthy spices that adds warmth, mild sweetness, and potent fragrance to a dish. Garam masala, typically a North Indian spice blend, is used extensively throughout India, with some regional variations in ingredients and proportions. There is no single classic garam masala recipe. Between my mom and I, we have about three or four garam masala recipes that we make depending on the season, for special occasions, or for certain recipes. My easy garam masala is a simple combination of eight whole spices and works well for almost any recipe that calls for it and can be used year-round.

MAKES 1 heaping cup (100 g)

½ cup (60 g) cumin seeds
¼ cup (20 g) coriander seeds
12 green cardamom pods
1 tablespoon cloves
4 large cinnamon sticks
4 black cardamom pods
4 mace flowers
2 teaspoons grated nutmeg

Dry-roast all the spices except the nutmeg in a small skillet over low to medium heat for 5 minutes, stirring continuously. Cool the spices to room temperature, combine grated nutmeg, and grind to a fine powder in a spice grinder. Store in an airtight container in the pantry.

NUTMEG (JAIPHAL): A whole nutmeg keeps forever, and I grate a small amount with a Microplane grater to add a warm, nutty aroma. I use nutmeg in both savory and sweet dishes and also in spice blends like garam masala and chai masala.

NIGELLA SEEDS (KALONJI): Nigella seeds are tiny black seeds with a distinctive warm, smoky, and nutty flavor. Their potent anti-inflammatory properties and antioxidants help calm and strengthen digestion.

CAROM SEEDS (AJWAIN): Carom seeds have a piercing peppery flavor and amazing antibacterial and anti-inflammatory properties. As a digestive aid, they are especially used in fried dishes in order to prevent bloating and gas.

SAFFRON (KESAR): The carefully harvested dried stigma of the *Crocus sativus* flower is the most expensive spice in the world. It is widely cultivated in India in the Kashmir Valley and used in North Indian desserts and special rice dishes like biryani. Saffron has antiseptic properties, as well as being a powerful antioxidant and mood booster.

INDIAN BAY LEAF (TEJ PATTA): The Indian bay leaf is different from the bay laurel used in Mediterranean cuisine. Tej patta is commonly used in its dried form. The leaves are paper thin and olive green in color with three veins running down their length. Tej patta is often used in savory Indian dishes like rice pilaf, biryani, North Indian dal recipes, and spice blends for its aroma and medicinal properties. I also keep a couple of dried tej patta in my rice storage bins, just as my mom does, to prevent bugs in the grains.

To Soak or Not to Soak

Most, but not all, of the recipes in this book require some prep work of washing and soaking the rice or dal. Washing and rinsing the rice and dal removes the powdery starches on the surface of the grains. Many recipes may need just a few minutes of soak time, while others may require an overnight soak before actual cooking begins. While this may seem daunting at first, it will become effortless with some practice. If the recipe requires a 20- to 30-minute soak, I do this step first as I gather other ingredients or begin chopping if needed. And by that time, the rice or dal is soaked enough to begin cooking.

Let's discuss this topic a little more. Some people insist that rice and dal should always be washed/rinsed and soaked before cooking, while others skip this step altogether. Because of the way I was taught and have seen my mom cook all my life, this is a crucial and nonnegotiable step, whether I am cooking the dal or beans in a pot on the stove or in a pressure cooker. Soaking not only hydrates and plumps up the hard dal or rice kernels, it reduces the cooking time and also reduces the antinutrients, such as lectins and phytates, which helps us absorb and digest the nutrients better.

AYURVEDIC MEALTIME PRAYER

अन्नब्रह्मा रसोविष्णुः
पक्तो देवो महेश्वरः ।
एवम् ज्ञक्त्व तु यो भुन्क्ते
अन्न दोषो न लिप्यते ।।

anna* brahma rasovisnuh
pakto devo mahesvarah
evam jnaktva ti yo bhunkte
anna doso na lipyate

The creative energy in the food is Brahma,
The nourishing energy in the body is Vishnu,
The transformation of food into pure
consciousness is Shiva,
If you know this, then any impurities in the
food you eat will never become a part of you.

anna is the Sanskrit word for cooked rice

MOONG

MOONG

SANSKRIT NAME: Mudga
OTHER INDIAN NAMES: Mung / Mag / Moog / Pachhai
Payaru / Pachhai Pesalu / Hesaru Bele / Cheru Payaru
ENGLISH NAMES: Mung / Mung Bean / Green Gram
BOTANICAL NAME: *Vigna radiata*

Moong is referred to as the Indian maharani (queen) of legumes with an illustrious lineage going back thousands of years. Archaeological evidence proves that moong has been growing in India since 1800 BCE, with its remains found in many archaeological sites across southern India. Moong is also mentioned in several classical ancient texts of Ayurveda as a nourishing food for both the healthy and sick. It has a sweet, astringent taste, is light and cold in potency, and alleviates kapha and pitta dosha. Among its many healing properties in Ayurveda, it bestows a clear vision and provides nourishment to tissues. Rich in B vitamins, folate, trace minerals like iron and zinc, plant-based proteins, and essential amino acids, moong is also high in complex carbohydrates and dietary fiber with a low glycemic index, making it an excellent choice in controlling elevated blood glucose in diabetes, prediabetes, and conditions like insulin resistance. The carbohydrates present in moong beans are easily digestible, causing less flatulence as compared to other legumes.

Three common forms of moong are used in Indian cooking: whole, sprouted, and split. Both whole and sprouted moong beans are used in different curries, and sprouted moong beans are also added to salads (Sprouted Moong Bean Salad, page 64). I typically have moong beans sprouting on my kitchen counter or a box of sprouted moong beans in my refrigerator waiting to be used.

When the moong bean is split into two it is called moong dal and is available both with and without its outer skin. Moong dal with its outer green skin intact is called *chilka moong dal* or "green split moong dal" and the peeled variety is *dhuli moong dal* or "yellow split moong dal." The yellow split moong dal is the easiest to digest and was the first dal I introduced to both my kids when they were ready for solid foods.

This dal is an important gentle protein used in the clinical setting in many therapeutic diets in hospitals all over India. During my years as a clinical dietitian in India, I worked with the yellow split moong dal most often for post-surgical and recovery patients when they were ready to eat solid meals, from moong dal broth (see Sukhi Moong Dal, page 48) to a watered-down moong dal to soft Dheeli Khichdi (page 188), and regular meals. So one can say the yellow split moong dal is equally nourishing to the gentle tummies of babies as well as the weak digestive state of the frail and sick and everyone in between.

If you are new to the world of dals, I invite you to begin your journey by investing in a jar of just the yellow split moong dal. Get familiar with the recipes using this simple but mighty dal before building your dal cabinet.

SUKHI MOONG DAL

SPLIT YELLOW MOONG DAL TEMPERED WITH SPICES

We begin the journey into the world of dal with my mom's recipe for *sukhi moong dal*. This was my dad's favorite moong dal dish and Mom cooked it almost every single week, serving it with warm rotis (Indian flat bread); and leftovers would end up in our school lunch boxes, rolled inside the roti along with a smear of chutney or achaar (Indian pickle). It can also be served with tortillas, smeared on toasted sourdough bread, or nestled atop a bed of greens for a fun twist on a salad. *Sukhi* means "dry," and this recipe uses the yellow split moong dal, which is the split and peeled form of whole moong beans. This variety is one of the easiest dals to cook and also to digest. It requires the least amount of soaking time, so this dish can be prepped and cooked in under 30 minutes. If you can cook pasta, I promise you can make this hearty sukhi dal just as easily. It's also a zero-waste recipe—even the water in which the dal is cooked is put to good use (see Tips)!

PERFECT PAIRING
Serve with Hara Bhara Pulav (page 168) and Gajar ka Achaar (page 221).

SERVES 4

SOAK TIME
10 to 15 minutes

---

1 cup (200 g) dhuli moong dal/ yellow split moong dal

5 cups (1.2 L) water

1 teaspoon fine sea salt

½ teaspoon ground turmeric

2 tablespoons (30 g) ghee or oil, such as peanut, avocado, grapeseed, olive, or sunflower

⅛ teaspoon hing/asafoetida powder

1 teaspoon cumin seeds

GARNISH

½ teaspoon Kashmiri red chili powder

½ teaspoon toasted ground cumin

½ teaspoon ground coriander

½ teaspoon amchur/dried mango powder

½ cup (30 g) finely chopped cilantro (leaves and tender stems)

Rinse the yellow split moong dal in a fine-mesh sieve under cold running water until the water runs clear, about a minute. Transfer to a medium bowl, add water to cover by 2 inches (5 cm), and soak for 10 to 15 minutes. Drain.

In a 3-quart (3 L) pot, combine the soaked dal, water, salt, and turmeric. Bring to a boil, skimming off any foam. Reduce the heat to medium, partially cover, and cook until the dal softens when pressed between the fingers but still holds its shape and is not mushy, 10 to 12 minutes.

Drain off the cooking liquid and save (see Tips). Transfer the dal to a serving bowl.

In a medium skillet, heat the ghee, add the asafoetida followed by cumin seeds, and let sizzle for a few seconds. Pour this hot mixture over the bowl of cooked yellow moong dal. Garnish with Kashmiri powder, ground cumin, ground coriander, mango powder, and cilantro leaves.

TIPS
The drained dal cooking liquid makes a lovely broth. Garnish with chopped cilantro and a dash of lime juice, making this a zero-waste dish.

If you overcook the dal (unintentionally or intentionally), you can retain the liquid in the dal and cook to soup consistency and proceed with the tempering as directed.

AYURVEDA NOTES

Yellow moong dal is sweet and astringent in taste and cooling in potency. It is tridoshic in nature but mainly calms vata and pitta dosha. It can be enjoyed all year long and should be a staple in our pantries.

- **VATA** Add extra ground coriander. Favor ghee or peanut oil.
- **PITTA** Add extra cilantro; avoid Kashmiri powder. Favor ghee or olive oil.
- **KAPHA** Replace Kashmiri powder with ground black pepper. Favor sunflower oil or ghee.

PAASI PARUPPU BEAN PORIYAL

SAUTÉED MOONG DAL WITH GREEN BEANS

Poriyal is a South Indian word in the Tamil language that refers to a dish of chopped or grated vegetables and dals that are sautéed with spices and grated coconut. This is one of the classic combinations: French green beans and yellow split moong dal (*paasi paruppu*) traditionally cooked in coconut or sesame oil and mild spices. I find a soak time of 30 minutes to 1 hour allows the dal to adequately hydrate before it is cooked with the green beans. This dish is not heavily spiced and comes together in less than 30 minutes once the dal is soaked and ready to cook.

PERFECT PAIRING It makes for a hearty side to serve alongside Matta Coconut Rice (page 164), Tiffin Sambhar (page 120), Nimmakaya Rasam (page 122), or any other soupy dal.

SERVES 4

SOAK TIME 30 minutes to 1 hour

TIP
While bean and dal poriyal is a classic combination, swap green beans with chopped carrots, beet, or cabbage based on seasonal availability.

Rinse the yellow split moong dal in a fine-mesh sieve under cold running water until the water runs clear, about a minute. Transfer to a medium bowl, add water to cover by 2 inches (5 cm), and soak for 30 minutes to 1 hour. Drain and set aside.

In a large skillet, heat the oil over medium heat. Add the asafoetida and mustard seeds and sizzle for 10 seconds. Add the whole chiles (if using) and fresh curry leaves and sizzle for 10 seconds. Add the soaked dal and stir in the turmeric and ½ cup (120 ml) of the water. Cover the pan and cook over medium heat until the dal softens slightly but still retains its shape, 3 to 4 minutes.

Add the chopped green beans and salt, mix well, and add the remaining ¼ cup (60 ml) water if needed. Cover and cook over medium heat until the beans are crisp-tender, 5 to 7 minutes. Sprinkle with the Kashmiri powder and shredded coconut, mix well, and simmer for 3 to 4 minutes uncovered.

Serve warm.

- ½ cup (100 g) dhuli moong dal/ yellow split moong dal
- 2 tablespoons coconut or sesame oil
- ⅛ teaspoon hing/asafoetida powder
- 1 teaspoon black mustard seeds
- 2 dried red chiles (optional), such as Byadagi or Guntur Sannam
- 8 to 10 fresh curry leaves
- ¼ teaspoon ground turmeric
- ¾ cup (180 ml) water
- 1 pound (450 g) French green beans, ends trimmed, cut into ¼-inch (6 mm) pieces
- 1 teaspoon fine sea salt
- ¼ teaspoon Kashmiri red chili powder
- ¼ cup (20 g) unsweetened shredded coconut (fresh or thawed frozen)

AYURVEDA NOTES

In summer, use cooling coconut oil, and in cooler months of fall, winter, and early springtime, use the warming sesame oil to create a balanced Ayurvedic dish. Overall, this dish is tridoshic.
- **PITTA** Skip the dried red chiles.
- **KAPHA** Reduce or skip the shredded coconut due to its heavy nature.

KUMBAKONAM KADAPPA

SOUTH INDIAN MOONG DAL AND POTATO STEW

This special stew of moong dal, potatoes, and subtle spices comes from the small town of Kumbakonam in the Tanjore district of South India, where it is a served alongside rice, pooris, or even idlis or dosas (page 199). The Kumbakonam kadappa uses a combination of coconut and white poppy seeds to create a thick gravy balanced with aromatic spices like fennel seeds, bay leaves, and cinnamon.

I was introduced to this unique stew during a South Indian wedding, and since then I have made it on special occasions and crave it during the fall season, when the body seeks moisture and a grounding quality because of the excess wind and dryness in the environment.

PERFECT PAIRING
Serve with steamed rice or alongside Masala Dosa (page 199).

SERVES 4

SOAK TIME
15 to 20 minutes

½ cup (100 g) dhuli moong dal/yellow split moong dal

4 cups (960 ml) water

1 medium-large russet potato, peeled and cut into ½-inch (1.3 cm) pieces

1 teaspoon fine sea salt

¼ teaspoon ground turmeric

SPICE PASTE

½ cup (40 g) unsweetened dried shredded coconut

1 tablespoon white poppy seeds

¾ cup (180 ml) water

2 teaspoons fennel seeds

1 Thai green chile, roughly chopped

3 garlic cloves, peeled but whole

1-inch (2.5 cm) piece fresh ginger, peeled and roughly chopped

TADKA

3 whole cloves

1-inch (2.5 cm) piece cinnamon stick

1 tablespoon coconut oil

1 teaspoon black mustard seeds

1 star anise

1 tej patta/dried Indian bay leaf

8 to 10 fresh curry leaves (optional)

1 medium white onion, thinly sliced, or 1 cup pearl onions, peeled but whole

GARNISH

¼ cup (15 g) finely chopped cilantro (leaves and tender stems)

Juice of 1 lemon (as needed)

Rinse the yellow split moong dal in a fine-mesh sieve under cold running water until the water runs clear, about a minute. Transfer to a medium bowl, add water to cover by 2 inches (5 cm), and soak for 15 to 20 minutes. Drain.

In a 3-quart (3 L) pot, combine the soaked dal, 3 cups (720 ml) of the water, potatoes, salt, and turmeric. Bring to a boil, skimming off any foam. Reduce the heat to medium, partially cover, and cook until the dal and potatoes are soft, 20 to 30 minutes.

Use a hand whisk to coarsely mash the potatoes and blend the dal well. Simmer over very low heat until ready to serve.

Make the spice paste: In a small bowl, soak the dried coconut and white poppy seeds in the water for 10 minutes. Transfer everything (including the soaking water) to a blender. Add the fennel seeds, green chile, garlic, and ginger and puree. Set aside.

Make the tadka: Coarsely grind the whole cloves and cinnamon stick in a mortar and pestle. Set aside.

Continued—

In a large skillet, heat the oil over medium heat. Add the mustard seeds and sizzle for 10 to 15 seconds. Add the ground cloves/cinnamon mixture and the whole star anise and sizzle for 10 to 15 seconds, reducing the heat if necessary so the spices don't burn. Add the bay leaf, curry leaves (if using), and onion and cook over medium heat until the onions are soft and translucent, 5 to 7 minutes.

Stir in the spice paste, cook for 2 minutes, then add the cooked dal and potatoes with all the liquid. Add the remaining 1 cup (240 ml) water and mix well. Bring to a boil, reduce the heat, and simmer for 10 to 15 minutes.

Season to taste with salt. Add the cilantro and lemon juice to taste just before serving.

TIPS

To cook the soaked dal and potatoes in an electric pressure cooker, pressure-cook on high for 3 minutes. Let the pressure release naturally before opening the lid. Use a hand whisk to coarsely mash the potatoes and blend the dal well.

For a heartier version, add other vegetables, such as chayote, sweet potatoes, or carrots, in place of or in combination with russet potato.

AYURVEDA NOTES

- **VATA** Mix carrots and chayote with the russet potato to balance vata.
- **PITTA** Reduce or omit the Thai green chile. Use lime instead of lemon.
- **KAPHA** The warming, pungent spices balance kapha.

MOONG DAL HALWA

SLOW-COOKED SWEET MOONG DAL WITH GHEE AND SPICES

I associate this decadent dessert with winter, wedding season, and warm snuggles. While you'll typically find it on wintertime party menus in North India and Rajasthan, I like to make a big batch with the arrival of cooler weather, dividing it into smaller portions to be refrigerated in an airtight container for up to two weeks or frozen for a few months. Heat up individual portions and enjoy by itself or with a scoop of vanilla, almond, or pistachio ice cream for a fun combination.

SERVES 12

SOAK TIME 30 minutes to 1 hour

Rinse the yellow split moong dal in a fine-mesh sieve under cold running water until the water runs clear, about a minute. Transfer to a medium bowl, add water to cover by 2 inches (5 cm), and soak for 30 minutes to 1 hour.

Drain and transfer the dal to a blender or use an immersion blender, adding 2 to 3 tablespoons (30 to 45 ml) water as needed to grind to a semi-coarse paste.

In a 5- to 6-quart (5 to 6 L) heavy-bottomed pot or Dutch oven, heat ¾ cup (172 g) of the ghee over medium heat. Add the ground moong dal to the pan, rinse the empty blender jar with a couple of tablespoons of water to remove every bit of the moong dal mixture, and add to the pan. Stir constantly to incorporate the ghee into the moong dal mixture. Adjust the heat to medium-low and cook, constantly stirring so the moong dal mixture does not stick to the sides or to the bottom of the pan, until the dal is a grainy coarse-sand texture, 15 to 20 minutes. The dal will first start to dry and the texture will change from a wet paste to thick dough before turning into coarse sand. Keep the heat at medium-low and resist the temptation to speed the process by increasing the heat. All the moisture needs to be cooked out, and the ghee will start to separate from the moong dal mixture.

Once the dal mixture is golden brown, similar to the color of peanut butter, reduce the heat and carefully add the milk and saffron strands with all its soaking liquid. Keep stirring constantly and with caution, as the ghee may start to splutter once the liquid is added. Adjust the heat to medium and continue stirring until the entire liquid is absorbed, 10 to 12 minutes.

Continued—

1 cup (200 g) dhuli moong dal/yellow
  split moong dal
1 cup (230 g) ghee
3 cups (720 ml) whole milk, at room
  temperature
10 to 12 saffron strands soaked in
  2 tablespoons warm milk
1 cup (200 g) sugar
1 teaspoon ground cardamom
3 tablespoons sliced almonds
10 to 12 pistachios, chopped

Stir in the sugar and cardamom; the mixture will become loose again as the sugar melts. Maintain the heat at medium or medium-low and continue stirring; the mixture will start to thicken again after about 2 minutes. It may start to stick to the bottom and the mixture may be sticky. Add the remaining ¼ cup (58 g) ghee, which will add a beautiful sheen to the halwa and keep the mixture from sticking to the pan. Continue to stir until the halwa stops sticking to the sides of the pan and the ghee begins to separate from the mixture, an additional 10 to 12 minutes.

Add the sliced almonds and pistachios and mix in with the halwa. Reserve a few pieces to garnish on top before serving. Serve warm.

TIP

Make it vegan with almond milk instead of whole milk and sunflower or avocado oil instead of ghee.

AYURVEDA NOTES | *The sweet, heavy nature of this dish will pacify vata and pitta, but kapha should enjoy it in moderation.*

Halwa

Halwa (sometimes spelled halva, halava) originates from the Arabic word *hulw*, meaning "sweet," and came to India via Persia. Not to be confused with the Middle Eastern tahini-based dessert halvah, India's halwa is made from grains (such as classic suji, or semolina), nuts (like almonds or walnuts), sweet vegetables (like carrots, pumpkin, bottle gourd), fruits (like pineapple or apple), or pulses (such as moong or chickpeas).

There are many regional variations, personal preferences, and heirloom recipes that dictate halwa recipes, but generally speaking, the main ingredient is cooked in good-quality ghee, milk or water, and sugar. Aromatic spices like cardamom and saffron are popular in many halwa recipes, with a final garnish of slivered nuts and dried rose petals.

DAL MORADABADI

CREAMY YELLOW MOONG DAL TOPPED WITH CHUTNEYS

Dal Moradabadi is a popular street food from Moradabad in Uttar Pradesh, typically enjoyed as an on-the-go breakfast or served at parties as a *chaat*, or appetizer. This dish is entirely customizable. It's a perfect canvas for different garnishes, including sweet and spicy chutneys, chopped onions, tomatoes, and aromatic spices—my kids refer to it as a "loaded dal queso minus the cheese," enjoying it with tortilla chips on the side, although you can certainly top it with shredded cheese for your own version.

SERVES 6

SOAK TIME
10 to 15 minutes

TIPS

Substitute chopped daikon radish and/or grated carrot for the raw red onion and tomato.

To cook the soaked dal in an electric pressure cooker, pressure-cook on high for 3 minutes. Let the pressure release naturally before opening the lid. Whisk the dal smooth with a hand whisk or immersion blender. Adjust water as needed and keep the dal warm until ready to serve.

Rinse the yellow split moong dal in a fine-mesh sieve under cold running water until the water runs clear, about a minute. Transfer to a medium bowl, add water to cover by 2 inches (5 cm), and soak for 10 to 15 minutes. Drain.

In a 3-quart (3 L) pot, combine the soaked dal, water, salt, and turmeric. Bring to a boil, skimming off any foam. Reduce the heat to medium, partially cover, and cook until very soft, 20 to 30 minutes.

Remove from the heat and whisk to a smooth paste by hand or with an immersion blender. Return to the stovetop and simmer over low heat to thicken to a creamy sauce-like consistency. If the dal becomes too thick as it simmers, add up to 1 cup (240 ml) water as needed.

To serve, ladle ½ to ¾ cup (120 to 180 ml) of warm thick dal into shallow bowls. Sprinkle with a couple of pinches of each of the ground spices and a dab of butter, then mix well. Top with a spoonful or two of chopped raw onions and tomatoes, followed by drizzles of both chutneys. Garnish with fresh ginger, cilantro, a lemon wedge, and a sprinkle of pomegranate arils.

Enjoy a bowl of Dal Moradabadi by itself or with some chips or bread crisps on the side.

1 cup (200 g) dhuli moong dal/ yellow split moong dal
3 cups (720 ml) water, plus more as needed
1 teaspoon fine sea salt
1 teaspoon ground turmeric

ACCOMPANIMENTS

1 tablespoon ground toasted cumin
1 tablespoon Kashmiri red chili powder
1 tablespoon amchur/dried mango powder
2 tablespoons chilled unsalted butter, cut into 1-teaspoon cubes
1 medium red onion, finely chopped
1 medium tomato, finely chopped
1 cup Hari Chutney (page 214)
1 cup Imli Khajur ki Chutney (page 215)
2-inch (5 cm) piece fresh ginger, peeled and julienned
¼ cup (15 g) finely chopped cilantro (leaves and tender stems)
1 lemon, cut into wedges
½ cup (90 g) pomegranate arils (when in season)

AYURVEDA NOTES

- **VATA** Soft heavy foods soothe vata. Limit raw nightshades like tomato and onion (see Tips).
- **PITTA** Reduce the Kashmiri powder. Use tomato and raw onion toppings sparingly. Swap lemon juice for lime.
- **KAPHA** Ginger and red onions add pungency to balance the dal's heaviness.

MUGACHI KOSHIMBIR

SPLIT MOONG DAL TOSSED WITH VEGGIES AND TEMPERED SPICES

This fuss-free and easy-to-assemble salad is yet another example of how versatile a jar of yellow split moong dal can be in any pantry. The soaked dal combined with seasonal raw veggies with a tempering of spices delivers a refreshing salad that can be enjoyed as a side or main dish. I was surprised by the delightful texture and taste of uncooked soaked dal in this salad when I first tried it in a small local restaurant in Pune, a robust city close to Mumbai in my home state of Maharashtra. Since the moong dal is consumed in an un-cooked form, it should be soaked for about 2 hours so it has adequate time to soften. The tempered spices (tadka) are essential to help with digestion, in addition to building flavor in the dish.

SERVES 4

SOAK TIME 2 hours

TIPS

Try grated daikon radish, finely chopped kale or spinach, or other seasonal vegetables to create your personal combination.

In place of or in addition to coconut, add crushed roasted peanuts.

Rinse the yellow split moong dal in a fine-mesh sieve under cold running water until the water runs clear, up to a minute. Transfer to a medium bowl, add water to cover by 2 inches (5 cm), and soak for 2 hours.

Drain and place in a large bowl with the carrots, cucumber, coconut, green chile (if using), lemon juice, and cilantro. Mix well.

Make the tadka: In a small skillet, heat the oil over medium heat. Add the asafoetida and sizzle for 5 to 10 seconds. Add the cumin seeds and curry leaves (if using) and immediately pour over the salad. Toss the ingredients together. Add the salt just before serving (if you add it earlier, it will release the water from the vegetables and make the salad a bit soggy).

½ cup (100 g) dhuli moong dal/ yellow split moong dal

1 medium carrot, grated

1 Persian cucumber, finely chopped

¼ cup (20 g) unsweetened shredded coconut (fresh or thawed frozen)

1 Thai green chile (optional), finely chopped

2 tablespoons lemon juice

½ cup (30 g) finely chopped cilantro (leaves and tender stems)

TADKA

1½ tablespoons oil, such as peanut, olive, or avocado

⅛ teaspoon hing/asafoetida powder

1 teaspoon cumin seeds

8 to 10 fresh curry leaves (optional)

1 teaspoon fine sea salt, for serving

AYURVEDA NOTES

- **VATA** Balance the raw veggies with extra oil. May include crushed peanuts in addition to coconut.
- **PITTA** Reduce or omit Thai green chile; use lime juice instead of lemon.
- **KAPHA** Add more seasonal raw veggies. Use Thai green chile to balance cucumber's heavy hydrophilic quality.

SHALGAM WALI DAL

SPICED TURNIPS WITH MOONG DAL

This delightfully rustic dal with a sharp kick of mustard oil topped with Kashmiri-style roasted spiced turnips is especially comforting during cold winter months. *Shalgam*, or turnips, are a cool-weather crop that does not require a long growing season. Mildly spicy when raw, turnips turn sweet, earthy, and nutty once cooked. They are abundantly grown in the northern Indian state of Kashmir and used in a variety of ways in its local cuisine.

Instead of cooking the dal with turnips, this dish is inspired by the traditional Kashmiri dish Tao Gogji, a dry-spiced turnip stir-fry layered on top of the green split moong dal that are cooked with the turnip greens. The use of mustard oil complements the turnips, which belong to the Brassicaceae cruciferous family.

PERFECT PAIRING Serve alone or alongside cooked basmati rice (see Rice 101, page 152), Bhuga Chawar (page 163), or Jeera Rice (page 156), with Gajar ka Achaar (page 221) on the side.

SERVES 4

SOAK TIME 30 minutes to 1 hour

TIPS

Try this recipe with yellow split moong dal or orange split masoor dal. Reduce the soak time to 10 to 15 minutes and the cook time to under 30 minutes on the stovetop or 2 minutes on high in a pressure cooker.

Substitute olive, avocado, or any vegetable oil for the mustard oil.

Try daikon radish with its greens in place of turnips and turnip greens.

To cook the dal in an electric pressure cooker, select Sauté and cook the turnip greens with spices as directed. Add the turmeric, Kashmiri powder, soaked dal, water, and salt and pressure-cook on high for 3 minutes. Let the pressure release naturally before opening the lid. Mix well and let it stay on the Warm setting until served.

Continued—

AYURVEDA NOTES

- **VATA** Cut back on the green chile and Kashmiri powder if they cause dryness.
- **PITTA** Use avocado or olive oil instead of mustard oil. Reduce or skip the Thai green chile.
- **KAPHA** Favor mustard oil. Reduce the salt to ½ teaspoon in both the dal and turnips.

1 cup (200 g) chilka moong dal/green split
   moong dal
2 tablespoons mustard oil
⅛ teaspoon hing/asafoetida powder
1 teaspoon black mustard seeds
1-inch (2.5 cm) piece fresh ginger, finely chopped
2 garlic cloves, finely chopped
1 Thai green chile, finely chopped
2 cups (150 g) finely chopped turnip greens
¼ teaspoon ground turmeric
½ teaspoon Kashmiri red chili powder
4 cups (960 ml) water
1 teaspoon fine sea salt
SPICED TURNIPS
2 tablespoons mustard oil
⅛ teaspoon hing/asafoetida powder
1 teaspoon cumin seeds
4 whole cloves, coarsely crushed
1 pound (450 g) turnips, peeled and finely diced
1 teaspoon fine sea salt
½ teaspoon sugar
1 teaspoon Kashmiri red chili powder
1 teaspoon ground coriander
1 teaspoon amchur/dried mango powder
½ teaspoon ground ginger
½ teaspoon garam masala (page 40)
2 tablespoons finely chopped cilantro (leaves
   and tender stems)

Rinse the green split moong dal in a fine-mesh sieve under cold running water until the water runs clear, about a minute. Transfer to a medium bowl, add water to cover by 2 inches (5 cm), and soak for 30 minutes to 1 hour. Drain and set aside.

In a 3-quart (3 L) pot, heat the mustard oil over medium heat. Add the asafoetida and black mustard seeds and sizzle for 10 seconds. Add the ginger, garlic, and chile and sizzle for a few seconds. Add the turnip greens and sauté for 3 to 4 minutes, until wilted. Add the turmeric, Kashmiri powder, dal, water, and salt. Mix well and cook, covered, over medium heat until the dal is soft and mushy, about 30 minutes. Keep at a simmer over low heat until ready to serve.

Make the spiced turnips: In a large skillet, heat the mustard oil over medium heat. Add the asafoetida, cumin seeds, and cloves, sizzling for a few seconds. Add the diced turnips, salt, and sugar, mixing well. Spread evenly, cover, and cook until the turnips brown all over, 3 to 4 minutes, turning the turnips occasionally. Once lightly roasted, add the Kashmiri powder, coriander, mango powder, ginger, and garam masala. Mix well to coat the turnips. Sprinkle with a couple of tablespoons of water as needed if the pan gets too dry and the spices are starting to burn. Cook over low heat for another couple of minutes, then sprinkle with the cilantro.

Ladle the green split moong dal into individual bowls and top with a scoop of the spiced turnips. Serve warm.

SHEPUCHI DAL

GREEN MOONG DAL WITH FRESH DILL

The aromatic fresh dill combined with a moong dal is a fuss-free everyday dal, especially in the western regional cuisine of Maharashtra, where I am from, or its bordering state of Karnataka, where this dish is called *sabsige soppu dal*. Dill is packed with many essential nutrients, including vitamin C, magnesium, and vitamin A. Due to its carminative properties, adding this dal with fresh dill to the weekly menu really supports overall digestion. Feel free to reduce the amount of dill by half for a less pronounced flavor.

PERFECT PAIRING Serve with cooked short- or medium-grain rice (such as Ambemohar, Indrayani, or Sona Masoori) or serve alongside Hara Bhara Pulav (page 168).

SERVES 4

SOAK TIME 30 minutes to 1 hour

Rinse the green split moong dal in a fine-mesh sieve under cold running water until the water runs clear, about a minute. Transfer to a medium bowl, add water to cover by 2 inches (5 cm), and soak for 30 minutes to 1 hour. Drain.

In a 3-quart (3 L) pot, combine the dal, water, salt, and turmeric. Bring to a boil, skimming off any foam. Reduce the heat to medium, partially cover, and cook until the dal is soft and mushy, about 30 minutes. Keep at a simmer over low heat until ready to serve.

In a small skillet, heat 1 tablespoon of the ghee over medium heat. Add the asafoetida, mustard seeds, cumin seeds, and green chiles and sizzle for a few seconds. Stir in the dill and green onions and cook for a couple of minutes to soften the dill.

Transfer the mixture to the cooked dal, mix well, and season with salt to taste. Continue to simmer over low heat. The dal should be a soupy consistency, so adjust with up to a cup of water as needed.

In the same skillet, heat the remaining 1 tablespoon ghee over medium heat. Add the garlic and sauté until golden brown, about 1 minute. Reduce the heat and stir in the Kashmiri powder, then immediately pour the mixture over the dal. Add lemon juice and serve warm.

¾ cup (150 g) chilka moong dal/ green split moong dal

4 cups (960 ml) water, plus more as needed

1 teaspoon fine sea salt

½ teaspoon ground turmeric

2 tablespoons (30 g) ghee

⅛ teaspoon hing/asafoetida powder

1 teaspoon black mustard seeds

1 teaspoon cumin seeds

2 Thai green chiles, halved lengthwise

1 cup (45 g) finely chopped fresh dill leaves

½ cup (50 g) green onions, both white and green parts, thinly sliced

3 garlic cloves, thinly sliced

½ teaspoon Kashmiri red chili powder or deggi mirch

Juice of 1 lemon

TIPS

Try this recipe with yellow split moong dal or orange split masoor dal. Reduce the soak time to 10 to 15 minutes and the cook time to less than 30 minutes on the stovetop or 2 minutes in a pressure cooker.

To cook the dal in an electric pressure cooker, pressure-cook the soaked dal on high for 3 minutes. Let the pressure release naturally before opening the lid. Mix well and keep it on the Warm setting until serving.

Make it vegan with peanut, avocado, sunflower, or olive oil instead of ghee.

AYURVEDA NOTES

- **VATA** Reduce the chiles if pungency causes dryness or indigestion.
- **PITTA** Reduce or omit the Thai green chile. Use lime instead of lemon.
- **KAPHA** Use ground black pepper instead of Kashmiri powder.

SPROUTED MOONG BEAN SALAD

Sprouted beans with tender shoots are full of prana, an Ayurvedic term meaning life-force energy, so when you are eating sprouts, you are eating the life-force energy needed to create a full-grown healthy plant. During sprouting, digestive enzymes are activated, the nutritional quality of proteins is enhanced, and vitamins and minerals are increased. I make my signature sprouted moong salad on repeat during warm weather for family and friends, sprouting the beans for no more than 2 days or until the shoots are between ¼ and ½ inch (6 mm and 1.3 cm) in length, and then giving the sprouted moong beans a quick blanch in boiling water with salt and turmeric to hydrate them and infuse a grounding, rather than airy, quality to them.

SERVES 6

SOAK TIME 8 hours or overnight

SPROUT TIME 1 to 2 days

SPROUTED BEANS

1 cup (200 g) whole green moong beans

SALAD

1 teaspoon fine sea salt

½ teaspoon ground turmeric

1 Persian or hothouse cucumber, chopped, with skin on

1 cup (150 g) halved cherry tomatoes

1 medium bell pepper, any color, chopped

1 medium carrot, chopped

½ cup (60 g) chopped red radishes

½ cup (30 g) finely chopped cilantro (leaves and tender stems)

½ cup (30 g) finely chopped mint

2 tablespoons extra-virgin olive oil

2 tablespoons lime juice

1 tablespoon grated lime zest

1 teaspoon ground toasted cumin

1 teaspoon kala namak/Indian black salt

½ cup (60 g) dried cranberries

½ cup (60 g) pumpkin seeds, toasted

Sprout the beans: Place the moong beans in a bowl and cover with about 3 inches (7.5 cm) water and soak for at least 8 hours or overnight.

Drain and rinse. Place the beans in the center of a cheesecloth, about the size of a dish towel, and tie the cloth tightly to form a bundle. Place the bundle in a fine-mesh sieve or colander, then place the colander inside a large bowl to catch any extra liquid. Cover the colander with a lid or dish towel and leave on the kitchen countertop.

Remove the bundle and shower the beans with water through the cloth a couple of times a day for 1 to 2 days, placing it back into the sieve in the bowl. Continue the process until small shoots between ¼ inch (6 mm) and ½ inch (1.3 cm) are formed. If you are not ready to use the fresh sprouts immediately, transfer to an airtight container and refrigerate them for up to 3 days. Rinse the sprouts well before cooking.

Make the salad: Bring a medium pot of water to a boil. Add the salt and turmeric. Add the sprouted moong beans and blanch for 1 minute. Drain and transfer the sprouts to a large bowl and let cool to room temperature.

Add the cucumber, tomatoes, bell pepper, carrot, radishes, cilantro, mint, oil, lime juice, lime zest, cumin, and black salt. Toss well and garnish with dried cranberries and toasted pumpkin seeds.

Chill the salad until ready to serve.

TIPS

Change the chopped vegetables based on seasonal availability and personal preference.

When serving, ladle the sprouted moong bean salad over a bed of arugula for a mild peppery flavor.

AYURVEDA NOTES

- **VATA** Enjoy in moderation, preferably for lunch, when digestion is strong. Blanching the sprouts hydrates the beans and reduces vata.
- **PITTA** Overall balancing for pitta, though reduce the red radish to ¼ cup due to its pungency.
- **KAPHA** Excellent for kapha.

KHATTA MOONG

GREEN MOONG BEANS IN SPICED YOGURT

Beans and dals are combined with yogurt in traditional Indian cuisine to replace tomatoes in many classic regional dishes. Yogurt adds a pleasing sour flavor while the probiotics from the lacto-fermentation aid in digestion of the beans. *Khatta* (meaning sour) moong over plain steamed rice is a staple weeknight meal in the western regional cuisine of Gujarat, and I have been lucky to have several Gujarati friends share their versions of this simple wholesome curry. My version loads the classic khatta moong with leafy greens to make it extra nutritious for a busy weeknight meal.

PERFECT PAIRING Serve with plain steamed rice—short- or medium-grain—along with Haldi Adrak Mirch ka Achaar (page 222).

SERVES 4

SOAK TIME 2 to 4 hours

Rinse the whole green moong beans in a fine-mesh sieve under cold running water until the water runs clear, about a minute. Transfer to a medium bowl, cover with 3 inches (7.5 cm) water, and soak for 2 to 4 hours. Drain.

In a 3-quart (3 L) pot, combine the beans, 4 cups (960 ml) of the water, and 1 teaspoon of the salt. Bring to a boil, skimming off any foam. Reduce the heat to medium, partially cover, and cook until the beans are soft but still intact, 30 to 45 minutes. Keep at a simmer over low heat.

In a small bowl, whisk the chickpea flour and yogurt into a smooth paste. Add the remaining 1 cup (240 ml) water, coriander, turmeric, and remaining ½ teaspoon salt and whisk well. Stir into the pot of beans and cook over medium-low heat for about 5 minutes, to the consistency of a thick soup.

TIPS

Use unsweetened soy yogurt for a vegan version.

To cook the soaked beans in an electric pressure cooker, pressure-cook on high for 5 minutes. Let the pressure release naturally before opening the lid. Change the setting to Warm, add the spiced yogurt mixture, and then proceed as directed.

Make the tadka: In a medium skillet, heat the oil over medium heat. Add the asafoetida, cumin seeds, and mustard seeds and sizzle for 10 to 15 seconds. Add the ginger, garlic, curry leaves (if using), green chiles, and Kashmiri powder and stir for a minute until fragrant, adjusting the heat as necessary to avoid burning.

Make the spiced greens: Add the greens to the skillet with the tadka and sauté for a couple of minutes to wilt, then add to the pot of moong beans, mixing well. Season with salt to taste. Serve warm, topped with the cilantro.

1 cup (200 g) whole green moong beans

5 cups (1.2 L) water

1½ teaspoons fine sea salt

2 tablespoons besan/chickpea flour

½ cup (115 g) plain yogurt

1 teaspoon ground coriander

½ teaspoon ground turmeric

TADKA

2 tablespoons oil, such as peanut, avocado, or grapeseed

⅛ teaspoon hing/asafoetida powder

1 teaspoon cumin seeds

1 teaspoon black mustard seeds

1 tablespoon minced fresh ginger

2 garlic cloves, minced

8 to 10 fresh curry leaves (optional)

2 Thai green chiles, halved lengthwise

½ teaspoon Kashmiri red chili powder

SPICED GREENS

2 cups (150 g) finely chopped spinach, Swiss chard, or seasonal greens

Fine sea salt

¼ cup (15 g) finely chopped cilantro (leaves and tender stems)

AYURVEDA NOTES

- **VATA** Favor peanut oil. Reduce Thai green chile if it causes dryness.
- **PITTA** Reduce or omit garlic and chile. Use avocado oil and Swiss chard for greens.
- **KAPHA** Favor grapeseed oil. Use mustard greens, kale, or spinach for greens.

MASOOR

MASOOR

SANSKRIT NAMES: Masura / Mangalaya
OTHER INDIAN NAMES: Masoori / Misur Paruppu /
Kesaribele / Chuvanna Parippu
ENGLISH NAME: Lentil
BOTANICAL NAME: *Lens culinaris*

Akkha masoor (whole brown lentils) and masoor dal (split red lentils) are some of the oldest pulses of the Indian subcontinent and mentioned in the early Vedic texts. Masoor is known to have Persian origins and is associated with the Mughlai and Awadhi cuisines of India. It is equally popular in the eastern Bengali cuisine. Some Hindu communities avoid masoor as they consider consuming masoor dal equivalent to meat due to spiritual bias. Despite this unfortunate prejudice, split red masoor dal is one of the easiest to cook and is the one dal that can sometimes be made successfully without prior soaking. Even though the split variety starts off as a reddish orange color, it turns yellow when cooked.

Masoor, like all lentils, is a rich source of vitamins, protein, and minerals, such as calcium and magnesium. Its low glycemic index prevents sudden spikes in blood sugar levels and is therefore ideal for individuals with diabetes and insulin resistance. The dal not only tastes delicious but is also an excellent exfoliant for skin and used in a variety of skin-care products ranging from face mask and scrubs to face packs.

From an Ayurvedic perspective, whole brown lentils, or akkha masoor, are astringent in taste, with a heating potency and pungent *vipaka* (see page 26). Its rough, heavy qualities pacify kapha dosha, increase or decrease pitta, and can aggravate vata dosha when consumed in excess. On the other hand, the split red lentils, or masoor dal, are soft and light and cooling in potency, with a sweet and astringent taste and sweet post-digestive effect.

LOADED MASOOR DAL HUMMUS

We love all kinds of hummus in our home and always have a couple of different varieties in our fridge to use as a spread for sandwiches or a dip with chips and veggies. While a classic hummus with chickpeas is super delicious, it can be a bit heavy to digest. Over the years I have made hummus with a variety of split dal, but the one with masoor dal is our favorite. Carrots and beets bring a mild sweetness and add to the vibrant color of this light-to-digest dal hummus. Load it up with herbs, microgreens, and chopped veggies and you now have a fancy dip to impress any crowd.

SERVES 6

SOAK TIME
30 minutes to 1 hour

TIPS
Replace split red lentils with yellow split moong dal and cook with ground turmeric and golden beets for a yellow-hued hummus.

Change the garnishes according to the seasons and/or personal preference.

Rinse the split red lentils in a fine-mesh sieve under cold running water until the water runs clear, about a minute. Transfer to a medium bowl, add water to cover by 2 inches (5 cm), and soak for 30 minutes to 1 hour. Drain.

In a 3-quart (3 L) pot, combine the lentils, water, beet, carrot, and salt. Bring to a boil, skimming off any foam. Reduce the heat to medium, partially cover, and cook until the dal and vegetables are soft and mushy and the most of the liquid is reduced, 20 to 25 minutes.

Transfer the contents of the pot to a blender along with the garlic, olive oil, tahini, and lemon juice and puree until smooth.

Spoon the hummus onto a plate and garnish with optional toppings of choice. Serve at room temperature or chilled.

½ cup (90 g) masoor dal/split red lentils
1½ cups (360 ml) water
½ medium beet (60 g), cubed
½ medium carrot (40 g), cubed
1 teaspoon fine sea salt
4 garlic cloves, peeled but whole
¼ cup (60 ml) extra-virgin olive oil
2 tablespoons well-stirred tahini
1 tablespoon lemon juice
OPTIONAL TOPPINGS
¼ cup (40 g) finely chopped Persian or English cucumber
¼ cup (40 g) halved cherry tomatoes
¼ cup (40 g) finely chopped red radishes
¼ cup (10 g) microgreens
¼ cup (10 g) finely chopped fresh parsley
2 tablespoons roasted pumpkin seeds
1 teaspoon sumac
1 teaspoon ground toasted cumin
1 teaspoon Kashmiri red chili powder

AYURVEDA NOTES

- **VATA** Use cucumber, pumpkin seeds, sumac, and cumin as toppings, with an extra drizzle of olive oil.
- **PITTA** Skip the Kashmiri powder garnish. Opt for a garnish of cucumbers and microgreens.
- **KAPHA** Skip cucumbers as a topping.

SPICED MASOOR MINESTRONE

Minestrone soup is popular for its mix-match style of vegetables, with beans and pasta added to the vegetarian version to help make up the body of the soup. This quinoa masoor minestrone is my play on the traditional vegetarian minestrone soup and makes quite a regular appearance on our weeknight menu, especially during cooler winter and spring months. This soup is a one-pot complete meal in itself and is tri-doshic (suitable for all body constitutions) in nature. It is an excellent source of protein, vitamins, complex carbohydrates, and fiber. The spices used are warm and grounding and are excellent for the winter months.

SERVES 6

SOAK TIME 15 to 30 minutes

¾ cup (140 g) masoor dal/split red lentils
¼ cup (45 g) white quinoa
2 tablespoons oil, such as olive or sesame oil
⅛ teaspoon hing/asafoetida
1-inch (2.5 cm) piece fresh ginger, finely chopped
3 garlic cloves, finely chopped
2 bay leaves
1 teaspoon ground toasted cumin
1 teaspoon garam masala (page 40)
1 teaspoon ground turmeric
3 cups (about 400 g) chopped vegetables: a combination of carrots, zucchini, yellow squash, and/or butternut squash
2 cups (150 g) finely chopped seasonal leafy greens: spinach, kale, chard, carrot greens, beet greens
1 teaspoon fine sea salt, plus more to taste
½ teaspoon coarsely ground black pepper
6 cups (1.4 L) water
½ cup (20 g) thinly sliced fresh basil
Lemon wedges, for serving

Rinse the split red lentils in a fine-mesh sieve under cold running water until the water runs clear, about a minute. Transfer to a medium bowl, add water to cover by 2 inches (5 cm), and soak for 15 to 30 minutes.

Meanwhile, in a small skillet, dry-roast the quinoa over low heat for 3 to 4 minutes and set aside.

In a large Dutch oven or heavy-bottomed pot, heat the oil over medium heat. Add the asafoetida, ginger, garlic, and bay leaves and sauté for a few seconds. Stir in the cumin, garam masala, and turmeric. Add the chopped vegetables, leafy greens, salt, and pepper. Mix well and cook for 3 to 4 minutes while the greens reduce.

Drain the lentils and transfer to the pot of vegetables, along with the toasted quinoa. Stir in the water and bring to a boil. Reduce the heat to medium, partially cover, and cook until the dal and vegetables are soft, about 20 minutes.

Reduce the heat to a simmer and stir in the basil. Season with salt to taste and serve warm with wedges of lemon for squeezing.

AYURVEDA NOTES

- **VATA** Split red lentil's lightness can aggravate vata. Asafoetida, ginger, and ample liquid in soup help pacify vata.
- **PITTA** Favor olive oil over sesame. Opt for kale, chard, or beet greens. Serve with a lime instead of lemon.
- **KAPHA** Dry-roasting the quinoa enhances flavor and reduces kapha.

PINEAPPLE DAL

SWEET-AND-SOUR RED LENTIL PINEAPPLE CURRY

This is not your regular Indian dal. Many dal recipes use tomatoes or tamarind to add sourness, but the hero ingredient in this recipe is the ripe pineapple, adding a tropical vibe that complements the soft, creamy red lentils. I make pineapple dal often as an appetizer soup on Thai dinner night at my home—the sweet-and-sour flavor works well with an Asian stir-fry. Add half of the tempered spices (tadka) and pineapple to the cooked dal and reserve the rest to use as a topping when serving, for an extra layer of flavor.

PERFECT PAIRING Serve with Matta Coconut Rice (page 164), plain steamed rice, or Jeera Rice (page 156).

SERVES 4

SOAK TIME 15 to 30 minutes

Rinse the split red lentils in a fine-mesh sieve under cold running water until the water runs clear, about a minute. Transfer to a medium bowl, add water to cover by 2 inches (5 cm), and soak for 30 minutes to 1 hour. Drain.

In a 3-quart (3 L) pot, combine the lentils, water, 1 teaspoon of the salt, and ½ teaspoon of the turmeric. Bring to a boil, skimming off any foam. Reduce the heat to medium, partially cover, and cook until dal is soft and mushy, 20 to 25 minutes. Whisk well to a creamy consistency.

Make the tadka: In a small saucepan, heat the oil over medium heat. Add the mustard seeds and let sizzle for 15 to 30 seconds. Add the green chile (if using) and onions and sauté until the onions are translucent and light brown.

Add the pineapple, sugar, garam masala, and the remaining ½ teaspoon salt and ½ teaspoon turmeric. Mix well and cook until the pineapple is soft, 2 to 3 minutes. Add the cilantro and coconut and cook for another minute.

Measure out ½ cup (120 ml) of the spiced pineapple mixture and set aside for garnishing. Add the rest to the cooked dal. Simmer the pineapple dal over low heat for 5 minutes.

Serve each portion with a spoonful of the reserved spiced pineapple mixture.

TIPS

This recipe works well with other dals like yellow split moong dal or toor dal.

Add ½ cup seasonal bitter leafy greens, such as finely chopped kale, fenugreek leaves, or Swiss chard, when cooking the chile and onion.

1 cup (180 g) masoor dal/split red lentils

3 cups (720 ml) water

1½ teaspoons fine sea salt

1 teaspoon ground turmeric

TADKA

2 tablespoons oil, such as peanut, avocado, sunflower, or olive

1 teaspoon black mustard seeds

1 Thai green chile (optional), finely chopped

½ cup (65 g) finely chopped red onions

1 cup (175 g) finely chopped or crushed pineapple (very ripe fresh or canned)

1 tablespoon sugar

½ teaspoon garam masala (page 40)

¼ cup (10 g) finely chopped cilantro (leaves and tender stems)

2 tablespoons unsweetened shredded coconut (fresh, thawed frozen, or dried)

AYURVEDA NOTES

- **VATA** Reduce or omit Thai green chile.
- **PITTA** Favor avocado, sunflower, or olive oil. Omit the Thai green chile. Add seasonal bitter leafy greens to balance the heating potency of the pineapple (see Tips).
- **KAPHA** Favor sunflower oil. Add seasonal bitter leafy greens to balance the heavy nature of the pineapple (see Tips).

KOLHAPURI AKKHA MASOOR

FIERY MASOOR LENTIL CURRY

Akkha means "whole" in the Marathi language, and this recipe celebrates the Kolhapuri cuisine from my birth home state of Maharashtra. Known for its fiery flavors, the whole masoor is cooked with a special spice blend called goda masala, which is used in Maharashtrian cuisine, and a ground paste of sesame seeds, poppy seeds, and dried coconut. Jaggery and tamarind are added at the end for sweet and sour notes to balance the heat from the spice blend and creaminess from the seeds. If you are looking for a unique recipe to add to your dal roster, you have to give this robustly flavored brown lentil curry, or akkha masoor, a try.

PERFECT PAIRING Serve with plain steamed rice or Matta Coconut Rice (page 164).

SERVES 4

SOAK TIME 8 hours or overnight

Rinse the whole brown lentils in a fine-mesh sieve under cold running water until the water runs clear, about a minute. Transfer to a medium bowl, cover with 3 inches (7.5 cm) water, and soak for 8 hours or overnight. Drain.

In a 3-quart (3 L) pot, combine the lentils, water, salt, and turmeric. Bring to a boil, skimming off any foam. Reduce the heat to medium, partially cover, and cook until the whole masoor is soft when pressed between fingers but remains intact, 20 to 25 minutes.

Meanwhile, make the ground paste: In a medium skillet, heat the oil over medium heat. Add the onions and whole garlic cloves and sauté until golden brown, 8 to 10 minutes. Add the coconut flakes, sesame seeds, and poppy seeds to the pan and sauté until they start to turn light brown. Transfer the contents of the pan to a blender. Add the cilantro and green chile and grind to a thick paste, adding a couple of tablespoons of water as needed.

For the curry: In the same skillet, heat the oil over medium heat. Add the ground paste and stir for 3 to 4 minutes until the oil starts to separate.

Continued—

1 cup (190 g) akkha masoor/whole brown lentils
4 cups (960 ml) water
1 teaspoon fine sea salt
½ teaspoon ground turmeric
GROUND PASTE
2 tablespoons oil, such as peanut, sunflower, avocado, or grapeseed
1 large red onion, thinly sliced
4 garlic cloves, peeled but whole
½ cup (40 g) unsweetened coconut flakes
2 tablespoons white sesame seeds
2 tablespoons white poppy seeds
½ cup (30 g) cilantro (leaves and stems)
1 Thai green chile, halved
CURRY
2 tablespoons oil, such as peanut, sunflower, avocado, or grapeseed
1 cup (240 ml) water
2 tablespoons grated jaggery or jaggery powder
1 tablespoon tamarind concentrate
2 teaspoons goda masala (recipe follows)
½ teaspoon fine sea salt, plus more to taste
¼ cup (10 g) finely chopped cilantro (leaves and tender stems)

Add the water, jaggery, tamarind concentrate, goda masala, and salt and mix well. Cook over medium heat for a couple of minutes, then add to the cooked masoor. Add the cilantro and mix well. Season with salt to taste. Simmer over low heat until ready to serve.

TIPS

Substitute 1 teaspoon garam masala (page 40) for the goda masala.

To cook the soaked whole masoor in an electric pressure cooker, pressure-cook on high for 4 minutes. Let the pressure release naturally before opening the lid.

AYURVEDA NOTES

- **VATA** Reduce the Thai green chile if it causes pungency.
- **PITTA** Reduce or skip Thai green chile. Favor sunflower or avocado oil; use white onion in place of red.
- **KAPHA** Favor sunflower oil. Consume in moderation as tamarind and jaggery's sweet-sour flavors may aggravate kapha.

GODA MASALA
MAKES about 1 heaping cup (140 g)

1 teaspoon peanut, coconut, or sunflower oil
½ cup (40 g) coriander seeds
2 tablespoons cumin seeds
2 teaspoons caraway seeds
½ teaspoon black peppercorns
6 green cardamom pods
2 black cardamom pods
2-inch (5 cm) piece cinnamon stick
4 dried tej patta/Indian bay leaves
6 whole dried Byadagi red chiles
½ cup (50 g) dried coconut
¼ cup (30 g) white sesame seeds
1 tablespoon white poppy seeds

Heat the oil in a medium skillet over low heat. Add the coriander seeds, cumin seeds, caraway seeds, black peppercorns, green and black cardamom pods, cinnamon stick, bay leaves, and dried red chiles and slow-roast by stirring continuously, about 5 minutes. Transfer to a bowl to cool.

In the same pan, roast the coconut, sesame seeds, and poppy seeds over low heat for about 5 minutes, until the coconut turns light golden brown, stirring continuously. Remove from the heat and cool to room temperature.

Combine all the ingredients in a spice grinder and grind to a fine powder.

Store in an airtight container in the pantry.

CHANA

CHANA

SANSKRIT NAME: Chanaka
OTHER INDIAN NAMES: Channa / Chana Dal / Kabuli Chana /
Chholar / Harbara / Kadalai / Senagalu / Kadele / Kadala
ENGLISH NAMES: Bengal Gram / Chickpea / Garbanzo Bean
BOTANICAL NAME: *Cicer arietinum*

Chana has the chameleon-like culinary ability to transform into anything, from soup to fritters to decadent truffles. Typically known as chickpeas or garbanzo beans in the West, chana has been described as the pulse of health, with its origins tracing back for centuries in several Indian texts. The British first made its acquaintance in Bengal, the eastern region of India, calling it Bengal gram, and you'll find it both whole and split. In addition to the common larger variety of chickpea from the Mediterranean, known as *kabuli chana* in India, there is also a smaller variety of chickpeas with wrinkled dark-brown skin called *kala chana*, developed on the Indian subcontinent. Chana dal is the split and peeled version of whole kala chana. There is also a dry roasted variety of chana dal called *dalia chana* which is often added to chutneys and found in several savory Indian packaged snacks called *farsan*. Many Indian grocery stores also carry fresh green chana (chickpeas) in pods, which make a delightful addition to salads or can be steamed and served as a tasty snack.

Besan, also known as chickpea flour, is a pale-yellow flour made from chana dal (split and peeled chickpeas). It is used in a variety of ways in Indian cooking: as a thickener for sauces, batter for fried foods, and even as a substitute for eggs in certain recipes. Besan is extensively used for external Ayurvedic skin-care applications and is quite popular in the natural beauty industry as well. In many parts of northern and central India, the flour made from roasted Bengal gram, called *sattu* (see Sattu ka Sharbat, page 237) is popular with construction workers, farm laborers, and athletes as a high-protein energy drink. Like other pulses, it is an excellent source of plant protein and packed with several nutritive properties, especially B vitamins, dietary fiber, and minerals, such as calcium, iron, manganese, and magnesium.

From an Ayurvedic perspective, *chanaka* (or chana) are light, sweet with astringent taste, and cold in potency with unctuous qualities. Its intake balances pitta and kapha dosha, and excess may increase vata dosha.

AMRITSARI PINDI CHOLE

TEA-INFUSED SPICED CHICKPEAS

This North Indian preparation of chickpeas with a dried spice blend—called a chole—pays homage to the northwest frontier of both India and Pakistan. Sometimes referred to as Pindi chole or Amritsari Pindi chole, this North Indian dish originated from Rawalpindi, in present-day Pakistan, before the India-Pakistan partition. The soaked chickpeas are cooked with black tea leaves, imparting a distinct dark color and aromatic flavor; traditionally served as a popular street food with deep-fried fermented bread called *bhatura* or oven-baked bread called *kulche*, you can also serve it with warm naan, bread crisps, or sliced baguette. Or skip the bread and scoop the rustic Pindi chole over chilled Bibb lettuce or romaine hearts for nutrient-dense chickpea lettuce cups.

PERFECT PAIRING
Serve with Jeera Rice (page 156) alongside Gajar ka Achaar (page 221).

SERVES 4

SOAK TIME 8 hours or overnight

1½ cups (300 g) kabuli chana/dried chickpeas

4 cups (960 ml) water

2 teaspoons fine sea salt

1 tablespoon loose black tea (Assam or Darjeeling), tied into a sachet, or 2 tea bags

½ cup (110 g) ghee, avocado oil, or grapeseed oil

3 to 4 tablespoons (45 to 60 ml) chole masala (recipe follows)

2-inch (5 cm) piece fresh ginger, cut into thin matchsticks

2 to 3 Thai green chiles, julienned

¼ cup (15 g) finely chopped cilantro (leaves and tender stems)

Rinse the chickpeas in a fine-mesh sieve under cold running water until the water runs clear, about a minute. Transfer to a medium bowl, cover with 3 inches (7.5 cm) water, and soak for 8 hours or overnight. Drain.

In a 6-quart (6 L) Dutch oven, combine the chickpeas, water, 1 teaspoon of the salt, and the tea. Cover and cook over medium-high heat for about 45 minutes. Check on the water levels periodically. If the water level goes below the chickpeas, add more water to cover the beans, replace the lid, and return it to a boil, then reduce heat and continue to simmer until done. Check the chickpeas; they should be soft and mashed easily when pressed between your fingers and thumb but at the same time hold their shape quite well. If the chickpeas are still a bit hard, continue to cook for another 10 to 15 minutes and check them again. Once the beans are cooked, remove the tea sachet/bags and turn off the heat. Drain the tea liquid off the chickpeas and set aside in a separate bowl. Keep the chickpeas covered and set aside.

Heat a cast-iron skillet over medium heat. Add the ghee or oil. Transfer the chickpeas and about 3 tablespoons (45 g) of the chole masala and mix well. Add 1 cup (240 ml) of the reserved tea liquid and the remaining 1 teaspoon salt and simmer the chickpeas over low heat. The flavors will build with a slow simmer of at least 15 to 20 minutes. If the chickpeas become dry, add another cup of the tea liquid and add more of the chole masala. This dish doesn't have a lot of liquid, just enough to coat the beans and create a little bit of sauce.

Garnish with the ginger, green chiles, and cilantro.

Continued—

TIPS

To cook the chickpeas in an electric pressure cooker, combine the soaked chickpeas, salt, water, and tea sachet and pressure-cook on high for 7 minutes. Let the pressure release naturally before opening the lid. The chickpeas should be soft when pressed between thumb and fingers but still have their shape intact.

Use three 15-ounce (425 g) cans (about 4½ cups) chickpeas if short on time. Rinse the chickpeas under cold water. Heat 3 cups (720 ml) water in a pot and brew black tea for 5 minutes. Add the drained chickpeas to the pot and simmer for 15 to 20 minutes to darken the beans.

Any excess liquid from the chickpeas stores well in a refrigerator for up to 1 week and can be used in place of broth for other dishes.

AYURVEDA NOTES

- **VATA** The spices help to balance the vata quality of chickpeas. Add additional liquid to the final dish.
- **PITTA** Reduce or eliminate the Thai green chile and Kashmiri powder.
- **KAPHA** Reduce the salt and fat. Use grapeseed oil instead of ghee.

CHOLE MASALA (DRY CHOLE SPICE MIX)

MAKES about ¾ cup (80 g)

3 tablespoons (45 g) coriander seeds
2 tablespoons cumin seeds
1 tablespoon anardana/dried
    pomegranate seeds
2 teaspoons fenugreek seeds
1 teaspoon black peppercorns
½ teaspoon whole cloves
4 green cardamom pods
2 bay leaves
2-inch (5 cm) piece cinnamon stick
2 dried Kashmiri red chiles
2 black cardamom pods
1 star anise
1 blade of mace
1 tablespoon amchur/dried mango powder
2 teaspoons kala namak/Indian black salt
1 teaspoon Kashmiri red chili powder

In a cast-iron skillet, dry-roast all the spices except mango powder and Kashmiri powder over low heat until the aroma gets released, 5 to 6 minutes. Keep mixing constantly and be careful that the spices do not burn. Once lightly toasted, transfer to a bowl and allow to cool. Transfer the cooled spices, dried mango powder, and Kashmiri powder to a spice grinder or a blender and grind to a fine powder. Transfer to an airtight container and store for up to 3 months.

SAAG CHANA

CHICKPEA CURRY WITH SEASONAL GREENS

Saag refers to any leafy green vegetable cooked and blended into a coarse mixture along with aromatics and spices to make a thick curry. Using spinach as a base, I like to add a combination of mustard greens and fenugreek leaves during the cooler fall and winter months, switching to radish greens and beet greens in the springtime, but you can also just use spinach, either fresh or frozen.

PERFECT PAIRING Serve with steamed basmati rice, Jeera Rice (page 156), or Bhuga Chawar (page 163).

SERVES 4

SOAK TIME 8 hours or overnight

Rinse the chickpeas in a fine-mesh sieve under cold running water until the water runs clear, about a minute. Transfer to a medium bowl, cover with 3 inches (7.5 cm) water, and soak for 8 hours or overnight. Drain.

In a 6-quart (6 L) pot or Dutch oven, combine the chickpeas, water, and 1 teaspoon of the salt. Bring to a boil. Cover the pot and cook over medium-high heat for about 45 minutes. Add additional water to cover the chickpeas when cooking as needed. Check the chickpeas; they should be soft and mashed easily when pressed between your fingers and thumb but remain intact. If they are still a bit hard, continue to cook for another 10 to 15 minutes and check them again. Once the chickpeas are cooked, remove from the heat and set aside.

Meanwhile, in a mini food processor, combine the ginger, garlic, and chile and finely chop. Set aside.

In a large saucepan, heat the ghee over medium heat. Add the cumin seeds and allow them to sizzle. Add the onion and cook until translucent and lightly browned, 4 to 5 minutes. Add the tomatoes and season with the remaining ½ teaspoon salt and cook until specks of oil separate and start to appear on the edges of the tomato/onion mixture, 3 to 4 minutes. Add the garam masala, ground coriander, ground cumin, Kashmiri powder, and turmeric and cook for another 2 to 3 minutes.

Continued—

1 cup (200 g) kabuli chana/dried chickpeas

4 cups (960 ml) water

1½ teaspoons fine sea salt, plus more to taste

1-inch (2.5 cm) piece fresh ginger

3 garlic cloves, peeled but whole

½ to 1 serrano chile

¼ cup (60 g) ghee or oil, such as peanut, avocado, or grapeseed

1 teaspoon cumin seeds

1 medium red onion, finely chopped

2 medium tomatoes, finely chopped

1 teaspoon garam masala (page 40)

½ teaspoon ground coriander

½ teaspoon ground toasted cumin

½ teaspoon Kashmiri red chili powder

¼ teaspoon ground turmeric

10 cups (about 1 pound/500 g) spinach or a combination of spinach with other leafy greens of choice

⅓ cup (80 ml) heavy cream or coconut milk (optional)

Add the spinach to the tomato/onion mixture in batches. Add ¼ cup (60 ml) cooking liquid from the pot of cooked chickpeas. Partially cover and cook until the spinach is soft, 5 to 7 minutes.

Using an immersion blender, blitz the spinach gravy a few times to your liking; I prefer to have some texture to the spinach gravy, but you can puree it smooth if desired.

Drain the cooked chickpeas and reserve the cooking liquid. Add the chickpeas to the spinach gravy along with ¼ to ½ cup (60 to 120 ml) of the cooking liquid. Season with salt to taste. Stir well and simmer for another 5 minutes.

If you'd like a creamy saag chana, stir in the heavy cream or coconut milk before serving.

TIPS

To cook the soaked chickpeas in an electric pressure cooker, pressure-cook on high for 7 minutes. Let the pressure release naturally before opening the lid. The chickpeas should be soft when pressed between the thumb and fingers but still have their shape intact.

Combine the greens with paneer instead of chickpeas if desired.

Use seasonal greens along with herbs such as mint, cilantro, or parsley for added aromatics in the saag.

AYURVEDA NOTES

- **VATA** Favor spinach and mustard greens. Use peanut or mustard oil.
- **PITTA** Favor avocado or grapeseed oils. Reduce chile and Kashmiri powder. Favor beet greens, dandelion greens, and spinach.
- **KAPHA** Use mustard oil. Skip heavy cream or coconut milk.

BESAN KA CHILA

CHICKPEA PANCAKE WITH SEASONAL VEGETABLES

You'll find something called a tomato-onion omelet in many Indian vegetarian restaurants, especially in Mumbai—*chila*, an egg-free pancake made with besan (chickpea flour), cooked with chopped tomatoes, onions, and cilantro, and served with toast and spicy cilantro chutney and tomato ketchup on the side. The memory of enjoying a hot chila with my college friends and sipping chai is what warmed me when I was cooking for myself as a graduate student on cold, lonely evenings while studying for an exam. The base recipe is incredibly versatile and can be enjoyed for breakfast, lunch, dinner, or a nutritious after-school snack for kids. When my kids were young, I would grate seasonal veggies into the batter and cook the chila in fun shapes as you might with a sweet pancake batter, and I have made small ones to stuff inside a panini with vegetables and cheese.

PERFECT PAIRING
Serve with Hari Chutney (page 214), Thecha (page 218), and a glass of Pudina Jaljeera (page 229).

SERVES 4

TIPS
A smaller size of chila— about 4 inches (10 cm)— can be used as "burger" patty or in sandwiches grilled in a panini press along with other fillings.

Dredge a slice of sourdough bread in the batter and cook in a skillet as you would French toast—you may not even miss the eggy version!

Sift the besan into a bowl to ensure there are no lumps in the batter. Add the carrots, onions, tomatoes, spinach, chile, salt, cumin, ajwain, turmeric, Kashmiri powder, and asafoetida. Gradually add the water ½ cup (120 ml) at a time to get a smooth batter; make sure there are no lumps. The batter should be a thin pancake-batter consistency.

Heat a cast-iron skillet over medium heat. Brush ½ teaspoon of oil evenly around the surface of the pan to season it. Pour in ½ cup (120 ml) batter and spread with the back of a large spoon or ladle into a 6-inch (15 cm) round. Add ½ teaspoon oil around the perimeter of the chila and drizzle ½ teaspoon on top of the chila as it cooks for a couple of minutes. Once the edges turn slightly crisp, flip the chila over with a spatula and cook until browned and slightly crisp on both sides. Press down on the chila with the spatula so it cooks evenly and there are no raw pockets of batter in the center. Repeat with the rest of the batter. Serve warm.

1 cup (120 g) besan/chickpea flour
½ cup (50 g) finely shredded carrots
½ cup (70 g) chopped red onions
½ cup (70 g) chopped tomatoes
½ cup (110 g) chopped fresh spinach leaves
1 teaspoon finely chopped green chile
1 teaspoon fine sea salt
1 teaspoon cumin seeds
½ teaspoon ajwain/carom seeds
½ teaspoon ground turmeric
½ teaspoon Kashmiri red chili powder
⅛ teaspoon hing/asafoetida powder
1 to 1½ cups (240 to 360 ml) water
¼ cup (60 ml) sunflower or olive oil

AYURVEDA NOTES

Adding spices and vegetables balances the dry and heavy guna (quality) of besan. In the spring season, load up on green leafy vegetables like spinach and kale. Substitute finely chopped green onions for regular onions. Add cilantro leaves in summer along with onions and tomatoes. In cooler months, add shredded carrots and beets along with leafy greens.

- **VATA** Increase carom seeds to 1 teaspoon. Use shredded carrots or beets.
- **PITTA** Add green leafy vegetables like finely chopped kale, chard, cilantro, or parsley. Skip tomatoes and red onions and use white onions or leeks instead.
- **KAPHA** Add minced ginger and garlic. Use black pepper instead of Kashmiri powder.

KALA CHANA SUNDAL

BROWN CHICKPEAS AND COCONUT

Sundal is a popular snack prepared during several Hindu festivals, such as Navaratri and Ganesh Chaturti, as an offering to God, then shared with family and friends. This simple yet hearty dish can be served warm or cold, and a generous garnish of coconut adds a touch of sweetness to balance the tart flavors from green mango and lemon juice. The chickpeas can be boiled ahead of time, and the dish is completed by tempering the seasonings just before serving warm. If serving cold, prepare the entire dish and chill for a few hours before serving to allow the spices and flavors to meld.

PERFECT PAIRING Serve with Matta Coconut Rice (page 164) or Haldi Wale Chawal (page 159).

SERVES 4

SOAK TIME 8 hours or overnight

TIPS

Swap the kala chana for two 15-ounce (425 g) cans of chickpeas or cannellini beans (about 3 cups), 3 cups (550 g) boiled yellow split chana dal, or 3 cups (550 g) boiled peanuts for an equally mouthwatering savory sundal.

If unripe mangoes are not available or not in season, try combining kala chana sundal with chopped cucumbers, cherry tomatoes, thinly sliced onions, and red radishes for a hearty salad.

To cook the soaked chickpeas in an electric pressure cooker, pressure-cook on high for 7 minutes. Let the pressure release naturally before opening the lid. The kala chana should be soft when pressed between the thumb and fingers but still have their shape intact.

Rinse the kala chana in a fine-mesh sieve under cold running water until the water runs clear, about a minute. Transfer to a medium bowl, cover with 3 inches (7.5 cm) warm water, and soak for 8 hours or overnight. Drain.

In a 3-quart (3 L) saucepan, combine the kala chana, water, and salt. Bring to a boil. Reduce the heat to medium, partially cover, and cook until soft but still intact, 30 to 45 minutes. Drain the kala chana and set aside.

In the same saucepan, heat the oil over medium heat. Add the asafoetida, mustard seeds, urad dal, fresh green chiles, dried chile, and curry leaves. When the mustard seeds splutter and the urad dal is slightly golden brown, add the cooked kala chana to the saucepan and mix well. Add the green mango (if using) and coconut and combine thoroughly.

Remove from the heat and then add lemon juice. Serve warm or cold.

1 cup (175 g) kala chana/dark-brown chickpeas

3 cups (720 ml) water

1 teaspoon fine sea salt

1 tablespoon oil, such as coconut, peanut, or sunflower oil

¼ teaspoon hing/asafoetida powder

1 teaspoon black mustard seeds

1 teaspoon urad dal/split and peeled black gram

2 Thai green chiles, halved lengthwise

1 dried red chile

10 to 12 fresh curry leaves

½ cup (71 g) finely chopped green (unripe) mango (optional or when in season)

2 tablespoons unsweetened shredded coconut (fresh, thawed frozen, or dried)

1 tablespoon lemon juice

AYURVEDA NOTES

- **VATA** Choose peanut oil and enjoy this dish warm.
- **PITTA** Choose sunflower or coconut oil and enjoy this dish cold (or warm).
- **KAPHA** Enjoy this dish warm.

SAI BHAAJI

SPINACH AND SPLIT-CHICKPEA STEW

Sai (green) *bhaaji* (vegetable dish) is a classic Sindhi comfort dish prepared with spinach, dill, chana dal, and a combination of seasonal vegetables. Chana dal by itself can be a bit heavy to digest, but combining it with leafy greens and spices aids digestion. Sai bhaaji can be enjoyed from late spring through summer or when fresh greens are in season. It is traditionally served with Sindhi *bhuga chawar*, an aromatic basmati rice dish that is transformed to a rich golden-brown color as it slowly cooks with caramelized onions and spices.

PERFECT PAIRING Serve with Bhuga Chawar (page 163) or Jeera Rice (page 156) along with Khatta Meetha Nimbu ka Achaar (page 223).

SERVES 4

SOAK TIME 2 to 3 hours

¾ cup (150 g) chana dal/peeled and split chickpeas

2 tablespoons (30 g) ghee or oil, such as sunflower, peanut, olive, or grapeseed

⅛ teaspoon hing/asafoetida powder

1 teaspoon cumin seeds

1 teaspoon finely chopped fresh ginger

1 teaspoon finely chopped garlic

1 medium red onion, finely chopped

2 medium tomatoes, finely chopped

1½ teaspoons fine sea salt, plus more to taste

1 teaspoon ground coriander

½ teaspoon ground turmeric

½ teaspoon Kashmiri red chili powder

¼ teaspoon garam masala (page 40)

1 medium potato, cut into 1-inch (2.5 cm) cubes

1 medium carrot, peeled and cut into 1-inch (2.5 cm) pieces

1 cup (60 to 70 g) cubed Indian bottle gourd, pumpkin, or yellow squash

1 pound (500 g) fresh spinach, roughly chopped

1 cup (200 g) chopped sorrel leaves (optional)

½ cup (100 g) fresh fenugreek leaves (optional)

½ cup (20 g) chopped fresh dill

2 cups (480 ml) water

Rinse the chana dal in a fine-mesh sieve under cold running water until the water runs clear, about a minute. Transfer to a medium bowl, add water to cover by 2 inches (5 cm), and soak for 2 to 3 hours. Drain and set aside.

In a 4- to 6-quart (4 to 6 L) Dutch oven or saucepan, heat the ghee over medium-high heat. Add the asafoetida and cumin seeds and sizzle for 5 to 10 seconds. Add the ginger and garlic and cook until fragrant, 30 to 45 seconds. Add the onions and sauté until translucent, 4 to 5 minutes. Add the tomatoes and cook until softened, 2 to 3 minutes. Stir in the salt, coriander, turmeric, Kashmiri powder, and garam masala.

Add the soaked chana dal, potato, carrot, bottle gourd, spinach, sorrel (if using), fenugreek (if using), dill, and water. Increase the heat to high and bring to a rolling boil. Reduce the heat to low, cover, and simmer until the dal and vegetables are soft and tender, 30 to 45 minutes.

Gently mash the veggies and dal with a potato masher, hand whisk, or an immersion blender. If using an immersion blender, be careful to not turn it into a puree. You are looking for a stew that has the veggies and dal tender and soft and gently mashed. Season with salt to taste and serve warm.

TIPS

Although traditional sai bhaaji is only very gently mashed to retain some of the texture of the vegetables and chana dal, if you prefer a smoother texture, blitz with an immersion blender to a smooth puree.

To make in an electric pressure cooker, select Sauté, heat the ghee, and sizzle the spices and aromatics. Add the soaked dal, vegetables, herbs, and water and pressure-cook on high for 6 minutes. Let the pressure release naturally before opening the lid.

AYURVEDA NOTES

- **VATA** Use ¼ teaspoon asafoetida powder.
- **PITTA** Avoid tomatoes and peanut oil. Substitute white onions for red.
- **KAPHA** Use grapeseed oil or sunflower oil. Increase garam masala to ½ teaspoon.

INSTANT KHAMAN DHOKLA

Khaman dhokla, a traditional savory snack from the western state of Gujarat, has won the hearts of billions all over India and beyond. One of the first things I ever took to a potluck in America was my instant khaman dhokla. It was a massive hit and since then I have relied on this trusted appetizer at my get-togethers. The steamed spongy squares, made with an airy batter of chickpea flour and spices, fit right in next to platters of bruschetta, mac and cheese, spring rolls, and tossed salads. Savory, sweet, spicy, gluten-free, and packed with protein and fiber, khaman dhokla appeals to diverse palates and all ages.

While there are special dhokla steamers available, a large pot with a lid that will fit an 8-inch (20 cm) cake pan will work just as well for steaming.

PERFECT PAIRING
Serve with Hari Chutney (page 214) on the side.

MAKES 16 to 18 pieces (2 inches/5 cm wide)

Make the instant khaman dhokla batter: Sift the chickpea flour and turmeric into a medium bowl to aerate the flour and ensure there are no lumps in the batter.

In another bowl, combine the water, oil, lemon juice, sugar, and salt. Grind the ginger and green chile to a paste in a mortar and pestle. Add the paste to the wet ingredients and mix well.

Pour the spiced water mixture into the dry ingredients and whisk well for 30 to 40 seconds until the batter is smooth and there are no lumps. The batter should have a flowing consistency but be thick enough that it coats the back of a spoon. Let the batter rest for 10 to 15 minutes.

Meanwhile, add 3 cups (720 ml) water to a pot large enough to hold an 8-inch (20 cm) cake pan. Place a steel ring or a steel cup placed upside down that is at least 2 inches (5 cm) in height and 4 to 5 inches (10 to 13 cm) in diameter in the center of the pot. Cover the pot with a lid and let the water come to a boil.

Coat an 8-inch (20 cm) cake pan with oil.

Add the fruit salt to the batter and whisk vigorously for 30 seconds. Working quickly, run the whisk around the bowl, including the sides, to mix it evenly. This will make the batter get frothy and bubbly. Immediately pour the batter into the oiled cake pan and place it inside the pot.

Continued—

INSTANT KHAMAN DHOKLA BATTER

1 cup (120 g) besan/chickpea flour
¼ teaspoon ground turmeric
½ cup + 2 tablespoons (150 ml) warm water
1½ tablespoons oil, such as peanut, sunflower, or avocado
1 tablespoon lemon juice
1 teaspoon sugar
1 teaspoon fine sea salt
1-inch (2.5 cm) piece fresh ginger
1 Thai green chile
Oil, to grease the cake pan
1 teaspoon fruit salt, such as Eno fruit salt

TADKA

2 teaspoons white sesame seeds
1 teaspoon black mustard seeds
3 Thai chiles, halved lengthwise
10 to 12 fresh curry leaves
1 teaspoon sugar
½ teaspoon fine sea salt
2 tablespoons oil, such as peanut, sunflower, or avocado
¼ cup (60 ml) water

GARNISH

1 tablespoon finely chopped cilantro
1 tablespoon unsweetened shredded coconut (fresh or thawed frozen)

Cover the pot and steam the khaman dhokla for 15 minutes over medium heat. Turn off the heat and uncover the pan to test the doneness by poking a knife into the center. If the knife comes out clean, the khaman dhokla is done.

Remove the pan from the steamer and let cool for 10 to 15 minutes. Then run a sharp knife around the sides of the pan. Place a serving plate on top of the pan and invert the pan and the plate to release the khaman dhokla. Cut into 2-inch (5 cm) pieces either before or after the tempered spices are poured over the khaman dhokla.

Make the tadka: In a small bowl, combine the sesame seeds, mustard seeds, chiles, curry leaves, sugar, and salt. In a small saucepan, heat the oil over medium heat. Add the spices to the hot oil, cover (or else the seeds and curry leaves will splatter everywhere), and temper the spices for about 30 seconds. Reduce the heat, uncover, add the water, and allow everything to heat for another 30 seconds. Remove from the heat.

Spoon the tempered spices and liquid generously over the khaman dhoklas. Garnish with chopped cilantro and coconut.

AYURVEDA NOTES

- **VATA** Reduce the chile if it causes dryness or indigestion. Favor peanut oil.
- **PITTA** Reduce the chile. Favor sunflower or avocado oil.
- **KAPHA** Favor sunflower oil.

BROCCOLI BESAN KI SUBZI

SAUTÉED BROCCOLI WITH SPICED CHICKPEA FLOUR

Growing up in India, I never knew what broccoli tasted like, so when I came to the US, I ate it for the first time. While I loved it raw in my salads, I never enjoyed it cooked—until my son discovered broccoli as a toddler at his Montessori school. His love for this cruciferous vegetable got me experimenting with different recipes, including substituting broccoli for the thinly sliced green bell peppers in one of my mom's recipes. It was an instant winner and continues to be on constant repeat in my home, coming together in less than 15 minutes and pairing well with any kind of dal and rice. Any leftovers can be wrapped up inside a roti burrito along with rice and beans on the side.

PERFECT PAIRING This is an effortless side to any dal and rice, but my son's favorite is to pair it with plain rice and Khatti Meethi Gujarati Dal (page 114).

SERVES 3 or 4

TIP
Swap the broccoli out for cauliflower, bell peppers, squash, okra, or any seasonal vegetable, and give them an extra oomph with the spiced chickpea coating.

In a small bowl, mix together the chickpea flour, turmeric, coriander, Kashmiri powder, and dried mango powder. Set aside.

Heat the oil in a wok or a wide skillet (so the broccoli florets have a large surface area to sauté in) over medium heat. Once the pan is hot, add the asafoetida, cumin seeds, ginger, and garlic and sauté for few seconds. Add the broccoli florets, sprinkle with salt, and stir well. Cover and cook for 2 to 3 minutes. Uncover, stir the broccoli florets, distribute the spiced chickpea mixture over the top, and sprinkle in the water. Cover and cook for another 3 to 4 minutes. The chickpea flour will cook from the trapped steam.

Uncover, stir well, and cook until the broccoli is slightly crisp and the chickpea flour softens and turns light brown, an additional minute or two.

This dish is best served immediately.

¼ cup (30 g) besan/chickpea flour
½ teaspoon ground turmeric
½ teaspoon ground coriander
½ teaspoon Kashmiri red chili powder
½ teaspoon amchur/dried mango powder
2 tablespoons oil, such as olive, avocado, or sunflower
⅛ teaspoon hing/asafoetida powder
1 teaspoon cumin seeds
1 tablespoon finely chopped fresh ginger
1 tablespoon finely chopped garlic
5 cups (about 1 pound/450 g) broccoli florets
1 teaspoon fine sea salt
2 tablespoons water

AYURVEDA NOTES

Broccoli, rich in nutrients and fiber, helps balance kapha. Ayurveda recommends steaming cruciferous vegetables over eating them raw. Combining pungent spices with the astringent chickpea mixture offers a balanced taste, ideal for spring. Including crucifers like broccoli helps counteract kapha's tendency to increase during the heavy, damp spring season.
- **VATA** Broccoli's astringency and cooling nature may challenge vata digestion. The digestive fire gets a boost from added spices, ginger, and garlic.
- **PITTA** Minimize the ginger and garlic.
- **KAPHA** Swap the Kashmiri powder for black pepper.

KANDE BHAJJI

CHICKPEA FLOUR–COATED ONION FRITTERS

A popular street food or teatime snack in Mumbai, *bhajjis* are also known as pakoras in other parts of India and can be made using a variety of vegetables and/or greens. While some pakora recipes call for the vegetable to be dunked in a chickpea batter and fried, the traditional *kande bhajji* served in Mumbai calls for a minimal amount of chickpea flour mixed with some rice flour, creating a perfectly crunchy, crispy bhajji. Change things up by using the kande bhajjis as a filling for sandwiches or in a hot dog bun drizzled with some chutney.

PERFECT PAIRING
Serve with Hari Chutney (page 214), Imli Khajur ki Chutney (page 215), and a cup of hot Masala Chai (page 238) on the side.

SERVES 4

Neutral oil, for deep-frying—such as sunflower or peanut

2 cups (250 g) thinly sliced red onions

¾ cup (90 g) besan/chickpea flour

2 tablespoons rice flour

1 teaspoon fine sea salt

1 teaspoon ground turmeric

½ teaspoon ground cumin

½ teaspoon Kashmiri red chili powder

⅛ teaspoon baking soda

2 to 4 tablespoons water, as needed

Line a large plate with paper towels and have it near the stove. Pour 3 inches (7.5 cm) neutral oil into a deep heavy-bottomed pan and heat over medium heat to about 350°F (177°C).

Meanwhile, separate the onion slices and place in a large bowl. Add the chickpea flour, rice flour, salt, turmeric, cumin, Kashmiri powder, baking soda, and a couple of tablespoons of water and massage the onion slices to help release some of the liquid; this will help the batter stick to them. The onions will continue to release some water as they sit in the bowl, so add any additional water 1 tablespoon at a time, only as needed.

To test if the oil is hot enough (if you don't have a deep-fry thermometer), put a drop of batter into the hot oil. If it rises up immediately, then you know the oil is ready to fry. If the batter sinks to the bottom or takes time to rise up in the oil, continue to heat the oil for an additional couple of minutes.

Drop rough clumps of onion slices very carefully into the hot oil. Some will separate and some of the slices will clump together. Fry until golden brown and crispy, 3 to 4 minutes. Use a spider skimmer to remove the fritters to the paper towels to catch any excess oil. Serve hot.

TIPS
You can use yellow or white onions instead of red for this recipe, but they tend to release more liquid and the bhajjis can become soggy quickly once fried.

When dropping the onion slices into the hot oil, do your best to separate them into small clumps. Bigger mounds of kande bhajji will have a chewy texture instead of crispy. Try different amounts as per personal preference.

If you are not a fan of onions, try the same recipe with other veggies like peppers, sliced okra, broccoli florets, pickled tomatoes, zucchini, or any other seasonal vegetable of choice.

AYURVEDA NOTES

Raw onions are pungent, heating, and heavy to digest. When cooked, onions have a sweet taste and can have a grounding effect, pacifying vata and pitta dosha. Kande bhajji makes a great snack, especially during the early spring or fall/winter months.
- **VATA** Sprinkle chaat masala over bhajjis before eating.
- **PITTA** Try white onions. Skip the Kashmiri powder.
- **KAPHA** Red onions are the ideal choice.

KOTHIMBIR WADI

CHICKPEA-AND-CILANTRO SAVORY BITES

Rich in protein and fiber and naturally gluten-free, chickpea flour is one of the most hardworking flours in my pantry. I put it to good use here in one of my favorite teatime snacks. This dish, called *kothimbir wadi*, is quite popular in my home state of Maharashtra, India. The spiced chickpea flour/cilantro mixture is first cooked and set to firm up in a loaf pan. Once cooled, the soft cake is cut into squares and fried, making it perfectly crisp on the outside and delicately spongy on the inside.

PERFECT PAIRING Serve with Thecha (page 218) or Hari Chutney (page 214) along with chilled Shikanji (page 230) or a hot cup of Masala Chai (page 238), depending on the mood and weather.

SERVES 4 to 6

TIPS

Try this recipe with seasonal greens instead of cilantro or in combination with cilantro.

Instead of a shallow-fry, you can bake or air-fry kothimbir wadi. Brush the squares with some oil and spread them on a baking sheet. Bake or air-fry at 375°F (190°C) for 12 to 15 minutes until golden brown.

Kothimbir wadi squares make a great alternative to falafel. Break the wadi into smaller pieces and stuff inside a pita pocket along with toppings.

Sift the chickpea flour and rice flour into a medium bowl. Add 1 cup (240 ml) of the water and the yogurt and whisk into a smooth batter. Set the batter aside.

Heat a heavy-bottomed pan over medium heat. Add 1 tablespoon of the oil. Add the crushed peanuts and fry for about a minute. Add the asafoetida, chile, and garlic and fry for a few seconds. Slowly add the remaining 1 cup (240 ml) water and let it come to a boil. Add the salt, sugar, and turmeric. Pour in the chickpea mixture and cook over medium-low heat for 5 minutes. The mixture will start to thicken and leave the sides of the pan as it comes together. Remove from the heat, add the chopped cilantro leaves, and mix well.

Grease a standard 8-by-4-inch (20-by-10 cm) loaf pan with oil. Transfer the chickpea mixture to the pan and press down. Allow the mixture to cool and set to a texture similar to medium firm tofu, 10 to 20 minutes. Cut into 3-inch (7.5 cm) squares.

In a cast-iron skillet, heat enough oil to coat the bottom of your pan. Add the squares and shallow-fry over medium heat until golden brown on both sides, 4 to 5 minutes. Garnish with white sesame seeds. Serve warm.

1 cup (120 g) besan/chickpea flour

1 tablespoon rice flour

2 cups (480 ml) water

1 tablespoon plain yogurt

¼ cup (60 ml) oil, such as peanut, avocado, or sunflower

2 tablespoons roasted peanuts, crushed

⅛ teaspoon hing/asafoetida powder

1 Thai green chile, finely chopped

1 teaspoon finely chopped garlic

1 teaspoon fine sea salt

1 teaspoon sugar

½ teaspoon ground turmeric

2 cups (140 g) packed finely chopped cilantro (leaves and tender stems)

Oil, for greasing and frying

2 teaspoons white sesame seeds

AYURVEDA NOTES

Besan has dry, rough, and heavy gunas (qualities). It pacifies pitta and kapha but can increase vata if overconsumed, leading to bloating. Ginger and garlic aid in digestion, while cilantro cools fiery pitta, especially in summer.

- **VATA** Use ¼ teaspoon hing/asafoetida.
- **PITTA** Cilantro leaves are excellent to pacify pitta.
- **KAPHA** Add seasonal greens like spinach or kale.

KHANDVI

SAVORY CHICKPEA FLOUR ROLL-UPS

Khandvi are savory roll-ups that are a delicate melt-in-your-mouth bite-sized snack, with a custard-like texture enhanced by a topping of crunchy black mustard seeds and curry leaves. One of my cherished memories of my dad is our Sunday morning outings to our favorite Gujarati *farsan ni dhukan* (a snack store selling fresh Gujarati snacks) in Mumbai to pick up *khaman dhoklas, jalebis, patra, fafda, papaya sambharo,* and khandvi to take home for an elaborate lazy breakfast with a cup of masala chai. My mom never made khandvi at home, as it was easier to buy it from the store, but here in the US, we don't have the luxury of farsan stores where fresh khandvi is prepared daily. This inspired me to make khandvi at home, and the biggest compliment I received was when my mom said that my khandvi rolls are just as good as store-bought. It's an absolute joy to make this much-loved snack of India, one that is less familiar to Westerners.

The thickness of the batter is very important. When undercooked, the batter will be runny, making it difficult to roll, while an overcooked thickened batter is difficult to spread into a thin layer. When the batter is cooked to a proper gel stage with a soft texture, it will spread into a thin layer and, once cooled, can easily be rolled into a neat cylinder. While cooking the khandvi batter can be intimidating for some, I assure you it is fun and easy—all it requires is 15 minutes of patient stirring. And if you have young kids, they will love to help roll the batter just as mine did. Grab the ingredients and let's get started.

PERFECT PAIRING
Have with a cup of hot Masala Chai (page 238) along with other snacks like Khaman Dhokla (page 95) and Kande Bhajji (page 98).

MAKES 32 khandvi rolls (1½ inches/4 cm wide)

Oil, for the pan

1 cup (120 g) besan/chickpea flour

1 cup (230 g) plain yogurt

2 cups (480 ml) water

1½ teaspoons fine sea salt

1 teaspoon minced fresh ginger

1 teaspoon minced green chile

½ teaspoon ground turmeric

TADKA

1½ tablespoons oil, such as peanut, sunflower, or avocado

⅛ teaspoon hing/asafoetida powder

1 teaspoon black mustard seeds

1 teaspoon white sesame seeds

2 Thai green chiles, quartered lengthwise

10 to 12 fresh curry leaves

GARNISH

2 tablespoons shredded coconut (fresh, thawed frozen, or dried)

2 tablespoons finely chopped cilantro (leaves and tender stems)

Prep a clean countertop or cutting board by lightly greasing the surface with oil or lining with a silicone mat. This is where the khandvi batter will be spread once cooked and ready. Set a roll of plastic wrap and a rolling pin nearby. If you prefer not to use plastic wrap, simply oiling the rolling pin should work as well. There is no time to waste once the batter is cooked, as it must be instantly spread, so it is important to have the countertop prepped and ready before cooking begins.

In a bowl, stir together the chickpea flour, yogurt, and 1 cup (240 ml) of the water. Whisk well to a smooth batter. Add the remaining 1 cup (240 ml) water, salt, ginger, chile, and turmeric and whisk well. Transfer the mixture to a blender and blitz it for a few seconds. This will ensure even mixing and a lump-free batter.

Strain the mixture through a fine-mesh sieve into a large pan. Cook over low heat, stirring constantly, until the batter doesn't fall off the spatula when lifted and resembles peanut butter, 10 to 12 minutes. It is very important to stir constantly while scraping the edges and bottom of the pan to ensure the batter doesn't stick to the pan. The tricky stage begins after the 10-minute mark, when the batter is thick but not quite ready. You will need a little more force to stir the batter vigorously so it continues to remain lump-free. Pay close attention to the consistency. Reduce the heat or remove the pan from the heat as you check the batter for its readiness. To do this, take a little batter and spread it on the back side of a clean steel spatula or steel plate. Let it cool for a minute and see if the edges lift easily and can be rolled. If not, cook for another minute and check again.

Once the khandvi batter reaches the right consistency, you need to work quickly. Transfer the cooked batter to the prepared counter or cutting board and spread very quickly with a silicone spatula. Spread as evenly as possible into a thin layer. You may notice a few small lumps or uneven surfaces. Don't worry. Place a sheet of plastic wrap over the batter. With a rolling pin, roll it as evenly as possible until it is 1/16 to 1/8 inch (2 to 3 mm) thick.

Carefully remove the plastic wrap. With a pizza cutter or sharp knife, trim off the uneven edges and create a neat rectangle, 16 by 24 inches (40 by 61 cm). Cut the khandvi sheet lengthwise into two strips, 8 by 24 inches (20 by 61 cm). Then cut those strips into 16 equal pieces, 8 by 1½ inches (20 by 4 cm). You will have 32 pieces in total. Carefully lift the short edge of each strip and firmly but gently roll the dough into a tight cylindrical shape. Transfer the khandvi rolls to a serving plate.

Make the tadka: In a small saucepan, heat the oil over medium heat. Add the asafoetida, mustard seeds, and sesame seeds and let them splutter in the hot oil for a few seconds. Reduce the heat and add the chiles and curry leaves and immediately spread the tempering over the khandvi rolls.

Serve khandvi warm, room temperature, or cold. Garnish with shredded coconut and chopped cilantro.

TIPS

For a vegan version, use soy yogurt plus 1 tablespoon lemon juice instead of plain yogurt.

If you overcooked the khandvi batter and it is not spreadable, return it to the pan and break it apart like a scrambled egg. Temper the spices and pour on top along with the garnish. You may not have khandvi rolls, but you have equally delicious khandvi scramble. You can even put some green scallions on top along with other veggies, like grated carrots and chopped peppers, to create a yummy hash. Enjoy as a side or use as a filling for tacos or sandwiches. Nothing goes to waste in the kitchen. Mishaps are miracles in disguise!

AYURVEDA NOTES

- **VATA** Use peanut oil and ¼ teaspoon asafoetida.
- **PITTA** Favor sunflower oil. Reduce or omit the green chile.
- **KAPHA** Favor sunflower oil. Be generous with the cilantro garnish.

SINDHI KADHI AND ALOO TUK

TART CHICKPEA AND VEGETABLE STEW

Sunday afternoons are made for enjoying Sindhi *kadhi*, *chawaran* (rice), and *aloo tuk* (recipe follows), a tradition common in many Sindhi homes, including mine when I was growing up. The tangy, hot, spicy, soupy kadhi is cooked with an assortment of vegetables and served with piping-hot rice and extra-crispy double-fried smashed potatoes (aloo tuk) on the side. It's nostalgia, culture, and warmth in every mouthful.

Not every Sindhi kadhi is the same. My mom's recipe uses only chickpea flour in the kadhi and she likes the addition of fresh tamarind pulp for tartness, while my aunt's Sindhi kadhi combines chickpea flour along with cooked toor dal and tangy tomatoes. No matter the variation, the inviting aroma of chickpea flour roasting in hot oil along with spices creates an ideal mood for a cozy family meal together—made even better when followed by an afternoon nap! It's worth it to look for either fresh or frozen drumstick pods from any Indian grocery store. To eat the cooked pods, open them up and scoop the pulp with your teeth, similar to eating steamed artichokes. Scooping and eating the drumstick pulp from the pods is a delectable experience everyone should try!

SERVES 4

---

5 tablespoons (75 ml) neutral oil

10 to 12 okra pods, ends trimmed, halved lengthwise

1 cup (120 g) besan/chickpea flour

6 cups (1.4 L) water

1 tablespoon tamarind concentrate

1½ teaspoons fine sea salt

½ teaspoon ground turmeric

10 to 12 guvar phali/cluster beans, ends trimmed, or French green beans

1 medium potato, cut into medium chunks

1 cup (80 g) cauliflower florets

8 to 10 fresh or frozen 3-inch (7.5 cm) long moringa/drumstick pods (optional)

TADKA

1 tablespoon oil, such as peanut, avocado, or sunflower

¼ teaspoon hing/asafoetida powder

1 teaspoon cumin seeds

1 teaspoon fenugreek seeds

2 Thai green chiles, halved lengthwise

10 to 12 fresh curry leaves (optional)

1 teaspoon Kashmiri red chili powder

Fine sea salt

GARNISH

2 tablespoons finely chopped cilantro (leaves and tender stems, optional)

Aloo Tuk (recipe follows)

In a 4-quart (4 L) pot, heat 1 tablespoon of the oil over medium heat. Add the okra and stir gently to coat evenly. Sauté until the okra softens with some brown spots, 2 to 3 minutes. Remove the okra to a bowl and set aside.

In the same pot, heat the remaining 4 tablespoons oil over medium heat. Add the chickpea flour and roast over medium-low heat, stirring constantly with a whisk, to a light caramel color, 5 to 6 minutes. Stirring ensures even roasting and keeps the chickpea flour from burning.

Reduce the heat, add 3 cups (720 ml) of the water, and whisk well, making sure there are no lumps. Add the remaining 3 cups (720 ml) water, tamarind concentrate, salt, and turmeric and whisk well. Add the beans, potato, cauliflower, and drumstick pods (if using) and bring to a boil. Reduce the heat to medium and cook until the vegetables soften, 10 to 12 minutes. Add the fried okra to the kadhi and simmer.

Continued—

Make the tadka: In a small saucepan, heat the oil over medium heat. Add the asafoetida, cumin seeds, and fenugreek seeds and let sizzle for a few seconds. Carefully add the green chiles, curry leaves (if using), and Kashmiri powder. Give it a quick mix. Pour the tadka into the kadhi pot and stir well. Season with salt to taste.

Serve warm, garnished with cilantro if using, alongside Aloo Tuk (page 107) on the side.

TIPS

Add seasonal vegetables of choice, such as baby eggplant or carrots.

Skip frying the okra and add it raw along with other vegetables to cook in the kadhi.

AYURVEDA NOTES

- **VATA** The sourness of tamarind is balancing. Favor peanut oil.
- **PITTA** Favor sunflower or avocado oil. Reduce the green chile and salt. Enjoy in moderation due to sourness of tamarind.
- **KAPHA** Use sunflower oil. Reduce the salt. Add plenty of seasonal vegetables. Enjoy in moderation as sour taste increases kapha secretions.

ALOO TUK:
DOUBLE-FRIED SMASHED POTATOES

SERVES 4 to 6

Sindhi kadhi and *chawaran* are incomplete without extra-crispy *aloo tuk* on the side. While aloo tuks are traditionally deep-fried, not just once but twice, you can opt for skillet-frying, air-frying, or baking in an oven. Aloo tuks should be crispy on the outside and soft and fluffy on the inside. For best results, use new potatoes as they soften faster and crisp better. You can keep the skin on the potatoes or peel them.

Wash the potatoes, peel or leave the skin on, cut them in halves, and soak in a bowl of cold salted water for 10 minutes. Drain and pat dry with a kitchen towel.

Pour about 3 inches (7.5 cm) of oil in a large pan or Dutch oven and heat to about 350°F (177°C).

Working in batches to avoid crowding the pan, add the potatoes and fry for 3 to 4 minutes over medium heat. The first round of frying is to cook the potatoes slightly but not to brown them. Remove with a slotted spoon to a plate lined with paper towels.

Once they are cool enough to handle, take each potato piece and place between a couple layers of paper towels and press down with your hands or use the bottom of a glass to carefully flatten it into a thick disc without breaking it.

Line a plate with paper towels and have it near the stove. Increase the oil temperature to about 375°F (190°C). Working in batches again, fry the smashed potatoes until crispy and golden brown on both sides, 4 to 5 minutes. Remove the potatoes with a slotted spoon to the paper towels to drain.

Arrange on a serving dish and generously sprinkle the ground spices, one at a time, evenly over the aloo tuks and serve.

1 pound (500 g) small
   new potatoes or baby
   potatoes
1 teaspoon fine sea salt
Neutral oil, for frying
GARNISH
Kala namak/Indian black
   salt or Himalayan pink
   rock salt
Ground coriander
Ground cumin
Amchur/dried mango
   powder
Kashmiri red chili powder

AYURVEDA NOTES

- **VATA** Substitute black pepper for the Kashmiri powder as it aids in digesting potatoes better.
- **PITTA** Eat in moderation. Garnish generously with digestive spices like coriander and cumin. Omit the Kashmiri powder.
- **KAPHA** Eat in moderation. Use sunflower oil and garnish with spices generously. Substitute black pepper for the Kashmiri powder for its kapha-pacifying properties.

BESAN LADDOOS

SWEET CHICKPEA-FLOUR TRUFFLES

Making *besan laddoos* for my family and friends is one of my favorite traditions each year during Diwali, the Indian festival of lights, when I make special homemade sweets and savory treats. Laddoos can be time-consuming to make, requiring constantly stirring chickpea flour with ghee on the stove until it roasts to a peanut butter–like color. However, my foolproof recipe uses the oven, no laborious stirring required! The addition of nuts and seeds adds a bit of crunch and makes these laddoos extra nutrient-dense, a perfect after-school snack and a great alternative to processed protein bars. Besan laddoos are traditionally prepared with a coarse variety of chickpea flour found in Indian grocery stores called *laddoo besan,* but regular besan works just fine.

MAKES 24 truffles

1½ cups (180 g) besan/
chickpea flour

½ cup (115 g) ghee,
or ½ cup (115 g)
unsalted butter,
melted

½ cup (50 g) ground
almonds

¼ cup (30 g) white
poppy seeds

¼ cup (30 g) hemp
hearts, plus 2
tablespoons for
garnish

½ teaspoon ground
cardamom

¾ cup (90 g)
powdered sugar

Preheat the oven to 350°F (180°C).

In a wide ovenproof glass or ceramic baking dish, mix together the chickpea flour and melted ghee. Place the dish in the oven and set a timer for 10 minutes.

Remove from the oven and stir the chickpea/ghee mixture really well so everything roasts evenly. At this stage you will begin to smell the aroma of chickpea flour as it heats up. Repeat this process in 10-minute increments one or two more times. The ghee will start to separate from the flour when it is roasted well, and the mixture will look like peanut butter in texture and color.

Let the mixture cool for 15 to 20 minutes at room temperature.

Once the chickpea mixture has cooled down slightly, add the ground almonds, poppy seeds, hemp hearts, and cardamom and mix well with your hands. Finally, add the powdered sugar and mix by hand.

Divide the mixture into 24 portions; I like to use a 1-tablespoon cookie scoop to portion the mixture. Shape the laddoos into a tight ball with the palm of your hands by pressing firmly. Sprinkle a few hemp hearts on top of each laddoo.

Allow the laddoos to rest for 1 hour and the ghee will firm them up a bit. There is no need to refrigerate the laddoos; store in an airtight container for up to 3 to 4 weeks.

TIPS
Skip the nuts and seeds to make this recipe nut- and seed-free.

You can also add other nuts like cashews or pistachios.

TOOR

TOOR

SANSKRIT NAMES: Adhaki / Tuvara / Tuvarika / Shanapushpika
OTHER INDIAN NAMES: Arhar / Tuvar / Tur / Kandi Pappu /
Thuvara Paruppu / Togari Bele
ENGLISH NAMES: Pigeon Pea / Red Gram Dal / Congo Bean / Gungo Pea
BOTANICAL NAMES: *Cajanus Cajan / Cajanus Indicus*

Toor dal (commonly known in English as pigeon pea) is one of the most beloved dals of India and enjoyed in different ways all over the world. Cultivated in India for the last 3,500 years, toor can be found in regional recipes across India, from the quintessential Gujarati dal of the West (page 114) to the classic *dhaba dal tadka* (page 117), the ultimate comfort dal of the North, to the humble Odiya Dalma (page 119) of the East and the splendid *sambhar* (page 120) and *rasam* (page 122) of the South. If you have a cup of toor dal precooked with just salt and some ground turmeric ready, you can cook almost all the recipes in this chapter, including a few nontraditional recipes.

India is both the largest consumer and producer of toor, accounting for 90 percent of global production. One of the most nutritious pulses and the first legume to have its genome completely sequenced, toor has been gaining prominence internationally with growing evidence of its many health benefits, such as reducing the risk of type 2 diabetes and cardiovascular diseases with regular consumption. Like other legumes, toor is rich in fiber, protein, complex carbohydrates, and many essential nutrients.

Shelled fresh green pigeon peas, also known as *lilva tuvar*, are easily found in Indian grocery stores in the frozen section and cooked as a winter vegetable (see Lili Tuvar nu Shaak, page 127). It is quite popular in regional cuisine of Gujarat, a western state of India. The shelled fresh green pigeon peas can be added to salads or lightly steamed and enjoyed as a snack. Once dried, the mature pigeon peas are hulled and split to its most commonly consumed form, known as toor dal. You may sometimes find an oiled variety of toor dal in the store, which has been smeared with castor or mustard oil and dried for a few days before it is packed to preserve its shelf life; I do not recommend this variety, as it runs the risk of becoming rancid. I simply stock regular dried toor dal in my pantry.

The names for the pigeon pea in Indian languages originate from two Sanskrit words: *adhaki,* meaning "one-half," referring to the fact that the pigeon peas are almost always consumed after they have been hulled and split. The second Sanskrit name is *tuvara,* meaning "astringent," a reference to the flavor of the pigeon peas. Toor is considered one of the most nutritious foods in Ayurveda, with an astringent, sweet taste, and dry qualities that make it light to digest. It balances pitta and kapha dosha, and excess consumption can increase vata dosha.

KHATTI MEETHI GUJARATI DAL

SWEET AND TANGY TOOR DAL WITH PEANUTS

Both my mom and dad were raised in Ghatkopar, a suburb of Mumbai with a strong Gujarati community. They spoke fluent Gujarati and even knew how to read and write in the Gujarati language. Growing up, Gujarati dal was on the menu at home as often as Sindhi kadhi and sambhar, as my mom loved to cook a variety of regional cuisines for us. This recipe is reminiscent of my childhood flavors the way my mom made it and how I have made it my own over the years for my kids.

PERFECT PAIRING Serve with plain steamed short- or medium-grain rice, such as Ambemohar.

SERVES 4 to 6

SOAK TIME 30 minutes to 1 hour

---

1 cup (200 g) toor dal/split pigeon peas

5 cups (1.2 L) water

1 teaspoon fine sea salt

1½ teaspoons ground turmeric

1 medium tomato, chopped

¼ cup (50 g) packed jaggery powder, or 2 heaping tablespoons brown sugar

1 tablespoon lemon juice

2 teaspoons grated fresh ginger

1 teaspoon Kashmiri red chili powder

TADKA

2 tablespoons (30 g) ghee

⅓ cup (50 g) raw peanuts

⅛ teaspoon hing/asafoetida powder

1 teaspoon cumin seeds

1 teaspoon black mustard seeds

1 teaspoon fenugreek seeds

4 whole cloves

½ cinnamon stick, broken roughly into 1- to 2-inch (2.5 to 5 cm) pieces

2 dried Kashmiri red chiles, whole

8 to 10 fresh curry leaves

1 cup (240 ml) water (optional)

Fine sea salt, as needed

GARNISH

¼ cup (15 g) finely chopped cilantro

1 tablespoon unsweetened shredded coconut (fresh or thawed frozen)

Rinse the toor dal in a fine-mesh sieve under cold running water until the water runs clear, about a minute. Transfer to a medium bowl, add water to cover by 2 inches (5 cm), and soak for 30 minutes to 1 hour. Drain.

In a medium pot, combine the dal, water, salt, turmeric, and tomatoes. Bring to a boil, skimming off any foam. Reduce the heat to medium, partially cover, and and cook until the dal is soft and mushy when pressed between your fingers, about 40 minutes.

Puree the dal smooth using an immersion blender or a hand whisk. Add the jaggery, lemon juice, ginger, and Kashmiri powder, stirring until combined. Simmer the dal over low heat.

Make the tadka: In a small saucepan, heat the ghee over medium heat. Add the peanuts and fry them for a minute. Add the asafoetida, cumin seeds, mustard seeds, and fenugreek seeds, and let sizzle for a few seconds. Add the cloves, cinnamon stick, dried chiles, and curry leaves and fry for 10 to 15 seconds.

Pour the tadka (tempered spices) into the simmering pot of dal and stir. Add the water if needed for a good soupy consistency, similar to or slightly runnier than heavy cream. Bring the dal mixture to a final boil, then reduce the heat to a simmer until served. Season to taste with salt.

Garnish with cilantro and coconut and serve warm.

TIPS

Combine the soaked dal, salt, turmeric, and tomatoes and pressure-cook on high for 6 minutes in an electric pressure cooker. Let the pressure release naturally before opening the lid.

AYURVEDA NOTES

- **VATA** Cut back on the chiles and Kashmiri powder if they cause dryness.
- **PITTA** Substitute lime for lemon juice to reduce heat. Omit or reduce the Kashmiri powder and dried chiles. The garnish of cilantro and coconut is cooling and adds balance.
- **KAPHA** This dish's heating nature balances kapha, countering the heaviness of sugar and peanuts.

DHABA-STYLE EASY DAL FRY

RUSTIC TOOR DAL TEMPERED WITH FIERY SPICES

Dal fry is a popular Punjabi comfort food in homes, in restaurants, and at highway truck-stop eateries called *dhabas*. One of the best parts of taking a road trip in India is stopping at dhabas, where they usually have a signature dal fry served with jeera rice, naan (flatbread baked in a tandoor clay oven), thinly sliced red onions, and a lemon wedge. My mom made dal fry weekly, and I follow the same tradition in my home with a pre-cooked toor dal topped with fresh tadka (tempered spices) just before serving. This easy dal fry is perfect for a weeknight and goes well with rice, roti (Indian flatbread cooked on a stovetop pan), naan, or a crusty sourdough toast on the side. The bold flavors from the tadka complement the thick, luscious consistency of the dal fry, thanks to the addition of a couple of tablespoons of split masoor dal.

PERFECT PAIRING
Serve with plain steamed basmati rice, Jeera Rice (page 156), or Sindhi Dum Biryani (page 173).

SERVES 4

SOAK TIME
30 minutes to 1 hour

Combine the toor and masoor dal in a fine-mesh sieve and rinse under cold running water until the water runs clear, about a minute. Transfer to a medium bowl, add water to cover by 2 inches (5 cm), and soak for 30 minutes to 1 hour. Drain.

In a 3-quart (3 L) pot, combine the dal, water, salt, and turmeric. Partially cover and cook over medium heat, skimming off any foam, until the dal is soft and mushy when pressed between your fingers, about 40 minutes, uncovering the pot every 10 minutes to stir so that the dal doesn't stick to the bottom of the pan. Add more water as necessary; the consistency of the cooked dal should be thick and not very soupy.

In a large skillet, warm the ghee over medium heat. Add the cumin, Kashmiri chile, ginger, garlic, and green chiles and sauté for 30 to 40 seconds. Add the chopped onions and sauté, stirring regularly, until the onions are light golden brown, 5 to 6 minutes.

Stir in the tomatoes and salt and cook until the tomatoes soften, 3 to 4 minutes. Add the deggi mirch, turmeric, coriander, mango powder, and garam masala. Mix well and cook for another minute.

Continued—

1 cup (200 g) toor dal/split pigeon peas
2 tablespoons masoor dal/split red lentils
3 cups (720 ml) water
1 teaspoon fine sea salt
½ teaspoon ground turmeric

FIRST TADKA
2 tablespoons (30 g) ghee or unsalted butter
1 teaspoon cumin seeds
1 dried Kashmiri red chile
1-inch (2.5 cm) piece fresh ginger, finely chopped
3 garlic cloves, finely chopped
2 Thai green chiles, finely chopped
1 large red onion, finely chopped
½ pound (225 g) tomatoes, finely chopped
½ teaspoon fine sea salt, plus more to taste
1 teaspoon deggi mirch chili powder
½ teaspoon ground turmeric
½ teaspoon ground coriander
½ teaspoon amchur/dried mango powder
½ teaspoon garam masala (page 40)
1½ teaspoons kasuri methi/dried fenugreek leaves
2 tablespoons finely chopped cilantro (leaves and tender stems)

SECOND TADKA
1 tablespoon (15 g) ghee or unsalted butter
¼ teaspoon hing/asafoetida powder
1 small red onion, thinly sliced
½ teaspoon Kashmiri red chili powder

FOR SERVING
Thinly sliced red onions
Salt
Lemon wedges, for squeezing

Add the cooked dal to the skillet and mix well. Crush the fenugreek leaves between your palms and add to the pot, along with cilantro. Stir well and let the dal simmer over low heat for 5 to 10 minutes or until ready to serve. Season to taste with salt.

When ready to serve, make the second tadka: In a small skillet, warm the ghee over medium heat until hot. Add the asafoetida and onions and sauté, stirring constantly, until the onions are golden brown, 5 to 6 minutes. Add the Kashmiri powder and immediately pour over the dal fry.

Serve warm with sliced red onions, salt, and lemon wedges for squeezing. Squeeze lemon juice over the dal and red onions before eating.

TIPS

To cook the soaked dals in an electric pressure cooker, pressure-cook at high temperature for 6 minutes. Let the pressure release naturally before opening the lid.

For a vegan version, use peanut, sunflower, or vegetable oil of choice instead of ghee/butter.

AYURVEDA NOTES

- **VATA** Cooked onion aids vata digestion. Avoid raw onions as they can be heavy. Reduce chile powders if they cause dryness.
- **PITTA** Enjoy in moderation, especially on hot days. Reduce chile powders and Thai green chile. Use lime wedges instead of lemon.
- **KAPHA** This recipe is kapha-reducing, from toor dal to raw onion. Be mindful of ghee amounts for the tadka.

ODIYA DALMA

BENGALI-STYLE VEGETABLE STEW

A medley of hearty vegetables cooked with toor dal, this staple dish from the eastern state of Odisha—known for its rich heritage, temples, and beaches—highlights the use of pungent mustard oil and the traditional *panch phoran* (five-spice) blend used in north eastern Indian cuisine. It also has a connection with Lord Jagannath, the blue-hued avatar of Lord Vishnu, for its traditional offering of an elaborate feast of fifty-six dishes, called *chappan bhog*, using locally grown vegetables and pulses cooked in earthen pots. While there are many variations to *dalma*, I have tried my best to honor the temple dalma recipe without the use of onions or garlic, which is a common practice in Hindu culture when meals are prepared for sacred occasions as a way to maintain ritual purity.

PERFECT PAIRING
Serve with short- or medium-grain rice.

SERVES 4

SOAK TIME 30 minutes to 1 hour

Rinse the toor dal in a fine-mesh sieve under cold running water until the water runs clear, about a minute. Transfer to a medium bowl, add water to cover by 2 inches (5 cm), and soak for 30 minutes to 1 hour. Drain.

In a medium pot, combine the dal, water, turmeric, and salt and bring to a boil, skimming off any foam. Lower the heat to medium, partially cover, and cook for 15 to 20 minutes. The dal will begin to soften and cook about halfway.

Add the eggplants, potatoes, pumpkin, plantain, and daikon and continue to cook until the vegetables soften and the dal is soft and mushy when pressed between your fingers, 15 to 20 minutes. Stir in the coconut and reduce the heat to a simmer.

Make the Panch Phoran: In a small bowl, combine the cumin, mustard, fenugreek, fennel, and nigella seeds.

Make the tadka: In a small saucepan, heat the oil over medium heat until hot. Add the bay leaves and panch phoran spice mix. Let the spices sizzle for 30 to 40 seconds before pouring the tadka into the stew. Stir, season with salt to taste, and serve warm.

1 cup (200 g) toor dal/split pigeon peas

4 cups (960 ml) water

1 teaspoon ground turmeric

1 teaspoon fine sea salt

2 small fairy tale eggplants, cut into 1-inch (2.5 cm) pieces

4 small red potatoes, cut into 1-inch (2.5 cm) pieces

8 ounces (225 g) pumpkin, peeled, or yellow summer squash, cut into 1-inch (2.5 cm) pieces

9 ounces (250 g) green plantain, peeled and cut into 1-inch (2.5 cm) pieces

8 ounces (225 g) daikon radish, peeled and cut into 1-inch (2.5 cm) pieces

½ cup (40 g) unsweetened shredded coconut (fresh or thawed frozen)

PANCH PHORAN

½ teaspoon cumin seeds

½ teaspoon black mustard seeds

½ teaspoon fenugreek seeds

½ teaspoon fennel seeds

½ teaspoon nigella seeds

TADKA

2 tablespoons mustard oil or ghee

2 tej patta/Indian bay leaves

2½ teaspoons Panch Phoran

AYURVEDA NOTES

- **VATA** Favor sweet potato over red potato. Substitute carrots, beets, zucchini, squash, and/ or okra for the eggplant and daikon radish.
- **PITTA** Use avocado or olive oil instead of mustard oil. Favor peas, okra, yams, summer squash, and sweet potatoes over daikon radish and eggplant.
- **KAPHA** Favor summer squash and white potato over pumpkin and sweet potato/yam for a lighter dish.

TIFFIN SAMBHAR

SOUTH INDIAN TOOR DAL

Sambhar is an integral part of the traditional South Indian meal, which also includes rice and other side dishes. Made with pigeon peas, vegetables, tamarind, and spices, sambhar is consumed regularly in homes and restaurants across India.

Tiffin refers to snack time between meals in South India. This is my go-to recipe to serve with idlis, dosas, and vadai. You can certainly cook dal and vegetables in one pot, but I like to cook the vegetables and dal in two separate pots and combine them with the sambhar spice paste. The spice paste gives an authentic taste and a much better texture to the sambhar. If you don't have time to make the paste, use 1 tablespoon store-bought sambhar powder instead. I change the vegetables seasonally and sometimes only use one vegetable to highlight its distinct flavor, such as pearl onions, pumpkin, or daikon radish.

PERFECT PAIRING
Serve with dosas (page 199), Medu Vada (page 137), or plain rice (see Rice 101, page 152).

SERVES 4

SOAK TIME 30 minutes to 1 hour

POT ONE
1 cup (200 g) toor dal/split pigeon peas
4 cups (960 ml) water
1 teaspoon fine sea salt
1 teaspoon ground turmeric

POT TWO
1 tablespoon sesame oil or coconut oil
¼ teaspoon hing/asafoetida powder
½ teaspoon fenugreek seeds
1 teaspoon black mustard seeds
10 to 12 fresh curry leaves
4 ounces (115 g) baby pearl onions or tiny shallots (8 to 10), peeled
4 okra pods, ends trimmed, cut into 1-inch (2.5 cm) pieces
8 ounces (225 g) pumpkin, peeled and cut into 1-inch (2.5 cm) pieces
Ten 3-inch (7.5 cm) moringa/drumstick pods (optional)
3 cups (720 ml) water
½ teaspoon fine sea salt
1½ tablespoons tamarind concentrate
1 tablespoon tightly packed jaggery powder or brown sugar

SPICE PASTE
1 tablespoon sesame oil or coconut oil
1 tablespoon chana dal/peeled and split chickpeas
1 tablespoon dhuli urad dal/peeled split black gram
1 tablespoon coriander seeds
½ teaspoon cumin seeds
½ teaspoon black peppercorns
3 dried red chiles, such as Byadagi or Kashmiri
¼ cup (20 g) unsweetened shredded coconut
1 medium tomato, roughly chopped
1 small red onion, roughly chopped
1 cup (240 ml) water

GARNISH
2 tablespoons finely chopped cilantro (leaves and tender stems)
Fine sea salt

To cook the soaked dal in an electric pressure cooker, pressure-cook on high for 6 minutes. Let the pressure release naturally before opening the lid.

Use coconut oil in summertime, as it is cooling. Use sesame oil in spring, fall, and winter for its warming qualities.

Some vegetables that work well in a sambhar are daikon radish, amaranth leaves, spinach, squash, eggplant, ash gourd, bottle gourd, and plantain. Use any or a combination according to season and availability.

For pot one: Rinse the toor dal in a fine-mesh sieve under cold running water until the water runs clear, about a minute. Transfer to a medium bowl, add water to cover by 2 inches (5 cm), and soak for 30 minutes to 1 hour. Drain.

In a 3-quart (3 L) pot, combine the soaked dal, water, salt, and turmeric. Partially cover and cook over medium heat, skimming off any foam, until the dal is soft and mushy, about 40 minutes. Remove from the heat and use a whisk or immersion blender to puree the dal to a smooth consistency.

When the dal is about halfway done: In another 3-quart (3 L) pot, heat the oil over medium heat. Add the asafoetida, fenugreek seeds, and mustard seeds and let them sizzle for a minute. Add the fresh curry leaves, baby pearl onions, okra, pumpkin, and drumstick pods (if using). Add the water and salt and cook the vegetables until soft, about 20 minutes.

Add the pureed toor dal to the vegetables along with the tamarind concentrate and jaggery and stir well. Simmer over low heat.

Meanwhile, make the spice paste: In a medium skillet, heat the oil over medium heat. Add the chana dal and urad dal and fry to golden brown, 1 to 2 minutes. Add the coriander seeds, cumin seeds, peppercorns, and whole chiles and sauté for a minute. Add the coconut and sauté until golden brown, about 1 minute. Add the tomato and onion and sauté for an additional 3 to 4 minutes. Transfer all the ingredients from the skillet to a blender and add the water. Remove the steam vent from the blender lid and grind to a smooth paste.

Stir the spice paste into the cooked vegetables and dal. Bring everything to a boil, then reduce the heat and simmer over low until ready to serve.

Garnish the sambhar with the cilantro. Stir well and season to taste with salt.

AYURVEDA NOTES

- **VATA** Favor sesame oil. Decrease the chile powder and whole red chiles.
- **PITTA** Favor coconut oil. Decrease or skip the chile powder and whole red chiles.
- **KAPHA** Vegetables and spices balance kapha, but use oil in moderation.

NIMMAKAYA RASAM

LEMON PEPPER–SPICED DAL BROTH

Rasam is derived from the Sanskrit word *rasa*, which means essence, juice, or extract. It is a tangy, spicy broth that is an essential part of the traditional South Indian cuisine. It is also called *saar, saaru, chaaru,* and *pulusu* in other South Indian languages. While it is typically made with tomatoes or tamarind, I find the combination of lemon (*nimmakaya* or *nimbu*) and pepper in this rasam recipe easy and well balanced. It is one I keep in my culinary arsenal to support my family's immune health on a regular basis. The spices not only pack a fiery flavor but also come in handy with digestive issues, upper respiratory ailments, fevers, and the flu.

SERVES 4

SOAK TIME 30 minutes to 1 hour

¼ cup (50 g) toor dal/split pigeon peas
6 cups (1.4 L) water
½ teaspoon fine sea salt
¼ teaspoon ground turmeric
SPICE PASTE
4 to 5 garlic cloves, peeled but whole
½-inch (1.3 cm) piece fresh ginger, roughly chopped
1 Thai green chile or ½ serrano chile
½ cup (20 g) finely chopped cilantro (leaves and tender stems)
2 teaspoons cumin seeds
¼ teaspoon black peppercorns
TADKA
1 tablespoon sesame oil or vegetable oil of choice
⅛ teaspoon hing/asafoetida powder
1 teaspoon black mustard seeds
10 to 12 fresh curry leaves
1 medium tomato, diced
½ teaspoon fine sea salt
¼ teaspoon ground turmeric
¼ teaspoon Kashmiri red chili powder
Grated zest and juice of 1 lemon
1 tablespoon finely chopped cilantro (leaves and tender stems)
1 tablespoon unsweetened shredded coconut (fresh or thawed frozen), optional
4 thin lemon slices

Rinse the toor dal in a fine-mesh sieve under cold running water until the water runs clear, about a minute. Transfer to a medium bowl, add water to cover by 2 inches (5 cm), and soak for 30 minutes to 1 hour. Drain.

In a 3-quart (3 L) pot, combine the soaked dal, 3 cups (720 ml) of the water, salt, and turmeric and bring to a boil, skimming off any foam. Lower the heat, partially cover, and cook until soft and mushy, about 40 minutes.

Make a coarse paste of garlic, ginger, chile, cilantro, cumin seeds, and peppercorns using a mortar and pestle or a small spice grinder. Set aside.

Make the tadka: In another 3-quart (3 L) pot, heat the oil over medium heat. Add the asafoetida, mustard seeds, and curry leaves. Be careful as the seeds and leaves will splutter in the hot oil. Add the spice paste and fry for about 1 minute over medium heat. Add the tomato, salt, turmeric, and Kashmiri powder. Sauté for about 1 minute.

Add the cooked dal along with the cooking liquid to the pot with the tadka. Add the the remaining 3 cups (720 ml) water, increase the heat to medium-high, and let the rasam boil for a few minutes. Reduce the heat and puree the rasam with an immersion blender until smooth. Continue to cook the rasam over medium-low heat for 5 more minutes for the flavors to meld.

Remove from the heat and stir in the lemon zest, lemon juice, cilantro, and coconut. Garnish with lemon slices, season to taste, and serve hot.

AYURVEDA NOTES

- **VATA** Cut back on the chiles.
- **PITTA** Reduce or skip the green chiles and Kashmiri powder. Opt for avocado or sunflower oil instead of sesame oil. Use lime instead of lemon.
- **KAPHA** Use grapeseed oil for the tadka. Skip the shredded coconut garnish.

METHI MALAI SULTANI DAL

CREAMY TOOR DAL WITH SEASONAL GREENS

This rich and creamy dal is inspired by two popular North Indian dishes. *Sultani dal* is a yogurt-based stew reserved for special occasions from the Mughlai/Awadhi cuisine, while *methi mattar malai* combines seasonal fenugreek leaves with cream and milk. The addition of bitter fenugreek leaves in the sultani dal cuts the heaviness from the cream and is especially warming during cooler months.

PERFECT PAIRING Serve with Jeera Rice (page 156) or Hara Bhara Pulav (page 168) along with Gajar ka Achaar (page 221).

SERVES 4

SOAK TIME 30 minutes to 1 hour

---

1 cup (200 g) toor dal/split pigeon peas

1 tablespoon ghee

2 cups (480 ml) water

1 cup (240 ml) whole milk

½ teaspoon fine sea salt

2 whole cloves

1 green cardamom pod

TADKA

2 tablespoons ghee

2 teaspoons oil, such as peanut, sunflower, avocado, or grapeseed

1 teaspoon shahi jeera/caraway seeds

3 garlic cloves, finely chopped

1 medium red onion, finely chopped

1 cup (85 g) finely chopped fenugreek (leaves and tender stalks), fresh or thawed frozen

1 small cinnamon stick

½ teaspoon ground turmeric

½ teaspoon deggi mirch chili powder

½ teaspoon ground coriander

½ teaspoon fine sea salt

½ cup (115 g) plain yogurt, whisked smooth

2 tablespoons finely chopped cilantro (leaves and tender stems)

1 tablespoon finely chopped mint

½ cup (120 ml) water

GARNISH

1 tablespoon ghee

4 garlic cloves, thinly sliced

Fine sea salt

2 tablespoons heavy cream

¼ teaspoon coarsely crushed black pepper

¼ teaspoon freshly grated nutmeg

1 tablespoon finely chopped cilantro (leaves and tender stems)

Rinse the toor dal in a fine-mesh sieve under cold running water until the water runs clear, about a minute. Transfer to a medium bowl, add water to cover by 2 inches (5 cm), and soak for 30 minutes to 1 hour. Drain.

In a 3-quart (3 L) pot or Dutch oven, heat the ghee over medium heat. Add the soaked dal and sauté for 30 to 40 seconds. Stir in the water, milk, salt, cloves, and cardamom pod. Bring to a boil, partially cover, and cook until the dal is soft and mushy, about 40 minutes. Check periodically to give a quick stir and make sure the dal is not sticking to the bottom of the pot.

Meanwhile, make the tadka: In a medium skillet, heat the ghee and oil over medium heat. Add the caraway seeds and let sizzle for 10 to 15 seconds. Add the garlic

TIPS

For a vegan dish, use oil (peanut, sunflower, avocado, grapeseed) instead of ghee. And instead of milk, use cashew paste. Soak ¾ cup (90 g) cashews in 2 cups (480 ml) water for a couple of hours. Grind the cashews along with the soaking water to a thin paste. Cook the dal with just water, salt, and turmeric. Add the cashew paste once the dal is cooked. Whisk well and proceed with the tempering.

In place of fenugreek leaves, use seasonal greens, such as finely chopped kale, Swiss chard, or dandelion greens.

If you are unable to find caraway seeds, substitute cumin seeds.

To make this in an electric pressure cooker, select Sauté and cook the soaked dal in the ghee before adding the cooking liquids and spices. Pressure-cook on high for 6 minutes. Let the pressure release naturally before opening the lid and proceeding with next steps.

and onion and cook until the onions begin to turn golden brown, 5 to 7 minutes. Add the fenugreek and fry until it reduces in quantity and most of the water is cooked off, 3 to 4 minutes. Stir in the cinnamon stick, turmeric, deggi mirch, coriander, and salt. Stir well. Add the whisked yogurt, cilantro, and mint and stir constantly for 2 to 3 minutes until the yogurt is well cooked and thickened in consistency. Look for specks of oil/ghee to separate from the mixture and start to float on top and at the edges.

Transfer this mixture to the pot with the cooked dal. Mix everything well. Add the water to the skillet and stir well to clean out any residual yogurt mixture in the pan, then pour that liquid into the pot of dal. (Keep the skillet for the next step.) Cook the dal for an additional 5 to 10 minutes over medium-low heat.

In the same skillet, heat the ghee over medium heat. Add the garlic and fry for a minute or so until golden brown. Pour the garlic over the cooked dal. This dal is traditionally thick in consistency, but you can thin with water to your own preference. Season to taste with salt.

To serve, add a drizzle of heavy cream and sprinkle with the black pepper and nutmeg. Garnish with the cilantro.

AYURVEDA NOTES

- **VATA** Toor dal, dairy, and spices are nourishing for vata.
- **PITTA** Cut back on the deggi mirch powder. Opt for sunflower or avocado oil.
- **KAPHA** Due to dairy's heaviness, enjoy in moderation. Use sunflower or grapeseed oil for the tadka.

LILI TUVAR NU SHAAK

FRESH PIGEON PEAS IN A GARLICKY GREEN SAUCE

Shaak, also known as *sabji/subzi* in Hindi, is a Gujarati term for an everyday stir-fried vegetable dish. A fall/winter specialty in many Gujarati households when freshly harvested pigeon peas in the pod (*tuvar lilva*) are available in the market, the shelled peas are cooked with a green paste of cilantro, fresh green garlic, coconut, peanuts, and spices. In America, I rarely find fresh garlic or even fresh tuvar lilva during winter months in my Indian grocery stores, so I use regular garlic with garlic chives and grab a bag of frozen shelled tuvar peas or frozen shelled green peas to make this dish. The garlicky green paste resembles Italian pesto, making a flavorful spread on toast, a dip with crudités, or a sauce for hot pasta.

PERFECT PAIRING

Serve as a side dish with Khatti Meethi Gujarati Dal (page 114) and rice.

SERVES 4

In a 3-quart (3 L) saucepan, combine the fresh peas, water, and salt and boil until soft, 5 to 7 minutes. Remove from the heat and set aside in their cooking liquid.

Make the green paste: In a food processor, combine the cilantro, coconut, water, garlic, chiles, and ginger and process to a fine paste. Transfer the paste to a bowl and stir in the peanuts, sesame seeds, coriander, salt, cumin, and turmeric.

Make the tadka: In a large skillet, warm the oil over medium heat. Once the oil is hot, add the cumin seeds, carom seeds, and asafoetida and let sizzle for 10 to 15 seconds. Add the boiled tuvar peas, their cooking liquid, and the green paste. Mix well, then stir in the garam masala and sugar and cook over medium-low heat for 4 to 5 minutes, stirring well to make sure it doesn't stick to the pan.

Remove from the heat, season to taste with salt, and stir in the garlic chives, cilantro, and lemon juice. Serve warm.

12 ounces (340 g) fresh or frozen shelled tuvar peas/pigeon peas or shelled green peas

3 cups (720 ml) water

½ teaspoon fine sea salt

GREEN PASTE

1 cup (65 g) tightly packed roughly chopped cilantro (leaves and tender stems)

½ cup (40 g) unsweetened shredded coconut (fresh or thawed frozen)

½ cup (120 ml) water

6 garlic cloves, peeled but whole

2 Thai green chiles, halved

1-inch (2.5 cm) piece fresh ginger, peeled and roughly chopped

½ cup (80 g) roasted peanuts, coarsely ground

2 tablespoons white sesame seeds

2 teaspoons ground coriander

1½ teaspoons fine sea salt

1 teaspoon ground toasted cumin

½ teaspoon ground turmeric

TADKA

¼ cup (60 ml) neutral oil, such as peanut, grapeseed, or avocado

1 teaspoon cumin seeds

½ teaspoon ajwain/carom seeds

¼ teaspoon hing/asafoetida powder

¼ teaspoon garam masala (page 40)

1 tablespoon sugar

GARNISH

½ cup (25 g) finely chopped garlic chives

¼ cup (15 g) finely chopped cilantro (leaves and tender stems)

1 tablespoon lemon juice

AYURVEDA NOTES

- **VATA** Peanuts, sesame seeds, and garlic are nourishing for vata. If pungency causes dryness or indigestion, reduce Thai green chile.
- **PITTA** Use grapeseed or avocado oil for the tadka. Reduce or omit Thai green chile. Use lime juice instead of lemon.
- **KAPHA** Use grapeseed oil for the tadka.

TOOR DAL KESARI

SWEET TOOR DAL PINEAPPLE PORRIDGE

Of the numerous Hindu festivals celebrated in my home, the ten-day festivities honoring Lord Ganesha, the beloved elephant god, is one that is extremely special. During each day of the Ganesh Chaturti festival, I prepare special dessert offerings to share with friends and family. On one of those days, I had planned to make the traditional *kesari*, a warm porridge prepared with semolina, sugar, water, and crushed pineapple, but learned at the last minute that one of the guests coming over was extremely sensitive to gluten. The previous day I had accidentally cooked excess amounts of toor dal and I was wondering how I was going to use it all. Sometimes the best opportunity is waiting in disguise, and my miscalculation became part of a divine plan leading to the creation of a new dish: swapping the wheat-based semolina with toor dal, I created a gluten-free and protein-rich dessert.

PERFECT PAIRING Add this to any festive menus or serve with biryani (page 173) or pulav (page 168).

SERVES 8 to 10

SOAK TIME 30 minutes to 1 hour

½ cup (100 g) toor dal/
  split pigeon peas
3 cups (720 ml) water
¼ teaspoon fine sea salt
¼ teaspoon ground
  turmeric
1 cup (200 g) cane sugar
1 cup (240 ml) water
6 to 8 saffron strands
½ teaspoon ground
  cardamom
1 cup (100 g) almond flour
1 tablespoon (15 g) ghee or
  unsalted butter, melted
¼ cup (60 g) crushed
  pineapple, fresh or
  canned
GARNISH
2 tablespoons coconut
  flakes, sweetened or
  unsweetened
2 tablespoons slivered
  almonds

Rinse the toor dal in a fine-mesh sieve under cold running water until the water runs clear, about a minute. Transfer to a medium bowl, add water to cover by 2 inches (5 cm), and soak for 30 minutes to 1 hour. Drain.

In a 3-quart (3 L) heavy-bottomed pot, combine the dal, water, salt, and turmeric. Partially cover and cook over medium heat, skimming any foam, until the dal is soft and mushy when checked by pressing between thumb and forefinger, about 40 minutes. Drain in a fine-mesh sieve and set aside.

In the same pot, combine the sugar, water, saffron strands, and cardamom. Bring to a boil over medium-high heat, stirring occasionally. Reduce the heat to a simmer and cook until the syrup reaches the "thread stage," about 5 minutes. To test, press a drop of syrup between the backs of two metal spoons and pull them apart; if the syrup is ready, a thin thread will form. Exercise caution in this step as the syrup is hot.

Add the cooked dal, almond flour, and ghee to the syrup and stir constantly for 5 minutes over medium-low heat until all the liquid is cooked off. Add the pineapple and mix well for an additional minute or so.

Serve warm and garnish with coconut flakes and slivered almonds.

TIPS

For a vegan version, use vegan butter or coconut oil.

Garnish with caramelized pineapple slices instead or in addition to coconut and almonds.

Try the same recipe with cooked chana dal or moong dal as per preference.

AYURVEDA NOTES

- **VATA** These ingredients are nourishing and vata-pacifying.
- **PITTA** Cooling sweetness balances toor dal and pineapple's heat.
- **KAPHA** Due to heaviness and sweetness, enjoy in moderation.

URAD

URAD

SANSKRIT NAME: Masha
OTHER INDIAN NAMES: Kali Urad / Kali Maa / Arad /
Mashkalai / Udid / Ulundu / Minumu / Uddu / Uzhinnu
ENGLISH NAMES: Urad Bean / Black Gram / Matpe Bean
BOTANICAL NAME: *Vigna mungo*

Urad, or black gram, appears in several ancient Indian texts dating to the Vedic period, and its remains have been found in several archaeological sites all over India, confirming its rich ancient lineage. Urad bean, or *Vigna mungo*, belongs to the botanical genus *Vigna*, also known as the *Phaseolus* genus. Since the skin that covers the urad bean is black, it is commonly referred to as black gram in India. Like its sister, moong bean, when the skin strips off the urad bean in the hulling process, the inner body is a different color—a beautiful pale cream.

Three varieties of urad dal are commonly used in Indian cuisine. First there is whole urad (unpeeled), which is enjoyed in rich stews like Dal Makhani (page 134). *Chilka urad dal*, its split (but unpeeled) version, is devoured equally in a variety of dal recipes such as Chaunsa Dal (page 135) from the northern state of Uttarakhand and Biulir Dal (page 136) of West Bengal. The third is the pale cream-colored split and peeled version, also called *dhuli urad dal*, which is used in a variety of ways in many regional Indian cuisines. One of

the popular ways is to create a deep-fried snack called *vada* in the South, *bade* in the North. The dhuli urad dal is also an essential ingredient that causes the fermentation and rise of batters found in various classical South Indian recipes like dosas.

In ancient India, one of the most fascinating uses of this little black legume was as a measure of weight, especially for weighing precious metals like gold and silver. The Sanskrit name for black gram is *masha*, which incidentally is also an ancient unit of weight. One masha is the weight equivalent of one grain of black gram, and sixteen mashas is equivalent to one *tola* or 11.7 grams.

The Ayurvedic properties of urad dal include a sweet taste with heavy, soft, unctuous qualities and slightly heating in potency. It is an excellent calming food for vata dosha and vata types can consume it frequently, while excess consumption can aggravate pitta and kapha disorders. It's also a nutritional powerhouse, helping to build strong muscles by providing plenty of protein, iron, copper, magnesium, and zinc, as well as being a rich source of fiber, with digestive and laxative properties.

DAL MAKHANI

NORTH INDIAN CREAMY URAD DAL

Makhani means "buttery," an apt description for this signature North Indian stew slow-cooked in butter or ghee to a satin-smooth texture and topped with cream to accentuate the unctuousness of black gram.

As a mom of two very athletic kids, dal makhani is simmering in my kitchen on repeat, especially ahead of their intense tennis tournament weekends. My kids lovingly refer to dal makhani as "muscle dal," as it is a great dietary choice for muscle repair, maintenance, and growth from Ayurvedic perspective.

PERFECT PAIRING Serve with plain basmati rice or Jeera Rice (page 156) along with Gajar ka Achaar (page 221).

SERVES 4 to 6

SOAK TIME 8 hours or overnight

---

1 cup (200 g) whole black urad/
  whole black gram
¼ cup (44 g) rajma/red kidney beans
5 cups (1.2 L) water
1 teaspoon fine sea salt
¼ teaspoon baking soda

SPICE MIXTURE
½ cup (115 g) ghee or unsalted butter
⅛ teaspoon hing/asafoetida powder
1 teaspoon cumin seeds
2 bay leaves
2-inch (5 cm) piece fresh ginger,
  peeled and roughly chopped
4 garlic cloves, peeled but whole
1 medium red onion, pureed
3 medium tomatoes, pureed
1 teaspoon fine sea salt
1 teaspoon ground toasted cumin
½ teaspoon ground turmeric
½ teaspoon garam masala (page 40)
½ teaspoon Kashmiri red chili powder
¼ cup (60 ml) heavy cream
¼ cup (15 g) loosely packed finely
  chopped cilantro

Rinse the urad and kidney beans in a fine-mesh sieve under cold running water until the water runs clear, about a minute. Transfer to a medium bowl, cover with 3 inches (7.5 cm) water, and soak 8 hours or overnight. Drain.

In a 4-quart (4 L) heavy-bottomed pot or Dutch oven, bring the water to a boil. Add the beans, salt, and baking soda. Cover and cook over medium heat until soft and tender, 1 to 1½ hours. Uncover and stir occasionally and adjust water levels as needed.

Make the spice mixture: In a large skillet, heat the ghee over medium heat. Add the asafoetida, cumin, and bay leaves and fry for 10 to 15 seconds. Add the ginger and garlic and cook for 30 seconds. Add the pureed onion and cook until the onion has dried out a little and is a nice light-brown color, about 5 minutes.

Add the tomato puree and cook for 3 to 4 minutes. Add the salt, cumin, turmeric, garam masala, and Kashmiri powder and cook for another minute or two.

Add the spice mixture to the cooked beans. Stir and let the dal simmer for another 30 to 40 minutes.

Season with salt to taste. Stir in the cream and garnish with finely chopped cilantro leaves just before serving. Serve warm.

TIPS
To cook the soaked urad and kidney beans in an electric pressure cooker, pressure-cook on high for 15 minutes. Let the pressure release naturally before opening the lid.

AYURVEDA NOTES

The predominant qualities of urad beans (masha) are unctuous, heating, heavy, strength-promoting, and vata-alleviating. While urad is generally heavier to digest, the addition of ginger, garlic, asafoetida, and garam masala helps ease of digestion of this dish.

- **VATA** Urad and spices are excellent for vata.
- **PITTA** Reduce the Kashmiri powder. Enjoy in moderation due to its heating qualities.
- **KAPHA** Increase the ginger and cumin. Due to heaviness of urad dal and cream, enjoy in moderation.

CHAUNSA DAL

GARHWALI-STYLE DAL

Garhwal is one of the two major regions of the mountainous northern Indian state of Uttarakhand. Garhwali cuisine, also referred to as *pahadi*, meaning "from the hills," is unpretentious and based on seasonal ingredients, with distinct summer and winter menus. *Chaunsa dal*, also called *chainsoo dal*, is enjoyed particularly during the cooler months with fresh rice or millet bread on the side, along with seasonal vegetables and chutneys. A traditional chaunsa recipe doesn't have any green leafy vegetables, but I love to include seasonal greens like spinach, amaranth greens, daikon radish greens, or carrot greens to add another depth of flavor to this dish.

PERFECT PAIRING
Serve with plain basmati rice, Jeera Rice (page 156), or Bhuga Chawar (page 163) along with Haldi Adrak Mirch ka Achaar (page 222).

SERVES 4

Rinse the dal in a fine-mesh sieve under running water until the water runs clear, about a minute. Spread the dal over a kitchen towel and pat dry.

Heat a large skillet over medium heat. Transfer the dal to the skillet and stir constantly to dry-roast it for 4 to 5 minutes until it is completely dry and lightly toasted. Turn the heat off and set the dal aside to cool to room temperature. Once cooled, grind it in a blender to a fine powder. Set aside.

Using a mortar and pestle, grind together the peppercorns, coriander seeds, ginger, and garlic cloves to a coarse paste. Set aside.

In a 4-quart (4 L) saucepan, heat the mustard oil over medium heat. Add the asafoetida, mustard seeds, and whole chiles and fry for a few seconds. Add the ground spice paste and fry for a minute. Add the dal powder and stir well with the oil and spices. Add the corn flour, salt, Kashmiri powder, and turmeric and mix well. If adding seasonal greens to the dal, add them now and mix into the dal mixture. Finally, add the water to the pan, stir well, cover, and cook over medium heat until the dal is cooked to a thick puree, 20 to 30 minutes. Open the lid every 10 minutes to stir the dal to ensure it doesn't stick to the bottom. Adjust the heat and water as needed.

Season with salt to taste. Serve warm.

1 cup (200 g) chilka urad dal/
  unpeeled split black gram
8 black peppercorns
1 teaspoon coriander seeds
1-inch (2.5 cm) piece fresh ginger,
  peeled and roughly chopped
6 garlic cloves, peeled but whole
¼ cup (60 ml) mustard oil
¼ teaspoon hing/asafoetida powder
1 teaspoon black mustard seeds
2 dried Kashmiri red chiles
2 tablespoons yellow corn flour
1 teaspoon fine sea salt
1 teaspoon Kashmiri red chili
  powder
½ teaspoon ground turmeric
3 cups (90 g) seasonal greens
  (optional)
4 cups (960 ml) water

AYURVEDA NOTES

- **VATA** Decrease whole red chiles and Kashmiri powder. Add vata-pacifying greens like mustard and spinach.
- **PITTA** Mustard oil is heating, so use olive, avocado, grapeseed, or sunflower oil instead. Reduce the whole red chiles and Kashmiri powder.
- **KAPHA** Include seasonal greens. This dish is beneficial for kapha due to mustard oil's heat, digestive spices, and dry, light corn flour.

BIULIR DAL

BENGALI-STYLE URAD DAL WITH FENNEL SEEDS AND SPICES

This prized Bengali recipe celebrates the unctuous quality of urad dal with simple spices. Dry-roasting the dal before cooking brings out its nutty flavor. It also reduces the heavy quality of urad dal and helps in digestion, along with the addition of spices like fennel seeds and ginger. Another unique feature is the use of mustard oil, which is often used in Bengali cuisine and is quite potent in flavor but complements urad dal beautifully.

PERFECT PAIRING Serve with plain or Jeera Rice (page 156) along with Haldi Adrak Mirch ka Achaar (page 222).

SERVES 4

---

1 cup (200 g) dhuli urad dal/peeled split black gram

4 cups (960 ml) water, plus more as needed

1 teaspoon fine sea salt

1½ teaspoons fennel seeds

1 tablespoon roughly chopped fresh ginger

TADKA

2 tablespoons mustard oil

2 dried red chiles

2 bay leaves

2 Thai green chiles, halved lengthwise

¼ teaspoon hing/asafoetida powder

¼ cup (60 ml) water

1 tablespoon lemon juice

TIPS

To cook the dal in an electric pressure cooker, pressure-cook on high for 3 minutes. Let the pressure release naturally before opening the lid.

For added richness, add a tablespoon of ghee once the dal is simmering just before it is ready to be served.

In a large dry skillet, dry-roast the dal over medium heat until slightly toasted to a light golden-brown color, 4 to 5 minutes. Immediately remove from the heat, transfer to a fine-mesh sieve, and rinse under cold water.

Transfer the dal to a large saucepan. Add the water and salt, cover, and cook over medium-high heat until the dal is tender but still lightly firm, 30 to 40 minutes. Check on the dal every 10 minutes or so to give it a gentle stir so it doesn't stick to the bottom of the pan, adding another ½ cup (120 ml) water as necessary. Whisk the cooked dal gently to mash some of it so that it thickens slightly. Set aside.

Meanwhile, using a mortar and pestle, crush the fresh ginger with 1 teaspoon of the fennel seeds. Add a couple of teaspoons of water to make a paste. Set aside.

Make the tadka: In a small saucepan, heat the mustard oil over medium heat until hot. Add the whole dried red chiles, the bay leaves, and green chiles. Fry for a few seconds, then add the remaining ½ teaspoon fennel seeds and the asafoetida and fry for another few seconds. Add fennel/ginger paste along with the water and braise the spices over medium heat for about 2 minutes.

Pour the tempered spices into the pot of cooked dal and let it simmer for 5 minutes. Stir in the lemon juice just before serving.

AYURVEDA NOTES

- **VATA** Reduce the amount of dried red chiles and Thai green chiles if they cause dryness or indigestion.
- **PITTA** Reduce the dried red chiles and Thai green chiles.
- **KAPHA** The dish's heat and digestive spices balance the heavy and smooth qualities of urad dal effectively for kapha.

MEDU VADA

CRISPY URAD FRITTERS

One of the most popular forms of *vada* is *medu vada*, the savory doughnut from South India. By tradition, medu vadas are dunked in piping hot sambhar (page 120) and served with coconut chutney on the side. Shaping the vada into a doughnut shape and carefully dropping into hot oil requires some practice. If this intimidates you, simply drop a spoonful of batter in the oil or use a small cookie scoop. If you want to skip deep-frying altogether, you can follow the no-fry method I share in the recipe for Dahi Bhalle Chaat (page 140).

PERFECT PAIRING Serve the medu vadas with hot Tiffin Sambhar (page 120) for dunking and Nariyal ki Chutney (page 216) on the side. Or for a "rasam vada," dunk the vadas in spiced Nimmakaya Rasam (page 122).

SERVES 4

SOAK TIME 4 to 5 hours

Rinse the dal in a fine-mesh sieve under cold running water until the water runs clear, about a minute. Transfer to a medium bowl, cover with 3 inches (7.5 cm) water, and soak for 4 to 5 hours.

Drain the dal and transfer to a high-powered blender. Add the salt and about ¼ cup (60 ml) ice cold water and grind on medium speed to avoid overheating the batter, scraping down the sides of the blender occasionally to ensure all the dal gets blended uniformly; add more water by the tablespoonful as necessary. The batter should be fluffy, smooth (no chunks of dal), and the consistency of a thick cake batter. To check the consistency of the batter, fill a small bowl with water. Take a little batter, form into a ball, and drop it into the water. If the consistency and texture of the batter is light and fluffy, the batter will float on top. If the batter is runny, add 1 to 2 tablespoons of rice flour and mix vigorously to help aerate the batter.

Transfer the batter to a bowl and stir in the cilantro, crushed black pepper, cumin seeds, curry leaves, green chiles, and asafoetida. Beat the batter by hand in a clockwise direction for 30 to 40 seconds; this will help aerate the batter. Rest the batter for 5 minutes.

Continued—

1 cup (200 g) dhuli urad dal/peeled split black gram

1½ teaspoons fine sea salt

¼ cup (60 ml) plus 2 to 3 tablespoons (30 to 45 ml) ice cold water, as needed

1 to 2 tablespoons rice flour, as needed

2 tablespoons finely chopped cilantro

1 teaspoon coarsely crushed black peppercorns

1 teaspoon cumin seeds

5 to 8 fresh curry leaves, roughly torn

2 Thai green chiles, finely chopped

¼ teaspoon hing/asafoetida powder

FOR FRYING

6 to 8 cups (1.5 to 2 L) peanut, sunflower, or vegetable oil

TIP

The vada batter can be made plain with just urad dal and salt. In addition, you can try adding chopped onions to the vada batter just before frying.

For Doughnut Shapes

METHOD 1 To make the traditional doughnut-shape medu vadas, keep a bowl of water next to you. Wet both your hands with water. Scoop about ¼ cup (60 ml) of vada batter onto one of your palms and make it into a ball. Slightly flatten the ball with your thumb. Make a hole in the center and gently slide the vada into the hot oil. Be extremely careful when doing this.

METHOD 2 Form the batter into a ball as in method 1 and place it on greased parchment paper or a silicone mat. Flatten it slightly and make a hole in the center. Dip your fingers in water and carefully lift the side or corner of the parchment sheet to carefully transfer the medu vada onto your fingers and gently slide it into the hot oil.

For Freeform Shapes

If the doughnut shape is not important to you, use your hands, a spoon, or a small cookie scoop to carefully drop about 1 tablespoon of the batter directly into the oil.

Line a tray with paper towels and have it near the stove. Pour about 3 inches (7.5 cm) of oil in a large pot or dutch oven and heat to 350°F (177°C). To check if the oil is hot enough, drop a small ball of batter in the oil. The batter must rise almost instantly without turning brown. If it gets too brown, the oil is too hot, so lower the heat to medium. Maintain the heat between 350°F and 375°F (177° and 190°C) for optimal frying of vadas.

Fry the vadas until they turn golden brown and crisp, 3 to 5 minutes depending on the size and shape of the vadas. Carefully turn them over with a slotted spoon and continue to fry on both sides. Continue to fry while turning them as needed. Once they are evenly crisp and golden on both sides, remove with a slotted spoon and transfer to the paper towels to drain.

Serve warm.

AYURVEDA NOTES

- **VATA** Favor peanut oil for frying; it strengthens and heats.
- **PITTA** Generally avoid or have fried foods in moderation. For frying, choose sunflower oil for its cooling nature and sweet taste. Reduce or skip Thai green chile.
- **KAPHA** Rarely consume fried foods due to heaviness; when preparing this dish, use sunflower oil for frying.

DAHI BHALLE CHAAT

SAVORY URAD DUMPLINGS IN SPICED YOGURT

Dahi bhalle are urad dal fritters dipped in spiced yogurt. When topped with chutneys and garnished with spices and herbs, you have transformed the dish into a *dahi bhalle chaat*. The bhalle are traditionally deep-fried, but I've included a no-fry method too.

PERFECT PAIRING Serve this chaat with Kande Bhajji (page 98) and Instant Khaman Dhoklas (page 95) along with a hot cup of Masala Chai (page 238).

SERVES 6

SOAK TIME 4 to 5 hours

BHALLES

1 cup (200 g) dhuli urad dal/peeled split black gram

1 teaspoon fine sea salt

¼ cup (60 ml) plus 2 to 3 tablespoons (30 to 45 ml) ice cold water, as needed

1 to 2 tablespoons rice flour, as needed

2 teaspoons minced fresh ginger

1 Thai green chile, minced

½ teaspoon ground toasted cumin

½ teaspoon ajwain/carom seeds

For deep-fry method: 6 to 8 cups (1.5 to 2 L) peanut, sunflower, or vegetable oil

For no-fry method: 3 tablespoons (45 ml) neutral oil

SPICED YOGURT

2 cups (460 g) plain yogurt

½ cup (120 ml) ice cold water

1 teaspoon sugar

½ teaspoon kala namak/Indian black salt

½ teaspoon ground toasted cumin

½ teaspoon chaat masala

¼ teaspoon Kashmiri red chili powder

ACCOMPANIMENTS

1 tablespoon Hari Chutney (page 214)

1 tablespoon Imli Khajur ki Chutney (page 215)

1 tablespoon julienned fresh ginger

1 to 2 tablespoons finely chopped cilantro

¼ cup fresh pomegranate arils (optional)

2 tablespoons fine sev/fried chickpea noodles (optional)

Kashmiri red chili powder

Ground toasted cumin

Chaat masala

Rinse the dal in a fine-mesh sieve under cold running water until the water runs clear, about a minute. Transfer to a medium bowl, cover with 3 inches (7.5 cm) water, and soak for 4 to 5 hours. Drain.

Transfer the dal to a high-powered blender. Add the salt and about ¼ cup (60 ml) ice cold water and grind on medium speed to a smooth, fluffy batter, adding more water by the tablespoonful as necessary. The batter should be smooth, the consistency of a thick cake batter. To test, fill a small bowl with water, then form a scoop of batter into a small ball, and drop it into the water. It should float. If the batter doesn't hold together, add 1 to 2 tablespoons of rice flour and mix vigorously to help aerate the batter.

Transfer the batter to a bowl and stir in the ginger, chile, cumin, and carom seeds. Beat the batter by hand in a clockwise direction for 30 to 40 seconds; this will help aerate the batter. Rest the batter for 5 minutes.

Continued—

Chaat

The word *chaat* means "to lick," but it is also used to describe a diverse category of savory and sweet snacks. Found not only on roadside eateries all across India as small quick bites, chaat dishes are also the main attraction at parties or gatherings and are showcased in upscale restaurants all over the world.

METHOD 1: DEEP-FRY Line a plate with paper towels and have it near the stove. Pour about 3 inches (7.5 cm) oil into a heavy-bottomed pot and heat to 350°F (177°C). Check if the oil is hot enough by dropping a small ball of batter into the oil. If it rises almost instantly without turning brown, it's ready. If the batter gets browned, the oil is too hot and the heat should be reduced. Maintain the frying temperature at 350° to 375°F (177° to 190°C).

Working in batches to not crowd the pan, use your fingers to drop small balls of batter carefully into the hot oil. (Alternatively, you can use two spoons or a small cookie scoop to drop small amounts of batter into the oil.) Fry the bhalle until they are golden brown and crispy on all sides, 2 to 3 minutes. With a spider or slotted spoon, transfer the fritters to the paper towels to drain.

METHOD 2: NO-FRY For this method you will need either a traditional appe or paniyaram pan, with spherical wells—similar to a Danish aebleskiver, a Dutch poffertjes pan, or a Japanese takoyaki pan. Heat the pan over medium heat. Add a few drops of oil to each cup of the pan and drop 1 to 2 tablespoons of bhalle batter in. Cover the pan with a lid, reduce the heat to medium-low, and cook until they are lightly golden on the bottom, 3 to 4 minutes. Carefully flip the bhalle balls over using either a chopstick or spoon and cook the other side for another 3 to 4 minutes. Transfer the cooked bhalle to a plate. Repeat with the remaining batter.

The key step after cooking or frying the bhalle is to soak them in a bowl filled with warm water for 5 to 10 minutes. This helps the bhalle get rid of some of the oil and makes them plump up from hydrating.

Meanwhile, make the spiced yogurt mixture: In a bowl, whisk together the yogurt, ice water, sugar, black salt, cumin, chaat masala, and Kashmiri powder.

Take one fritter at a time from the water and press between your palms to remove excess water. What you will be left with is a soft, spongy bhalle ready for its immersion in the spiced yogurt mixture. Arrange them in a shallow serving bowl or rimmed serving platter. Pour the spiced yogurt mixture over the pressed bhalle in the serving dish. Refrigerate until ready to serve.

When ready to serve, make a bhalle platter with small bowls of both chutneys, the ginger, cilantro, pomegranate seeds, and fine sev (if using). Everyone should garnish their own chaat how they like.

TIPS
Although sev is easily found in an Indian grocery store or purchased online, you could substitute some crushed tortilla chips or pita chips for the crunch factor essential in many chaat dishes.

Swap pomegranate arils with chopped red grapes based on seasonal availability.

AYURVEDA NOTES

- **VATA** Deep-fry with any oil. Top with plenty of digestive chutneys.
- **PITTA** Opt for the no-fry method. Favor sunflower oil. Reduce Thai green chile and Kashmiri powder.
- **KAPHA** Enjoy in moderation using the no-fry method. Use sunflower oil.

Urad Dal Vadas

SAVORY URAD DAL FRITTERS

If you come across the word *vada* in Indian cuisine, then it's some kind of savory snack in the form of a fritter and probably deep-fried. A typical vada uses a combination of dals and vegetables, along with regionally popular spices and herbs. Vadas are served alongside coconut chutney and dunked in piping hot dal soup like sambhar (page 120) or spiced broth like rasam (page 122) in South India. Soaking fried vadas in spiced yogurt is commonly referred to as *dahi* (yogurt) *vada* (fritter), and one of the popular street food dishes of North India is *dahi bhalle chaat*: layers of yogurt-dipped vada with various chutneys and other garnishes. Vadas are also added to spiced curry dishes, like the traditional Sindhi Kachori Curry (page 145), and when vadas are soaked in spiced water and fermented for a few days, it is called *kanji vadas*, a popular dish from the western state of Rajasthan.

Vadas may be referred as *vade*, *bara*, *wadeh*, *wada*, and *vadei* depending on the region of India, and its Sanskrit name, *vataka*, is mentioned in ancient texts like *Arthashastra*. While vadas can be made from different pulses and legumes, the slimy, unctuous texture of urad dal (black gram) is savored best in the form of deep-fried vada. There is a classic vada batter made with urad dal that, with minor variations, is transformed to create popular recipes across India.

SINDHI KACHORI CURRY

SAVORY DUMPLINGS IN SPICED TOMATO BROTH

Whenever Mom made *dahi bhalles* (page 140), she would fry an extra batch of the fluffy urad dal *kachoris* to add them to a traditional spiced tomato broth. The broth comes together in a few minutes, and the fried kachoris, or dumplings, are added to the piping hot broth just before serving. This recipe calls for dried kokum to accentuate the tanginess of the tomatoes. Kokum fruit is a member of the mangosteen family, indigenous to the Western Ghats of Maharashtra. The outer flesh of the fruit is dried and is commonly used to add sour flavor to dishes. Dried kokum is easily found in many Indian grocery stores or online. If you are unable to find it, you can simply add a squeeze of lime or lemon juice to give that sour punch. Serve the kachori curry by itself or over steamed rice.

SERVES 4 to 6

SOAK TIME
4 to 5 hours

Make the curry: In a large saucepan, heat the oil over medium heat. Add the asafoetida, mustard seeds, and fenugreek seeds and let sizzle in hot oil for a few seconds. Add the chickpea flour and roast over low heat until it changes to a light brown color, 3 to 4 minutes. Add the Kashmiri powder, turmeric, green chile, ginger, and fresh curry leaves and fry for another minute.

TIPS

Substitute 3 large tomatoes in place of both of the canned tomato ingredients used in the recipe.

Use 1 tablespoon of lemon or lime juice for the dried kokum.

Add the crushed tomatoes and canned tomato sauce and whisk well to get rid of any lumps of chickpea flour. Add the water, salt, and dried kokum (if using) and bring to a rolling boil while whisking regularly. Reduce the heat and let simmer for 15 minutes.

About 5 minutes before serving, add the urad dal kachoris to the hot tomato curry broth.

Serve garnished generously with the cilantro.

Bhalles (from Dahi Bhalle Chaat, page 140), made with the deep-fry method

CURRY

3 tablespoons (45 ml) oil (peanut, sunflower, or avocado) or ghee

¼ teaspoon hing/asafoetida powder

1 teaspoon black mustard seeds

¼ teaspoon fenugreek seeds

3 tablespoons (23 g) besan/chickpea flour

1 teaspoon Kashmiri red chili powder

½ teaspoon ground turmeric

1 Thai green chile, finely chopped

1-inch (2.5 cm) piece fresh ginger, finely chopped

8 to 10 fresh curry leaves

One 16-ounce (454 g) can no-salt-added crushed tomatoes

One 8-ounce (225 g) can tomato sauce

4 cups (960 ml) water

1 teaspoon fine sea salt

3 to 4 pieces dried kokum (optional)

¼ cup (10 g) finely chopped cilantro

AYURVEDA NOTES

Kokum aids digestion, cools the body, and pacifies pitta, reducing heat rash in summer.

- **VATA** If tomatoes weren't nightshades, their sweet-sour taste and warmth would benefit vata. However, nightshades can be problematic, especially for vata. Consume in moderation. Decrease the Kashmiri powder and Thai green chile if they cause dryness or indigestion.
- **PITTA** Use sunflower or avocado oil. Reduce the Kashmiri powder and Thai green chile.
- **KAPHA** Use sunflower oil. Enjoy in moderation. Skip the additional sour from kokum or lemon.

RICE /
CHAWAL

RICE / CHAWAL

SANSKRIT NAMES: Anna / Tandula / Dhanya / Vrihi
OTHER INDIAN NAMES: Choka / Chaul / Tandul /
Arisi / Biyyamu / Akki / Ari / Annam / Anna / Bhaat / Sadam /
Choru / Chawar
ENGLISH NAME: Rice
BOTANICAL NAME: *Oryza sativa*

According to the ancient Hindu Vedic texts, the entire universe is held within each grain of rice. Rice is intertwined with every aspect of life in India and revered by both the rich and poor. From *anna*, the Sanskrit word meaning "cooked rice," to *akshata*, meaning "unbroken raw rice," this beloved grain holds sacred status in traditional Indian kitchens and throughout Hindu culture. Whether I have less than 30 minutes to cook simple Jeera Rice (page 156) on a busy weeknight or I'm preparing an elaborate Dum Biryani (page 173) on a weekend, rice is an integral part of my daily life. It also comes to our rescue when one of us is under the weather, in the form of a simple Rice Kanji (page 155) or a comforting Dheeli Khichdi (page 188) for a gentle gut reset after we return from a few days of hectic travel.

Half a cup of cooked rice provides about 100 calories, 20 grams of carbohydrates, and 2.5 grams of highly digestible protein, is low fat and contains no trans fat, and is essentially sodium free.

Rice is the principal convalescent food in Ayurveda. Rice is enjoyed savory, sweet, and sometimes fermented to a delicious sour. It can be eaten with almost anything and enjoyed for breakfast, lunch, dinner, or as a snack in between meals. It is gentle enough to withstand digestion as delicate as a baby's or as frail as that of an aging grandmother. Because of this, in Ayurveda, rice is considered the perfect food—soothing, nourishing, and healing. Unlike the Western perspective, where the focus is on the quantitative properties such as calories, fiber, and nutrient content, Ayurveda takes into account who is eating it, when it is eaten, and how the *agni*, or digestive fire, reacts to it. The properties of rice are recognized by the type of rice, its age, the amount of water used for cooking, the duration of cooking, and the intensity of heat which defines its final outcome. Also, the addition of certain herbs and spices and combining with other food groups can change the therapeutic spectrum of rice preparation.

Plain cooked white rice has *madhu rasa* (sweet taste) and offers deep satisfaction. The sweetness of rice is so mild that you appreciate its relative sweetness if you eat something bitter and then some rice. The energetic impact on digestion, or *virya*, of rice is cooling. When consumed in moderation, aged rice is balancing in nature for all doshas. It is especially pacifying for vata and pitta dosha, but when eaten in large quantities, it can aggravate kapha dosha.

Types of Rice

India is home to at least 6,000 of the 40,000 varieties of rice cultivated worldwide. With over 300 indigenous aromatic varieties grown in India, rice is categorized based on its kernel length—small-, medium-, and long-grained—with thousands of regional varieties, each with its own distinct aroma, flavor, and associated recipes.

But when one thinks of Indian rice, basmati rice is likely what comes to mind first, and for good reason. India is the biggest producer of basmati rice in the world. Considered the queen of rice (*bas* means "fragrance" and *mati* means "queen"), basmati rice is one of the most celebrated Indian rice varieties. Held in high esteem in Ayurveda and Indian cuisine because of its aroma, ease of digestion, and peaceful sattvic (balanced, harmonious, and serene) effect on the mind, basmati rice is suitable year-round for all Ayurvedic body constitutions.

Long-grain basmati rice from India has less starch compared to other types of rice, and its starch content reduces as it ages. Therefore, in India, the price of aged basmati rice is higher than for fresh harvested rice. Both brown and white varieties are available, but traditional Indian cooking favors white basmati rice. Brown rice, however, does not store well, because of the presence of rice bran, which contains oil, causing brown rice to go rancid rather quickly. If using brown rice, it is better to buy fresh and in smaller quantities.

RICE AGES JUST AS WELL AS WINE!

Basmati rice is usually aged up to two years once harvested before it is packaged and shipped out to consumers. Aging begins preharvest and continues until it is ready to be consumed, enhancing volume expansion and water absorption, resulting in a superior quality of cooked rice. According to Ayurveda, rice aged for at least a year not only improves cooking quality and flavor but also is much easier to digest than freshly milled rice. It is therefore not surprising to see Indians buy a 10- or 20-pound rice bag at the grocery store to consume over several months, and it's not uncommon to store a year's supply of rice.

POPULAR RICE VARIETIES FROM DIFFERENT REGIONAL STATES IN INDIA

Short Grain
- Ambemohar (Maharashtra)
- Jeera Samba (Andhra Pradesh)
- Selam Samba (Tamil Nadu)
- Palakkad Matta (Kerala)
- Joha (Assam)

Medium Grain
- Balami (Odisha)
- Indrayani (Maharashtra)
- Surti Kolam (Gujarat, Tamil Nadu)
- Sona Masoori (Andhra Pradesh, Telangana, Karnataka)
- Ponni (Tamil Nadu)

Long Grain
- Basmati (Punjab, Haryana, Uttar Pradesh, Kashmir Valley, Dehradun)
- Sharbati (Punjab, Haryana)
- Pusa (Punjab, Haryana, Uttar Pradesh)
- Parmal (Punjab, Haryana, Uttar Pradesh)
- Miniket (West Bengal)

Perfectly Cooked Plain Rice

I remember making my first pot of plain rice on a snowy winter evening in my first American kitchen in Cleveland, Ohio. It was a clumpy mush, stuck to the bottom of the pot, and quite unpleasant to eat. I had watched my mom cook rice daily, throughout my entire childhood, with every grain separate, fluffy, and tender, and I naively thought this would be the simplest thing to prepare. It took several expensive international phone calls (they were not free back in the day!) home before I was finally able to enjoy a pot of rice that tasted just like Mom's.

We generally eat two to three varieties of rice throughout the week: medium- and short-grain during weekdays and long-grain during weekends. For plain rice, I do not add any salt or oil in cooking. Heat and water are all you need to cook rice and retain its distinct aroma. Once rice and water are combined and heat is introduced, avoid stirring so the grains don't break and release the starch.

RICE 101

There are four steps to perfectly cooked plain rice: rinse, soak, cook, rest (and fluff).

---

1. Rinse

Rinsing rice removes excess starch and helps make the texture of the cooked rice less sticky and fluffier. I believe rice should always be rinsed, except when it interferes with a specific recipe. Combine rice with double the amount of water in a bowl. Stir the rice in the water gently with your fingers. The water will become cloudy. Hold a hand over the rice and carefully discard most of the water into the sink or catch the discarded water in another bowl. (Alternatively, place the rice in a fine-mesh sieve under cold running tap water and catch the discarded water in a large bowl underneath. See Uses for Rice Water, page 154.) Repeat the rinsing process two to three times—sometimes six times depending on the rice—until the water in the bowl is clear.

---

2. Soak

Soak the rinsed rice in 2 to 3 inches (5 to 7.5 cm) of water. Set aside on the kitchen counter for a minimum of 20 minutes and up to 1 hour, though some varieties, like the unpolished indigenous Kerala red matta rice, require 1 hour of soak time for best results. Soaking any variety of rice plumps the grains and allows it to absorb water before the cooking process begins. Once cooked, the grains of rice are tender, and the rice cooks evenly without getting mushy.

3. Cook

Rice can be cooked in special rice cookers, pressure cookers, bamboo steamers, or even in an oven, but cooking rice on a stovetop is the most versatile, and my preferred method. Once you have learned it, you can make rice anytime, anywhere, without any special equipment. There are two common methods of cooking rice: the drain method and the absorb method.

Method 1: Drain Method

The drain method involves cooking rice in more than double the amount of water (this method is similar to cooking pasta). Once cooked, the water is discarded (see Uses for Rice Water, page 154). For this method, you don't need precise measurements of water. Transfer the soaked rice to a heavy-bottomed pot and add 4 to 5 parts water. Cook the rice uncovered for 15 to 20 minutes over medium heat until the rice grains are soft when pressed between your fingers but still hold their shape. It is best to avoid stirring the rice so the grains don't break and release the starch. Drain the cooked rice, return to the pot, and cover.

I prefer this method for my everyday plain rice—it's similar to how my mom has done it for most of her life. Because the excess starch released into the water gets discarded, this method also makes the rice feel much lighter when eaten, in my opinion, and tends to be easier to digest.

Method 2: Absorb Method

Using the Rice Cooking Chart below, in a medium saucepan, combine the specific amounts of rice and water and bring to a boil over high heat. Reduce the heat to medium and cook until all the liquid is fully absorbed and the rice is tender yet still slightly firm. The amount of water is important because if there is too much, the rice will cook to an unpleasant sticky mush, and if there is too little, the rice will not cook evenly.

Rice Cooking Chart	1 → 1 cup uncooked rice (about 200 g)	3 → 3 cups cooked rice	2–3 Comfortably serves about 2–3 people when accompanied by a dal and/or a vegetable.
Type	Long-grain basmati	Medium-grain and short-grain	Brown / Red matta
Rice-to-water ratio for cooking	1 cup rice, soaked, to 1½ cups water	1 cup rice, soaked, to 2 cups water	1 cup rice, soaked, to 3 cups water / 1 cup rice, soaked, to 4 cups water
Cook time (over medium heat)	About 15 minutes	15 to 30 minutes	30 to 40 minutes / 30 to 45 minutes

The cooking time and rice-to-water ratio are general guidelines for stovetop cooking. Actual times and water amount may vary depending on your stovetop cooking medium (gas/induction/electric), size of burner, the specific rice variety, rice brands, and age of raw rice. If rice is cooked in an electric pressure cooker, reduce the water amount from the table amount by half a cup and follow the cook time based on the electric pressure cooker instructions.

4. Rest and Fluff

Once the rice is cooked, turn off the heat, cover the pot with a tight lid, and allow the rice to rest for 10 to 15 minutes. The steam locks in the aroma while the starches cool down slightly, firming up the grains. Resist the urge to stir the rice as soon as it is cooked as the grains will break and get mushy. After resting, uncover the lid and lightly fluff the rice with a fork to create some volume before serving.

Uses for Rice Water

Transforming a cup of raw rice to cooked rice uses water at different stages, from the rinsing, to soaking, and finally to cooking. Instead of tossing all this water down the drain, collect it in a large bowl. Here are just some ways to use this nutrient-rich water and practice zero-waste cooking.

WATER THAT IS DISCARDED

. . . during rinsing rice 2 to 3 times

- This water may contain impurities, traces of pesticides if the rice is not organic, and some water-soluble vitamins.
- Use this water for plants—both indoors and outdoors. It contains a decent amount of NPK (nitrogen, phosphorus, and potassium), which are beneficial to the soil and plants.

. . . during soaking rice

- This water contains water-soluble vitamins and is natural micellar water (excellent for gently cleansing skin). It is very cooling when used externally.
- Wash your face with this water, especially during summer to relieve redness and burning sensation.
- Use this water to soak smelly plastic food containers and jars for 30 minutes to 1 hour. It is a natural deodorizer.

. . . after rice is cooked using the drain method

- This thick, starchy water left behind when rice is cooked is referred to as *kanji*.
- Rice Kanji (page 155) can be flavored with spices and herbs and consumed as a warm drink, especially when someone is unwell or recovering from an illness. It boosts energy and is gentle on digestion.
- Fill a spray bottle with kanji, dilute as needed, and use it to spray on cotton clothes before ironing.
- Rinsing hair with kanji—a tradition in many Indian households—can help with improving hair texture.

RICE KANJI

RICE PORRIDGE

The first mention of rice in the ancient Indian Vedic texts is in the form of *kanji*, with detailed recipes for special occasions and treating specific ailments. It's a simple rice porridge prepared by boiling rice in water, and the word *kanji*, from the South Indian Tamil language, has been Anglicized into the word *congee*, a rice dish found in cultures around the world. This humble dish has profound health benefits and is used in homes and even in hospitals in India as the first meal when recovering from an illness, surgery, or when the body simply needs a break. My version includes a couple of spices to help boost the digestive juices.

SERVES 4

SOAK TIME 20 to 30 minutes

Rinse the rice in a fine-mesh sieve under cold running water until the water runs clear, about a minute. Transfer to a medium bowl, add water to cover by 2 inches (5 cm), and soak for 20 to 30 minutes. Drain.

In a pot, combine the soaked rice and water and cook partially covered over medium heat until the rice becomes a soft mush or almost completely dissolved, 20 to 30 minutes. Halfway through the cooking process, add the black salt, cumin, and crushed carom seeds.

Sip on the kanji while it is nice and warm. Pour it into a thermos to keep it hot and ready to eat whenever you are hungry.

½ cup (113 g) short-grain or medium-grain rice
7 cups (1.6 L) water
½ teaspoon kala namak/Indian black salt
¼ teaspoon ground toasted cumin
¼ teaspoon crushed ajwain/carom seeds

AYURVEDA NOTES

Kanji is as nutritious as it is digestible and very useful as a short-term diet to quickly clear undigested food material (ama) from the system. A day of kanji or even one meal of kanji works wonders after any eating mishaps. This is a great food for fasting and to give the digestive system a small rest. It helps with apana vata (pelvic floor) imbalances and with bowel health.

- **VATA** If tolerated, add a teaspoon of ghee when serving.
- **PITTA** Add ¼ teaspoon ground coriander.
- **KAPHA** Add ¼ teaspoon turmeric and ¼ teaspoon black pepper.

JEERA RICE

CUMIN-SPICED RICE

Jeera (cumin seeds) have a wide variety of health benefits, from helping to boost digestion to anti-inflammatory properties. Sautéing the spices in ghee or oil releases the potent compounds within and elevates the flavor and aroma of the entire dish. Aged basmati rice contains less starch and therefore is an ideal choice for perfectly cooked jeera rice that is fluffy, nonsticky, and aromatic.

PERFECT PAIRING Serving warm jeera rice with piping hot dals like Dhaba-Style Easy Dal Fry (page 117) or Dal Makhani (page 134) is what makes weeknight dinners extra special, especially in many North Indian homes.

SERVES 2

SOAK TIME 20 to 30 minutes

- 1 cup (200 g) basmati rice
- 1 tablespoon (15 g) ghee or oil
- 1 teaspoon cumin seeds
- 1 dried or fresh bay leaf
- 1 star anise
- 2 green cardamom pods
- 3 to 4 black peppercorns
- 2 cups (480 ml) water
- 1 teaspoon fine sea salt
- ½ teaspoon ground toasted cumin

Rinse the rice in a fine-mesh sieve under cold running water until the water runs clear, about a minute. Transfer to a medium bowl, add water to cover by 2 inches (5 cm), and soak for 20 to 30 minutes. Drain.

In a 4-quart (4 L) heavy-bottomed saucepan, heat the ghee over medium heat. Add the cumin seeds, bay leaf, star anise, cardamom pods, and peppercorns and allow them to sizzle in the hot ghee for a few seconds. Add the drained basmati rice and gently fry the rice with the spices and ghee for a minute to bring out the aroma of the rice. Do not stir the rice vigorously as it will break the rice and can make it extra starchy.

Add the water, salt, and ground toasted cumin. Increase the heat to high and bring to a boil. Reduce the heat to medium-low, cover, and cook until the water is absorbed and the rice is cooked, 10 to 15 minutes. Turn off the heat and keep the rice covered in the pot for another 10 minutes. The steam will help the grains to expand and become fluffy.

TIPS

To make this vegan, use sunflower, avocado, grapeseed, or olive oil in place of the ghee.

Simply use whole cumin seeds, ground toasted cumin, and salt and skip the other spices.

Instead of cooking raw rice with the spices, you can use leftover plain cooked rice and combine with a mixture of whole cumin seeds and ground toasted cumin that have been first cooked/ warmed in hot ghee.

To make this a wholesome mixed-vegetable jeera pulao, add raw vegetables like shelled peas, chopped carrots, diced potatoes, or cauliflower florets to the pot and cook with the rice and spices.

AYURVEDA NOTES

- **VATA** Choose ghee over oil for cooking.
- **PITTA** Garnish generously with finely chopped cilantro.
- **KAPHA** Favor neutral oil, such as sunflower or avocado, over ghee.

HALDI WALE CHAWAL

TURMERIC LEMON RICE

My mom would often cook an extra cup of rice at dinnertime so she could make *haldi wale chawal* to pack for our school lunches the next morning. Frying the raw peanuts and dals, along with the spices and fresh curry leaves, in toasted sesame oil adds a distinct nuttiness to this dish. Fresh lemon juice and a generous garnish of cilantro provide a bright, herbaceous finish. Traditionally, a medium-grain rice variety, such as Surti Kolam or Sona Masoori, is used for this dish, but you can use any variety of white rice with equally satisfying results.

PERFECT PAIRING This can be enjoyed alone or with *sambhar* (page 120) or *rasam* (page 122) along with Gajar ka Achaar (page 221) on the side for an extra spicy kick.

SERVES 4

TIP
Omit both the chana and urad dals and instead add ½ cup shelled peas to the spices.

In a large skillet, heat the sesame oil over medium heat. Add the asafoetida, peanuts, urad dal, chana dal, and mustard seeds and fry for a minute until both the dals turn golden brown. Add the cashews and fry for a few seconds, followed by the green chiles, curry leaves, and turmeric and cook for a few seconds to temper the spices.

Add the cooked rice and mix well for a minute until the rice is coated uniformly. Pour the salt and lemon juice over the rice and mix again. Cover the pan to let the rice and spices steam and cook over medium-low heat for a couple of minutes. Season with more salt to taste. Uncover and garnish with cilantro leaves.

1½ tablespoons sesame oil

¼ teaspoon hing/asafoetida powder

2 tablespoons raw peanuts

1 teaspoon dhuli urad dal/peeled split black gram

1 teaspoon chana dal/peeled and split chickpeas

1 teaspoon brown mustard seeds

6 to 8 raw cashews

2 Thai green chiles, halved lengthwise

6 to 7 fresh curry leaves

1 teaspoon ground turmeric

3 cups (685 g) packed cooked medium-grain rice, such as Surti Kolam or Sona Masoori

1 teaspoon sea salt

2 tablespoons lemon juice

¼ cup (10 g) finely chopped cilantro (leaves and tender stems)

AYURVEDA NOTES

Lemons have heating potency (virya), so in summer, replace them with limes. Similarly, use sunflower oil instead of sesame oil.
- **VATA** Asafoetida is essential.
- **PITTA** Skip the green chiles. Add green peas. Use sunflower oil instead of sesame.
- **KAPHA** Add minced ginger to the tempered spices.

PULIYODHARAI

TAMARIND RICE

The secret to the best bowl of *puliyodharai* is all in the *pulikaichal,* or spiced tamarind paste. The aroma of the zesty tamarind brings back fond childhood memories of trading one of my mom's prized *parathas* (North Indian–style stuffed flatbreads) for a bowl of home-cooked tamarind rice with a friend during school lunch. You'll find different variations of tamarind rice across South India, each with a unique set of spices and regional name. My recipe is an ode to a Tamilian *pati* (grandma) who lived next door to us in Mumbai and who first introduced me to the aromas and flavors of authentic Tamil cuisine. You can use store-bought tamarind concentrate for this dish, but I encourage you to make your own tamarind pulp, if you can find the tamarind slab (compressed tamarind pods). The recipe for spiced tamarind paste can be doubled and used to make puliyodharai in an instant with leftover plain rice. Leftover tamarind paste can be stored in the refrigerator for up to a week.

PERFECT PAIRING
Puliyodharai holds its space alone or serve it with rasam (page 122) on the side.

SERVES 4

SOAK TIME
20 minutes

TAMARIND PULP
2 ounces (55 g) tamarind slab (see Tip), or 2 tablespoons store-bought tamarind concentrate
2 cups (480 ml) water

RICE
1½ cups (340 g) medium-grain rice, such as Surti Kolam, Sona Masoori, or jasmine
4 cups (960 ml) water
½ teaspoon fine sea salt

SPICE MIXTURE
3 dried red chiles
1 tablespoon chana dal/peeled and split chickpeas
1 tablespoon dhuli urad dal/peeled split black gram
1 tablespoon coriander seeds
1 tablespoon fenugreek seeds
1 tablespoon white sesame seeds

TADKA
¼ cup (60 ml) toasted sesame oil
¼ teaspoon hing/asafoetida powder
2 teaspoons black mustard seeds
2 tablespoons raw peanuts
1 tablespoon chana dal/peeled and split chickpeas
1 tablespoon dhuli urad dal/peeled split black gram
3 dried red chiles
10 to 15 curry leaves, fresh or dried
1 teaspoon fine sea salt
½ teaspoon ground turmeric

Prepare the tamarind pulp: In a small saucepan, combine the tamarind slab and water and bring to a boil. Remove from the heat and let the fruit soak and soften in the hot water for 20 minutes. Use your hands to squeeze the pulp and separate it from the seeds. Strain the pulp through a fine-mesh sieve, pressing the tamarind and squeezing out the pulp. (Alternatively, if you are short on time or unable to find tamarind slab, combine the water with the store-bought tamarind concentrate. Mix well and set aside.)

Cook the rice: Meanwhile, rinse the rice in a fine-mesh sieve under cold running water until the water runs clear, about a minute. Transfer to a medium bowl, add water to cover by 2 inches (5 cm), and soak for 20 to 30 minutes. Drain.

Continued—

Transfer the rice to a medium pot. Add the 4 cups (960 ml) water and bring to a boil over high heat. Reduce the heat to medium and cook partially covered until the rice is soft when pressed between fingers but retains its shape, 15 to 20 minutes. Drain the rice in a fine-mesh sieve, return to the pot, and keep covered for 5 minutes to let the rice rest as the steam continues to cook the rice.

Meanwhile, make the spice mixture: Heat a medium skillet over medium heat. Add the whole chiles and roast for a couple of minutes. Transfer to a bowl. Add both of the dals and roast until golden brown. Transfer to the bowl with the chiles. Add the coriander seeds, fenugreek seeds, and sesame seeds and dry-roast until lightly browned. Add to the bowl. Once they have cooled to room temperature, grind all the ingredients to a fine powder in a spice or coffee grinder. Set the spice mixture aside.

Make the tadka: In a large skillet, heat the sesame oil over medium heat. Add the asafoetida and mustard seeds. When they begin to crackle, add the raw peanuts, chana dal, urad dal, dried chiles, curry leaves, salt, and turmeric and fry for a minute or two. Once the dals are toasted to light golden brown, add the tamarind paste and bring to a boil. Add the spice mixture to the pan and cook over medium heat until the oil starts to separate and begins to float on top, 1 to 2 minutes.

Reduce the heat and transfer all the cooked rice to the pan and mix well. Season with salt to taste.

Turn off the heat and allow the puliyodharai to rest for a few minutes, covered, for the rice to take in all the flavors. Serve warm or at room temperature.

TIP
Dried tamarind pods are sold pressed into a block, so to get what you need here, loosen the compressed pulp and weigh out the 2 ounces (55 g) you need.

AYURVEDA NOTES

The sour taste of tamarind aids digestion, acts as a laxative, enhances focus, and boosts energy. This dish is vata-pacifying but increases pitta and kapha, so portion-control is key.

- **VATA** Reduce the red chiles if experiencing excess dryness.
- **PITTA** Enjoy this dish infrequently and in small quantities, balanced with cooling dishes.
- **KAPHA** While the pungent taste reduces kapha, the sour taste increases it, so indulge infrequently and in small portions.

BHUGA CHAWAR

RICE WITH CARAMELIZED ONION

A classic Sindhi recipe of basmati rice slow-cooked with spices and lovely dark-brown caramelized onions, signified by its name in the Sindhi language, in which *bhuga* means "cook until brown." While I was growing up, our Sunday dinners traditionally consisted of a warm bowl of *bhuga chawar* paired with *sai bhaaji*, a hearty stew prepared with chana dal, vegetables, and fresh spinach.

PERFECT PAIRING Bhuga Chawar and Sai Bhaaji (page 92) are a match made in heaven.

SERVES 2

SOAK TIME 20 to 30 minutes

Rinse the rice in a fine-mesh sieve under cold running water until the water runs clear, about a minute. Transfer to a medium bowl, add water to cover by 2 inches (5 cm), and soak for 20 to 30 minutes. Drain and set aside.

Heat a 4-quart (4 L) Dutch oven or heavy-bottomed pot over medium-high heat. Add the ghee and, once hot, add the bay leaf, peppercorns, cloves, star anise, cardamom pods, and cinnamon stick and fry for 30 to 40 seconds to allow the aromas to be released into the oil. Add the onions, reduce the heat to medium, and cook, stirring constantly, until the onions are a lovely medium dark brown, similar to milk chocolate, 8 to 12 minutes. The even browning of the onions will have a direct impact on the final dish color, so be patient and ensure the onions are being cooked evenly by scraping the edges and mixing well.

Add the soaked rice, water, salt, toasted cumin, and Kashmiri powder. Give everything a gentle stir as vigorous mixing once the rice is in the pot will break the wet rice and release its starch, resulting in a sticky cooked rice. Cover the pot and cook over medium heat for 10 minutes. Uncover and give one more gentle stir to ensure the rice is not sticking to the bottom. Reduce the heat to a simmer and cook the rice for another 10 minutes. Resist the temptation to keep stirring the rice as it cooks. The rice will absorb all the water as it cooks. The rice grains retain their shape once cooked and are soft when pressed between your thumb and index finger.

Turn off the heat and allow the rice to rest for 5 to 10 minutes. Then fluff the rice with a fork and serve warm.

1 cup (200 g) basmati rice

3 tablespoons (45 g) ghee or oil of your choice

1 bay leaf

4 or 5 black peppercorns

2 whole cloves

1 star anise

2 green cardamom pods

1-inch (2.5 cm) piece cinnamon stick

2 cups (455 g) finely chopped red onions

2 cups (480 ml) water

1½ teaspoons fine sea salt

1 teaspoon ground toasted cumin

½ teaspoon Kashmiri red chili powder

TIP

To make it a one-pot wholesome meal, add 1 cup of green peas (for protein) and mixed veggies, such as diced carrots, potatoes, and cauliflower, when you add the soaked rice to the pot.

AYURVEDA NOTES

Basmati rice is the most popular rice variety from India, aged before packaging to reduce starch content for easier digestion. Spices aid digestion further.
- **VATA** Use ghee for cooking this dish.
- **PITTA** Skip the Kashmiri powder.
- **KAPHA** Whole spices in this dish aid digestion of the grain.

MATTA COCONUT RICE

RED RICE COOKED WITH COCONUT AND SPICES

Red matta rice, also known as Palakkadan or Rosematta, is an indigenous variety of rice grown in the Palakkad district of Kerala, a southern coastal state in India. I was first introduced to red matta during my trip to Kerala for an Ayurvedic retreat, where the rice was served for both lunch and dinner. Since I wasn't used to this variety, it took a couple of days for me to develop a taste for the nutty aroma and chewy taste of this brownish-red rice. Red matta has more fiber and nutrients compared with white rice. Freshly grated coconut is a staple in many South Indian homes, but for those who don't regularly have it on hand, frozen grated coconut, which is easily found in an Indian grocery store, is a fine substitute.

PERFECT PAIRING
Serve as a side to a bowl of piping hot Tiffin Sambhar (page 120).

SERVES 2 or 3

SOAK TIME
1 to 2 hours

---

1 cup (237 g) Kerala red matta rice

5 cups (1.2 L) water

2 tablespoons coconut oil

¼ teaspoon hing/asafoetida powder

2 teaspoons black mustard seeds

2 teaspoons dhuli urad dal/peeled split black gram

2 teaspoons chana dal/peeled and split chickpeas

2 teaspoons minced fresh ginger

10 raw cashews

2 Thai green chiles, halved lengthwise

8 to 10 fresh curry leaves

1 teaspoon black peppercorns

1 cup (85 g) unsweetened shredded coconut (fresh, thawed frozen, or dried)

Rinse the rice in a fine-mesh sieve under cold running water until the water runs clear, about a minute. Transfer to a medium bowl, add water to cover by 2 inches (5 cm), and soak for 1 to 2 hours. Drain.

In a 4-quart (4 L) heavy-bottomed pot, combine the soaked rice and water and bring to a boil. Partially cover and cook over medium heat until the rice is soft but retains its shape, about 45 minutes.

Drain the rice in a sieve, return to the pot, cover, and let it rest and steam while you prepare the spices.

In a large skillet, heat the coconut oil over medium heat. Add the following ingredients in order, frying each for a few seconds before adding the next: asafoetida, mustard seeds, urad dal, chana dal, ginger, cashews, chiles, curry leaves, and black peppercorns.

Add the cooked matta rice and coconut to the spices and mix everything together. Serve warm.

TIPS
You can make coconut rice from any variety of white rice.

If you want to speed up cooking of the red matta rice, you can cook this rice in an electric pressure cooker. Soak the rice for 30 minutes. Drain and transfer to the pressure cooker along with 2½ cups of water. Pressure-cook on high for 10 minutes. Let the pressure release naturally. Drain off any excess water.

AYURVEDA NOTES

The Sanskrit term for matta rice is rakta shali. Rakta *means "naturally red" and shali means "rice." Red matta rice is tridoshic, which means it pacifies all three doshas—vata, pitta, and kapha.*
- **VATA** The spices are essential to balance vata.
- **PITTA** Coconut oil and grated coconut are cooling and ideal.
- **KAPHA** Enjoy in moderation.

KHICHU

SAVORY STEAMED RICE FLOUR DUMPLINGS

The name *khichu* is derived from the word *khinch*, which means "to pull" and describes the soft and supple nature of the rice flour dough. Khichu, a classic dish from Gujarat, the western state of India, is a popular teatime snack. The rice flour is first cooked in hot water, then formed into small doughnuts that are steamed into a soft spongy snack. Khichu is traditionally drizzled with peanut oil and an Indian pickled spice blend known as achaar masala. Here, I have garnished with *thecha* thinned with peanut oil.

PERFECT PAIRING Khichu topped with Thecha (page 218) and enjoyed with a cup of Masala Chai (page 238) is a delicious combination for lazy weekend teatime.

MAKES 8 khichus

In a 3-quart (3 L) saucepan, combine the water, chile, ginger, cumin seeds, sesame seeds, and carom seeds and bring to a rolling boil over medium-high heat. Mix in the salt and baking soda. Add the rice flour and stir with the handle of a wooden spoon. Reduce the heat to low and stir vigorously until it forms a lumpy dough.

Transfer the dough to a large platter. Knead the dough while it is still hot, but do so with the bottom of a metal cup or bowl. Add 2 tablespoons of the oil to the dough and knead until smooth, 4 to 5 minutes. As the dough cools, you can use your hands to knead as well.

Fill a steamer with water to come just below the basket or steamer plate. Heat the water to a rolling boil. Grease the basket or steamer plate with the remaining 1 tablespoon oil to prevent the khichu from sticking.

Divide the khichu dough into 8 equal portions. Wet your palms with water and shape the dough into a ball and then flatten slightly to a disc. Use your index finger to make a hole in the middle of each disc to form a kind of doughnut shape. Repeat for the remaining mixture and arrange the khichu in the steamer, leaving a ½-inch (1.3 cm) space between them for even steaming.

Cover and steam over medium heat for 15 minutes. Remove from the heat but leave the steamer covered for an additional 5 minutes.

Transfer the khichus to a plate. Drizzle with the thecha thinned out with a tablespoon of oil. Serve warm.

2½ cups (600 ml) water
1 teaspoon minced green chile
1 teaspoon minced fresh ginger
1 teaspoon cumin seeds
1 teaspoon sesame seeds
½ teaspoon ajwain/carom seeds
1 teaspoon fine sea salt
½ teaspoon baking soda
1 cup (160 g) fine rice flour
3 tablespoons (45 ml) peanut oil or neutral oil of choice

GARNISH

1 tablespoon thecha (page 218)
1 tablespoon peanut oil or olive oil

TIPS

Store leftover khichu in an airtight container in the refrigerator for up to 2 days. Quick-steam the khichu for a couple of minutes to serve warm.

Traditionally, khichu is made with fine rice flour, but I have made them with corn flour for a delicious and pretty yellow khichu.

AYURVEDA NOTES

Rice flour alone can be drying, and spices counterbalance this dryness.
- **VATA** Spices and steaming balance rice flour's dryness.
- **PITTA** Omit the green chile and use half the ginger. Skip spicy thecha and serve with mint cilantro chutney instead.
- **KAPHA** Replace the green chile with ground black pepper.

HARA BHARA PULAV

RICE PILAF WITH SEASONAL GREENS

Hara bhara pulav is a rich green rice pilaf packed with seasonal veggies in a wholesome one-pot dish. This green superfood dish is best when greens and vegetables are in their prime, from classic spinach and mildly pungent radish greens to beet greens, sweet carrot greens, peppery mustard greens, collard greens, and even leftover arugula from a salad mix. The green paste in this recipe is a delicious way to incorporate leafy vegetables for even the pickiest of eaters in your family. Like any rice pilaf, I prefer long-grain basmati for this.

PERFECT PAIRING
Serve with Panchmel Dal (page 205) or Dhaba-Style Easy Dal Fry (page 117).

SERVES 4

SOAK TIME 20 to 30 minutes

1½ cups (300 g) basmati rice

GREEN PASTE

2 cups (60 g) roughly chopped spinach

1 bunch (120 g) cilantro (leaves and tender stems)

1 medium red onion, roughly chopped

1 medium tomato, roughly chopped

1-inch (2.5 cm) piece fresh ginger, peeled

2 garlic cloves, peeled but whole

1 serrano chile, roughly chopped

TADKA

2 tablespoons vegetable oil

⅛ teaspoon hing/asafoetida powder

1 teaspoon cumin seeds

2 green cardamom pods

2 whole cloves

1-inch (2.5 cm) piece cinnamon stick

1 teaspoon ground turmeric

1 teaspoon ground coriander

PULAV

½ cup (115 g) frozen green peas, shelled edamame, or another shelled seasonal pea, such as fresh black-eyed peas

½ cup (115 g) chopped carrots

½ cup (115 g) cauliflower florets

½ cup (115 g) cubed unpeeled fingerling potatoes (blue and red variety)

2¾ cups (660 ml) water

1½ teaspoons fine sea salt

GARNISH

2 tablespoons dried cranberries

1 tablespoon pepitas or roasted pumpkin seeds

1½ teaspoons hemp hearts

Rinse the rice in a fine-mesh sieve under cold running water until the water runs clear, about a minute. Transfer to a medium bowl, add water to cover by 2 inches (5 cm), and soak for 20 to 30 minutes. Drain and set aside.

Make the green paste: In a blender, combine the spinach, cilantro, onion, tomato, ginger, garlic, and chile and puree.

Make the tadka: In a Dutch oven or 4-quart (4 L) heavy-bottomed pot, heat the oil over medium heat. Add the asafoetida, cumin seeds, cardamom pods, cloves, and cinnamon and fry for 15 to 20 seconds. Add the green paste and fry for 10 minutes until the water is evaporated and oil starts oozing out of the paste. Add the turmeric and coriander and fry for another minute.

TIPS

To make this dish in an electric pressure cooker, select Sauté and fry the spices and green paste as directed. Add the vegetables, pre-soaked rice, water, and salt. Pressure-cook on high for 5 minutes. Let the pressure release naturally before opening the lid.

To make a one-pot dish with complementary complete protein, reduce the amount of rice to 1 cup and add ½ cup split dal variety of choice.

If you want the dish to be soupy, increase the cooking liquid by ½ cup to create a masala khichdi–like consistency.

Make the pulav: Add the peas, carrots, cauliflower, and potatoes to the spice/paste mixture and stir well. Add the rice to the pot along with the water and salt and stir gently. Cover the pot and cook the rice pulav over medium heat until the rice is tender and all the liquid is absorbed, 15 to 20 minutes. Season with salt to taste. Cover and let the rice rest for 5 minutes for all the flavors to come together.

Fluff the pulav with a fork and transfer to a serving dish. Garnish with cranberries, pepitas, and hemp hearts and serve warm.

AYURVEDA NOTES

This one-pot dish has all six Ayurvedic tastes, which creates a harmonious balance. The green leafy vegetables and herbs especially provide the bitter taste that, according to Ayurveda, is one of the dominant tastes suggested for spring and summer months. Change the vegetables and spices based on the season and individual needs.

- **VATA** Limit the cauliflower.
- **PITTA** Omit the serrano chile. Substitute sunflower seeds for pumpkin seeds.
- **KAPHA** Limit the potatoes and carrots. Add black pepper.

AKKI ROTI

SAVORY RICE FLATBREAD

The first time I had *akki roti* was at my friend's home in Dallas. I remember distinctly the anise scent from the fresh dill leaves mingling with the mildly pungent aroma of scallions as my friend mixed them into her akki roti batter before cooking it into a soft and crispy savory rice pancake.

Akki means "rice flour" and *roti* means "flatbread." Traditionally, the akki roti dough is prepared by mixing rice flour with finely chopped vegetables, dill leaves, cilantro leaves, grated coconut, and spices along with water to form a soft dough. A handful of this gluten-free dough is carefully spread directly onto a hot griddle with your hands, which takes a bit of practice. Alternatively, you can spread the dough with a piece of banana leaf or parchment paper to help transfer it to the griddle.

PERFECT PAIRING
Serve with tomato garlic chutney.

SERVES 6

---

1 cup (160 g) fine rice flour
½ cup (32 g) finely chopped scallions
½ cup (50 g) grated carrots
½ cup (20 g) finely chopped fresh dill
½ cup (20 g) finely chopped cilantro
2 tablespoons grated coconut (fresh or dried)
1 tablespoon minced green Thai or serrano chile
1 tablespoon minced fresh ginger
1 teaspoon cumin seeds
1 teaspoon fine sea salt
5 tablespoons (75 ml) coconut oil
¾ cup (180 ml) warm water, plus 2 tablespoons if needed

In a wide bowl, combine the rice flour, scallions, carrots, dill, cilantro, grated coconut, green chiles, ginger, cumin seeds, salt, and 1 tablespoon of the coconut oil. Using your hands or a spatula, mix the ingredients together. Add warm water ¼ cup (60 ml) at a time to form a soft, loose dough. Cover the dough in the same bowl with a lid or cloth and let the dough rest for 10 to 15 minutes.

Keep a bowl of cold water near the stove to dip your fingers in as you spread the akki roti on the skillet. Heat a cast-iron skillet over medium heat and season the skillet with a couple of teaspoons of the coconut oil. Scoop out ½ cup (120 ml) of the akki roti dough with your hand or a ladle and place it in the center of the skillet. Dip your fingers in water and carefully spread the akki roti into a round, about 6 inches (15 cm) wide and ¼ inch (6 mm) thick. Take the handle of a spoon and make 3 to 5 holes in the akki roti. Drizzle a teaspoon of coconut oil around and in the holes on the akki roti. Cover the akki roti with a dome-shaped lid from a cooking pot that fits the size of the akki roti. Cook over medium heat until the edges start to crisp up, 3 to 4 minutes. Flip the akki roti over with a thin metal spatula and cook on the other side until it has golden-brown spots all over, for an additional 3 to 4 minutes. Repeat with the remaining dough and coconut oil.

Serve warm.

TIPS
In addition to grated carrot, use other seasonal vegetables, such as grated zucchini, yellow squash, or different colors of bell pepper.

Try this recipe with fresh green garlic, available during late winter and early spring. It adds a delightful pungency.

AYURVEDA NOTES

- **VATA** Use sesame oil in place of the coconut oil.
- **PITTA** Omit the green chiles.
- **KAPHA** Add ground black pepper. Use sesame or olive oil.

SINDHI DUM BIRYANI

A ROYAL RICE AND VEGETABLE CASSEROLE

For me, biryani will always be associated with Diwali, the Hindu New Year's celebration, which is when I'd help my mom prepare this special one-pot meal. Biryani comes from the Persian phrase *birinj biryani*, which means "fried before cooking." While biryani is traditionally identified with Islamic cuisine and cooked with meat, it has evolved alongside the diverse cultural and culinary traditions in India, and nowadays vegetarian versions are just as popular. Perfect for large gatherings or potlucks, biryani can easily feed a crowd and is worth the extra effort.

Similar to layered baked pasta dishes, biryani is created by layering marinated proteins or vegetables with partially cooked rice, fried onions, and aromatic herbs. The pot of biryani is then slow-cooked using *dum*. *Dum pukht* or "cooking on dum" refers to the ancient art of slow-cooking food in tightly sealed earthen pots. The pot can be sealed using raw wheat dough if the dum cooking is done on the stovetop. Alternatively, the biryani pot can be covered with heavy-duty aluminum foil for modern-day dum cooking in an oven. The steam inside the sealed container locks in the aromas and flavors. There are several regional variations of biryani, and this recipe honors my Sindhi lineage. The cornerstone of a Sindhi-style biryani is *sella* (parboiled) basmati rice, *aloo bukhara* (dried plums), sour yogurt (see Tips), and tomatoes, all of which combine to create a unique sour, spicy, and sweet dish. The bottom layer of the rice gets browned and crisp, much like a Persian *tahdig*.

PERFECT PAIRING
Biryani is usually served with dal fry or raita (yogurt dip) on the side.

SERVES 8

SOAK TIME 30 to 45 minutes

---

2 cups (400 g) basmati rice, preferably sella basmati rice (see Tips)

FRIED GARNISH LAYER
½ cup (115 g) ghee
½ cup (120 ml) oil, such as sunflower, peanut, avocado, or grapeseed
2 cups (230 g) thinly sliced onions
½ cup (115 g) raw cashew halves

VEGETABLE CURRY LAYER
1 bay leaf
1 star anise
Two 1-inch (2.5 cm) pieces Indian cinnamon sticks
3 green cardamom pods
4 black peppercorns
3 whole cloves
1 teaspoon caraway seeds
1-inch (2.5 cm) piece fresh ginger, peeled and minced
3 garlic cloves, peeled and minced
1 cup (240 ml) pureed red onion

1 cup (240 ml) fresh or canned tomato puree
1 tablespoon tomato paste
1 teaspoon fine sea salt
1 teaspoon Kashmiri red chili powder
1 teaspoon ground coriander
1 teaspoon ground turmeric
½ teaspoon garam masala (page 40)
1 cup (230 g) plain yogurt (see Tips)
6 to 8 aloo bukhara/Indian dried plums (see Tips)
2 cups (455 g) cubed potatoes (cut into 1-inch/2.5 cm pieces)
2 cups (160 g) cauliflower florets (1 to 1½ inches/2.5 to 4 cm)
1 cup (140 g) chopped green beans (cut into 2-inch/5 cm pieces)
1 cup (140 g) chopped carrots (cut into 1-inch/2.5 cm pieces)
⅓ cup (50 g) shelled green peas
½ cup (120 ml) water

RICE LAYER
8 cups (1.9 L) water
2 teaspoons salt
1 tablespoon oil, such as sunflower, peanut, avocado, or grapeseed
3 green cardamom pods
3 whole cloves
Two 1-inch (2.5 cm) pieces Indian cinnamon sticks
1 bay leaf

SAFFRON JHOL (LIQUID) LAYER
½ cup (120 ml) whole milk
¼ cup (60 ml) water
10 to 12 saffron strands
1 teaspoon kewra water (see Box) or rose water (optional)

ASSEMBLY
½ cup (20 g) finely chopped cilantro (leaves and tender stems)
½ cup (20 g) finely chopped mint (leaves and tender stems)

Continued—

Rinse the rice in a fine-mesh sieve under cold running water until the water runs clear, about a minute. Transfer to a medium bowl, add water to cover by 2 inches (5 cm), and soak for 30 to 45 minutes. Drain and set aside.

Meanwhile, make the fried garnish layer: Line a bowl with paper towels and have it near the stove. In a 6-quart (6 L) heavy-bottomed pot, heat the ghee and oil over medium heat. Add the onions and sauté, stirring regularly, until golden brown, 8 to 10 minutes. Transfer the fried onions to the paper towels to drain.

In the same oil/ghee, sauté the cashew pieces until golden brown, 3 to 4 minutes. Add the cashews to the fried onions and set aside. Pour the oil/ghee into a separate bowl and set aside for cooking other components of the biryani.

Make the vegetable curry layer: Add 6 tablespoons (85 g) of the reserved oil/ghee to the same large heavy-bottomed pot and heat over medium heat until hot. Add the bay leaf, star anise, cinnamon sticks, cardamom pods, peppercorns, cloves, and caraway seeds and fry for a few seconds. Add the ginger and garlic and sauté for a minute. Add the onion puree and sauté until golden brown, 8 to 10 minutes.

Once the onion puree is well cooked and starts to release oil, add the tomato puree and tomato paste and cook for another 5 minutes. Add the salt, Kashmiri powder, coriander, turmeric, and garam masala and fry for a few seconds. Add the yogurt and mix well. Add the dried plums, potatoes, cauliflower, green beans, carrots, peas, and water and give it a good stir. Cover the pot and cook over medium heat until the vegetables are partially cooked but still crunchy and firm, 3 to 4 minutes. Remove from the heat.

Make the rice layer: In a large pot, combine the water, salt, oil, cardamom pods, cloves, cinnamon sticks, and bay leaf. Bring to a rolling boil, add the soaked rice, and reduce the heat to medium. Cover and cook until the rice is almost cooked through but still has some bite, 5 to 6 minutes. Drain the rice in a fine-mesh sieve. Return the rice to the pot and set aside.

Make the saffron jhol (liquid) layer: In a small pan, combine the milk, water, saffron, and 1 tablespoon of the reserved oil/ghee. Warm this liquid for a minute or so and then turn off the heat. If using, add the kewra (or rose) water after the heat is turned off. Set aside.

Preheat the oven to 250°F (120°C).

TIPS

Sella basmati is a parboiled variety and retains the integrity of each grain of rice for cooking biryani. However, any variety of aged basmati rice will be equally fine to use for this dish.

The older and more sour your yogurt is (a couple of days old at least), the better it is for this dish.

If you can't find Indian dried plums, use 4 American dried plums (prunes), roughly chopped.

To make a dough seal for the biryani pot, combine 1½ cups (195 g) wheat flour with ½ to ¾ cup (120 to 180 ml) water to form a soft dough. Roll the dough into a thick rope long enough to go around the pot and seal the edges of the biryani pot. Cover the pot with a lid and press the dough against the lid to form a seal around the edge.

To make this vegan, replace the ghee with oil and replace the dairy yogurt with cashew yogurt.

Assemble the biryani layers: Add a couple of tablespoons of the reserved oil/ghee to the bottom of an ovenproof covered casserole or Dutch oven. Add a 1-inch (2.5 cm) layer of rice at the bottom of the pan. This will crisp up once the biryani is slow-cooked. Layer half of the vegetable curry over the rice, leaving some rice uncovered around the edges. Add half of the remaining rice on top of this. Sprinkle half of the fried onions and cashews, half of the cilantro and mint. Drizzle half of the saffron jhol liquid over this rice layer. Repeat the layers in the same order with the remaining components.

Cover the pot with a layer of aluminum foil before placing the lid on top. (Alternatively, put the lid of the Dutch oven on and then stick a thick roll of wheat dough all around the edge of the pot to seal it. See Tips.) Place the sealed biryani pot in the oven and cook for 20 to 25 minutes.

Remove from the oven and keep the biryani pot covered until ready to eat. Carefully uncover the lid and enjoy biryani warm.

AYURVEDA NOTES

While combining tomatoes and yogurt isn't ideal in Ayurveda, the addition of various spices in the biryani counterbalances any incompatibilities, especially since it's typically enjoyed on special occasions rather than regularly.

- **VATA** Cooked vegetables and cashews nourish vata. Many spices in the dish aid digestion of potatoes, which can be problematic for vata.
- **PITTA** Reduce the amount of Kashmiri powder and cinnamon.
- **KAPHA** Use sunflower oil, which is tridoshic. Enjoy the fried garnish in moderation.

Kewra Water

Kewra water is an aromatic extract distilled from pandanus flowers and leaves. Its sweet perfume quality is similar to rose water, but kewra is fruitier in aroma. It is the secret ingredient in a Sindhi biryani but can be easily substituted with rose water to add to the luxurious aroma of a traditional Sindhi biryani.

KANDE POHE

SAVORY SPICED RICE FLAKES

Kande pohe is, without a doubt, one of the most popular breakfasts served in India, a classic recipe from my birth state of Maharashtra. The Hindi word for these flattened rice flakes is *poha* while its Marathi language word is *pohe*. Poha is rice that is parboiled, rolled, flattened, and dried to produce compressed flakes, in both thin and thick varieties, and can be found in any Indian grocery store. Choosing the thick variety is key for a perfect bowl of kande pohe; my version includes onions, potatoes, and peanuts, but feel free to create your own.

PERFECT PAIRING Top with Kolhapuri Akkha Masoor (page 77) and garnish with onions, cilantro, and a squeeze of lime to make a complete and hearty meal.

SERVES 4

1½ cups thick poha/flattened rice flakes

2 tablespoons sunflower oil or avocado oil

⅛ teaspoon hing/asafoetida powder

1 teaspoon cumin seeds

1 teaspoon black mustard seeds

1 to 2 Thai green chiles, halved lengthwise

¼ cup unroasted peanuts

¾ cup (50 g) finely chopped red onion

¾ cup (150 g) peeled and chopped potatoes

1 teaspoon fine sea salt

1 teaspoon sugar

½ teaspoon ground turmeric

1 tablespoon lemon juice

¼ cup (10 g) finely chopped cilantro leaves

Rinse the poha in a fine-mesh sieve under running water a few times until it softens. Don't soak the poha. Leave it in the sieve and set aside to drain off any excess water.

In a large skillet, heat the oil over medium heat. Add the asafoetida and allow it to sizzle for 5 to 10 seconds. Add the cumin seeds, mustard seeds, and green chile and fry for a few seconds. Add the peanuts and fry for a minute or so. Add the onion and sauté until translucent and the oil starts to separate from the onions, 3 to 4 minutes. Add the potatoes and salt, cover, and cook until the potatoes are soft, 4 to 5 minutes. Uncover the pan and stir well.

Transfer the rinsed poha to the pan. Add the sugar, turmeric, and adjust for salt as needed. Mix well. Cover and cook over low heat for 2 to 3 minutes.

Stir in the lemon juice and serve warm, garnished with cilantro leaves.

TIPS

To make this a wholesome one-pot meal, add 1 cup green peas and other mixed veggies, such as diced carrots, corn, and chopped squash, when you add the potatoes.

Other optional garnishes include fine sev, crushed tortilla chips, and pomegranate arils in addition to the cilantro and lemon juice.

AYURVEDA NOTES

Poha, or flattened rice, can be heavy to digest and may increase kapha if consumed excessively. The spices used in the recipe help counterbalance its heavy qualities.

- **VATA** Use ghee for cooking this dish. Increase the quantity of vegetables.
- **PITTA** Omit the green chiles. Substitute white onion for the red onion.
- **KAPHA** Skip the potatoes. Add chopped ginger to the recipe and fry along with the cumin and mustard seeds.

MUMBAI BHELPURI

PUFFED RICE TOSSED WITH VEGGIES AND CHUTNEYS

Bhelpuri, or *bhel* for short, is one of India's most popular savory snacks, with regional variations found all over the country. Growing up, I loved making small talk with the street *chaat* vendor as he tossed together the crunchy puffed rice with my choice of vegetables, chutneys, and toppings, serving it up in a paper cone made of recycled newsprint, with a *papdi* (flat wheat crisp) as a spoon. It's a truly crowd-pleasing snack that can be personalized with different types of chutney and toppings. Most Indian stores carry bhel mix, which is puffed rice already roasted with salt, turmeric, and spices in case you want to skip the step of roasting the puffed rice.

PERFECT PAIRING
Serve with Shikanji (page 230) or Pudina Jaljeera (page 229) to drink.

SERVES 4

TIPS

Replace unripe mango with pomegranate arils.

If unable to find thin sev, crush tortilla chips to a coarse powder to use as garnish.

A nice size sturdy pita chip can be used as a spoon if desired, replacing a traditional Indian papdi.

Roast the puffed rice: In a wok or large pan, heat the oil over low heat. Add the puffed rice, salt, and turmeric and toast for 10 minutes. Transfer the puffed rice to a large mixing bowl to cool.

Assemble the dish: In a large bowl, mix together the potato, tomato, onion, all three chutneys, and the chaat masala. Stir well and then add the roasted puffed rice. Stir gently to combine.

Spoon into paper cones or bowls. Garnish with the mango, cilantro, and generous amounts of fine sev, and a handful of pomegranate arils. Serve immediately as the puffed rice will start to become soggy.

ROASTED PUFFED RICE

1 teaspoon avocado or sunflower oil

4 heaping cups (120 g) plain puffed rice

½ teaspoon salt

½ teaspoon ground turmeric

ASSEMBLY

1 cup (225 g) finely chopped boiled, peeled potato

1 cup (90 g) finely chopped red tomatoes

¾ cup (150 g) finely chopped red onion

2 tablespoons Hari Chutney (page 214)

2 tablespoons Imli Khajur ki Chutney (page 215)

1 tablespoon Thecha (page 218) thinned with 2 tablespoons water

1 teaspoon chaat masala

GARNISH

¼ cup (57 g) finely chopped green (unripe) mango

¼ cup (10 g) finely chopped cilantro

½ cup (115 g) fine sev/fried chickpea noodles

½ cup (90 g) pomegranate arils (when in season)

AYURVEDA NOTES

Bhelpuri is a delicious dish that has all six Ayurvedic tastes (shad rasas)—sweet (rice, dates, potatoes), sour (tomatoes, tamarind, mango), salt (chaat masala), bitter (cilantro, mint), pungent (onion, garlic), and astringent (sev, pomegranate). Puffed rice is dry and light and makes a great dish, especially for the spring season.

- **VATA** Boiled potatoes balance the dry quality of puffed rice.
- **PITTA** Avoid or limit the quantity of onions and thecha (chile garlic chutney).
- **KAPHA** Avoid or limit the quantity of potatoes and the imli khajur ki chutney (sweet date tamarind chutney).

KHAJUR KI KHEER

DATE AND RICE PUDDING

Khajur ki kheer is a variation of the classic Indian rice kheer, made by cooking rice and milk with dates and almonds. The kheer is slow-cooked without any refined sugar, offering a perfect bowl of nourishment, especially in the dry months of autumn. Rice, dates, and fresh raw milk are considered sattvic foods in Ayurveda, promoting energy, happiness, and balance. Dates are particularly revered in Ayurveda for their capacity to effectively contribute to the reserves of ojas: the subtle essence of vitality and immune health. If you have access to raw milk or nonhomogenized low-temp pasteurized milk where you live, I highly recommend it for this dish.

PERFECT PAIRING A small bowl of khajur ki kheer after a comforting dinner of Saag Chana (page 87) and Jeera Rice (page 156) is a perfect way to end a meal, especially during autumn months.

SERVES 4 to 6

SOAK TIME 20 to 30 minutes

½ cup (100 g) basmati rice
8 ounces (225 g) Medjool dates (about 12), chopped
5¼ cups (1.25 L) whole milk
½ cup (70 g) raw almonds
1 tablespoon (15 g) ghee
1 teaspoon ground cardamom
¼ teaspoon ground ginger
¼ teaspoon freshly grated nutmeg
¼ cup (21 g) sliced almonds

Rinse the rice in a fine-mesh sieve under cold running water until the water runs clear, about a minute. Transfer to a medium bowl, add water to cover by 2 inches (5 cm), and soak for 20 to 30 minutes. Drain and set aside.

Meanwhile, soak the chopped dates in 1 cup (240 ml) of the milk for 30 minutes. Soak the raw almonds in hot water for 30 minutes. Drain the almonds and remove the skins.

In a blender, combine the dates along with the soaking milk and the peeled almonds and puree until smooth. Set aside.

In a heavy-bottomed pan, heat the ghee over medium heat. Add the soaked rice and sauté for a couple of minutes to release the aroma. Stir in the remaining 4¼ cups (1 L) milk, adjust the heat to high, and let the milk come to a boil. Reduce the heat to medium and cook the rice until it is soft and starting to get mushy, 15 to 20 minutes. Stir regularly to make sure the rice doesn't stick to the bottom of the pan. When pressed between your fingers, the rice should be soft and tender.

Add the date/almond paste to the pan. Add the cardamom, ginger, and nutmeg to the pan. Mix well and cook with the rice and milk over medium heat for 15 minutes to thicken the kheer.

Serve warm or chilled, garnished with the sliced almonds.

TIPS
Use ½ cup (50 g) store-bought almond flour instead of raw almonds.

To make this plant-based, replace whole milk with oat milk and use a neutral oil like sunflower oil or rice bran oil instead of ghee.

AYURVEDA NOTES

Dates have a sweet taste (rasa) with cooling potency (virya), nourishing and energizing all three doshas, but can increase kapha in excess.
- **VATA** This dish is beneficial for pacifying and nourishing vata depletion.
- **PITTA** Use soaked and peeled almonds instead of store-bought almond flour if possible.
- **KAPHA** Enjoy in moderation.

SINDHI TAIRI

SWEET SPICED RICE WITH NUTS AND DRIED FRUITS

An aromatic sweet rice preparation, *tairi* is traditionally prepared during special Sindhi festivals such as Cheti Chand, which honors the birthday of Sindhi patron saint Jhulelal, an incarnation of the Hindu water god, Varun. The Cheti Chand festival is celebrated when the crescent moon appears on the second day of the Chaitra month, marking the arrival of spring. Traditional Sindhi cuisine is influenced by Persian, Arab, and Central Asian cooking traditions, so this dish embraces a diversity of flavors: coconut is a holy fruit for Hindus, while saffron, pistachios, and almonds are plentiful in Persian and Muslim cuisines. Similar dishes in other regional Indian cuisines include Kashmiri *zarda* and North Indian *meethe chawal*.

SERVES 4 to 6

SOAK TIME
20 minutes

---

1 cup (200 g) basmati rice

3 tablespoons (45 g) ghee or
    neutral oil of choice

2 tablespoons raw cashews

2 tablespoons sliced almonds

1 teaspoon fennel seeds

½-inch (1.3 cm) piece cinnamon
    stick

3 green cardamom pods

8 to 10 saffron strands soaked in 1
    tablespoon warm milk or water

2 tablespoons raisins

¼ teaspoon fine sea salt

⅛ teaspoon ground turmeric

2 cups (480 ml) water

¾ cup (170 g) cane sugar or
    turbinado sugar

2 tablespoons chopped pistachios

1 tablespoon unsweetened shredded
    coconut or coconut flakes

Rinse the rice in a fine-mesh sieve under cold running water until the water runs clear, about a minute. Transfer to a medium bowl, add water to cover by 2 inches (5 cm), and soak for 20 to 30 minutes. Drain and set aside.

In a 3-quart (3 L) heavy-bottomed pot, heat the ghee over medium heat. Add the cashews and sliced almonds and cook over low heat until lightly browned, 2 to 3 minutes. Remove with a slotted spoon and set aside.

In the same pot, fry the fennel seeds and cinnamon stick over low heat for 15 to 30 seconds. Smash the cardamom pods with a mortar and pestle to release the seeds from the pods. Add the cardamom seeds and the outer skin to the pot and fry with other spices.

Add the soaked rice and gently sauté the rice in the ghee for a minute. Add the soaked saffron strands along with their soaking liquid, the raisins, salt, turmeric, and water. Cover and cook over medium heat for 10 minutes.

Uncover the pot (the rice should be cooked halfway through), stir in the sugar, reduce the heat to low, and cook uncovered until the rice is tender and all of the liquid is absorbed, 5 to 10 minutes. Check for doneness by pressing a grain of rice between your fingers. The rice should be soft but still firm in shape.

Fluff the rice with a fork. Garnish with the pistachios and coconut. Remove from the heat, cover the pot, and set aside undisturbed for 10 to 15 minutes before serving.

TIP
To make it vegan, use neutral cooking oil such as avocado or sunflower oil instead of ghee.

AYURVEDA NOTES

- **VATA** The warming spices and nuts, raisins, and coconut make this a wonderful dish to nourish vata.
- **PITTA** Substitute almonds and sunflower seeds for the cashews and pistachios.
- **KAPHA** In addition to cinnamon, cardamom, and turmeric, add a couple of pinches of black pepper to support kapha.

GULAB PISTA PHIRNI

ROSE-PISTACHIO RICE PUDDING

The difference between *phirni* and *kheer*, traditional Indian rice pudding, is the texture and use of ground rice versus whole rice cooked in milk. Phirni, which is traditionally kept in clay pots or cups and best enjoyed cold, can be traced to India's ancient Mughlai cuisine with Persian influences. This thick, creamy pudding is slow-cooked with ground rice paste, sugar, nuts, and spices. I personally love the addition of dried rose petals and rose petal jam, called *gulkand*.

PERFECT PAIRING Serve with a meal of Dal Makhani (page 134) and Jeera Rice (page 156).

SERVES 6

SOAK TIME 30 minutes to 1 hour

TIPS

For a vegan version, use almond or oat milk instead of whole milk.

I use a brand of rose syrup called Kalvert, which can be found in Indian grocery stores. If unable to find the rose syrup, use 1 teaspoon food grade rose water and ½ teaspoon beet powder or a few drops of red food coloring for color.

Rinse the rice in a fine-mesh sieve under cold running water until the water runs clear, about a minute. Transfer to a medium bowl, add water to cover by 2 inches (5 cm), and soak for 30 minutes to 1 hour.

Drain well, then combine the rice and the ¼ cup (60 ml) water in a blender and blend to a paste.

In a medium Dutch oven or saucepan, bring the milk to a boil over medium heat. Reduce the heat to low, stir in the rice paste, and whisk constantly to avoid any lumps. Add the sugar and cardamom and keep stirring regularly until the mixture thickens, 20 to 30 minutes.

Add the rose petal jam and rose syrup and mix well. Remove from the heat and let the phirni cool to room temperature. Divide among individual cups or ramekins and garnish each with the chopped pistachios and dried rose petals. Refrigerate for a couple of hours or overnight until well chilled.

Serve chilled.

¼ cup (50 g) basmati rice
¼ cup (60 ml) water
4 cups (960 ml) whole milk
¾ cup (135 g) turbinado sugar
½ teaspoon ground cardamom
2 tablespoons gulkand/rose petal jam
2 tablespoons rose syrup (see Tips)
¼ cup (30 g) chopped pistachios
¼ cup (10 g) dried rose petals

AYURVEDA NOTES

Basmati rice is tridoshic. Rose is cooling and has a profound effect on the mind and body and emotions. Cardamom helps with the digestion of milk proteins. This dish is a perfect summertime dessert due to its cooling properties.
- **VATA** If vegan, use oat milk.
- **PITTA** Reduce the cardamom.
- **KAPHA** Use almond milk instead of dairy. Reduce the sugar, rose syrup, and rose jam.

COMBINING DALS + CHAWAL

Dal and rice complement each other effortlessly in any meal and create nutritional harmony through mutual supplementation as they form a complete protein when combined.

Countless traditional Indian recipes use more than one dal in a dish or a combination of dals and rice. For example, almost every region of India has its own version of khichdi that combines dal and rice to make a wholesome one-pot meal. There is the southern classic sweetened porridge of *chakkara pongal*; *dal pittha,* the savory dumplings from Bihar; and the classic combination of rice and dal to make the fermented batter for dosa, the traditional South Indian savory crepes.

DHEELI KHICHDI

AN AYURVEDIC GUT RESET MEAL

Khichdi—also known as *kitchari* or *kitcharee*—is a one-pot meal combining rice and yellow split moong dal that has gained popularity in the West with the emergence of Ayurveda and the practice of yoga. *Khichdi* means "mixture," and for an average Indian household, it's as basic a recipe as one can cook.

Dheeli khichdi is simple, light, and deeply nourishing; you could eat it at least once a week for a gentle gut reset or at any time when recovering from an illness or returning home from travel. As a kid, I would frown when Mom said she was making khichdi, as it meant either someone was sick or she needed a break from all the cooking. My dad, however, could eat khichdi every day—it was truly his favorite comfort meal, and his last meal on this earth was a bowl of my mom's *dheeli khichdi*.

Traditional homestyle dheeli khichdi uses medium- or short-grain rice, such as Surti Kolam, Indrayani, or Ambemohar instead of basmati rice, as it is much easier to digest. *Dheeli*, which means "loose," suggests a soft, mushy, pouring consistency, so if the khichdi thickens when it cools, loosen it with hot water as needed.

SERVES 4

SOAK TIME 30 minutes to 1 hour

---

1 cup (200 g) medium-grain rice, such as Indrayani, Sona Masoori, or Surti Kolam

¾ cup (150 g) dhuli moong dal/yellow split moong dal

5 cups (1.2 L) water

1 teaspoon fine sea salt

½ teaspoon ground turmeric

2 tablespoons (30 g) ghee

⅛ teaspoon hing/asafoetida powder

1 tablespoon cumin seeds

½ teaspoon freshly ground black pepper

Rinse the rice and dal in a fine-mesh sieve under cold running water until the water runs clear, about 1 minute. Transfer to a medium bowl, add water to cover by 2 inches (5 cm), and soak for 30 minutes to 1 hour. Drain.

Transfer the dal and rice to a 4-quart (4 L) pot. Add the water, salt, and turmeric and bring to a boil. Skim off and discard any foam from the surface. Reduce the heat to medium, partially cover, and cook until the dal and rice are soft and mushy, 20 to 25 minutes.

In a small pan, heat the ghee over medium heat. Add the asafoetida and cumin seeds and allow them to sizzle for a few seconds. Add the black pepper and immediately pour the hot spiced tempering over the pot of cooked khichdi. Season with salt to taste.

Add hot water to loosen to a soft pouring consistency as needed. Serve warm.

TIPS

To cook the soaked rice and dal in an electric pressure cooker, pressure-cook on high for 3 minutes. Let the pressure release naturally before opening the lid.

To make the dish vegan, use oil instead of ghee.

AYURVEDA NOTES

Khichdi is tridoshic, an Ayurvedic term meaning "suitable for all body types." The spices can be varied based on a person's body constitution. It is an extremely important dish in Ayurveda. This dish is very easy to digest and gives strength and vitality and nourishes all the tissues of our body. It is the preferred food when going through Ayurvedic cleansing, or panchakarma.

- **VATA** Add fresh lemon or lime juice and top with shredded coconut.
- **PITTA** Add lime juice, cilantro, and shredded coconut.
- **KAPHA** Include a small amount of spicy pickle on the side.

BISI BELE BHATH

RICE, DAL, AND VEGGIES SLOW-COOKED IN A SPECIAL SPICE BLEND

A traditional recipe from the southern state of Karnataka, *bisi bele bhath* translates literally to "hot dal rice." I like to make this slow-cooked dish on the weekend, with leftovers for a hearty meal the next day. I add vegetables of different textures and taste that build on the different layers of flavor from dal, rice, and the special spice blend. Carrots for sweetness, the crunch from green beans and green bell peppers, chayote for its mild crispness, and the sweet pungency from baby pearl onions are a must for my updated version, but feel free to choose vegetables from what is available locally. The true secret to a bisi bele bowl is its special spice blend—whether you use a store-bought bisi bele spice blend or make your own from scratch shared in the recipe.

PERFECT PAIRING
Serve with Khatta Meetha Nimbu ka Achaar (page 223) or sprinkle Javas Chutney (page 220) on top.

SERVES 4

SOAK TIME 2 hours

½ cup (100 g) toor dal/split pigeon peas

½ cup (100 g) medium-grain rice, such as Sona Masoori or Surti Kolam

4 cups (960 ml) water

1 teaspoon fine sea salt

½ teaspoon ground turmeric

VEGGIES

1 tablespoon oil, such as sesame, peanut, avocado, or grapeseed

1 medium green bell pepper, chopped

1 medium carrot, peeled and chopped

1 medium chayote or yellow squash, chopped

3½ ounces (100 g) green beans, cut into 1-inch (2.5 cm) pieces (about 1 cup)

4½ ounces (130 g) baby pearl onions, peeled and left whole

½ teaspoon fine sea salt

2 cups (480 ml) water

2 tablespoons tamarind concentrate

2 teaspoons grated jaggery or jaggery powder

¼ cup Bisi Bele Bhath Powder (recipe follows)

TADKA

3 tablespoons (45 g) ghee

⅛ teaspoon hing/asafoetida powder

1 teaspoon black mustard seeds

¼ cup (37 g) raw cashews, whole or broken pieces

¼ cup (30 g) raw peanuts

10 to 12 fresh curry leaves

Rinse the dal and rice in a fine-mesh sieve under cold running water until the water runs clear, about a minute. Transfer to a medium bowl, add water to cover by 2 inches (5 cm), and soak for about 2 hours. Drain.

Transfer the dal and rice to a 3-quart (3 L) pot. Add the water, salt, and turmeric and bring to a boil over high heat. Skim and discard any foam from the surface. Reduce the heat to medium, cover, and cook until the dal and rice are soft and mushy, 20 to 25 minutes.

Meanwhile, cook the veggies: In a large skillet, heat the oil over medium heat. Add the bell pepper, carrot, chayote, green beans, pearl onions, and salt and sauté for a minute. Add 1 cup (240 ml) of the water and cook the vegetables over medium heat to soften a bit but still hold their crunch, about 5 minutes.

While the veggies cook, in a small bowl, combine the tamarind concentrate, remaining 1 cup (240 ml) water, jaggery, and bisi bele bhath powder.

TIPS

To cook the soaked rice and dal in an electric pressure cooker, pressure-cook on high for 5 minutes. Let the pressure release naturally before opening the lid.

For a vegan version, use oil instead of ghee.

Change the vegetables seasonally. From summer to winter squash, scallions instead of pearl onions, golden beets instead of carrots, or zucchini instead of chayote.

Once the vegetables soften, add the tamarind mixture to the skillet and cook for 1 minute. Transfer the cooked dal and rice along with any liquid to the skillet with the vegetables and spices. Mix well and simmer for 5 minutes.

Make the tadka: In a small skillet, heat the ghee over medium heat. Add the asafoetida and mustard seeds and sizzle for a few seconds. Add the cashews and peanuts and sauté until golden brown, 1 to 2 minutes. Carefully add the fresh curry leaves as the moisture in the leaves will splutter in the ghee. Give a quick mix and immediately pour this tempering over the bisi bele bhath. Mix well and let the bisi bele bhath simmer until ready to serve.

The bisi bele bhath will thicken once cooled. To heat any leftovers, add a cup or more of hot water to bring it back to its creamy pouring consistency.

AYURVEDA NOTES

- **VATA** The cooked rice, dal, and veggies with spices are ideal for vata. Favor ghee over oil.
- **PITTA** Reduce the bisi bele bhath powder due to its heating potency. Use avocado or grapeseed oil.
- **KAPHA** Reduce the amount of tempering oil. The heat from bisi bele bhath powder balances the sweetness and sourness in this dish.

BISI BELE BHATH POWDER

MAKES about 1½ cups (180 g)

¼ cup (50 g) chana dal/peeled and split chickpeas
2 tablespoons urad dal/split black gram
½ cup (35 g) coriander seeds
1 tablespoon cumin seeds
½ teaspoon fenugreek seeds
½ teaspoon black peppercorns
4 whole cloves
2-inch (5 cm) piece cinnamon stick
4 green cardamom pods
10 dried red Byadagi chiles
5 dried red Guntur Sannam chiles
¼ cup (25 g) unsweetened shredded coconut
2 teaspoons white poppy seeds

In a medium skillet, dry-roast both dals over medium-low heat, stirring constantly, 3 to 4 minutes. Add the coriander seeds, cumin seeds, fenugreek seeds, peppercorns, cloves, cinnamon stick, cardamom pods, and both dried red chiles and roast for another 3 to 4 minutes. Reduce the heat, add the coconut and poppy seeds, and roast until the coconut turns light brown, an additional 3 to 4 minutes.

Let all the ingredients cool to room temperature. Grind to a fine powder in a spice grinder. Store in an airtight container in the pantry for up to 3 months.

HANDVO

SPICY SAVORY CAKE WITH RICE, DAL, AND VEGGIES

I call Gujarat's traditional *handvo* a spicy savory cake because I have been requested to make this instead of a traditional birthday cake more than once, and it's been a showstopper for several special occasions over the years in our family. It can be served as an appetizer, a side dish, or a main dish along with chutney. The savory cake is a combination of several dals, rice, and a generous quantity of veggies and spices. It appeals to diverse palates as it tends to remind people of an American cornbread, and the leftovers heat up well in a toaster oven or microwave and make for a filling lunchbox meal or after-school snack. It's the kind of dish that allows for experimentation and creativity, and I've enjoyed garnishing the top much like decorative focaccia breads.

PERFECT PAIRING Serve with Hari Chutney (page 214), Imli Khajur ki Chutney (page 215), or Thecha (page 218) on the side.

SERVES 8

SOAK TIME 6 to 8 hours

FERMENTATION TIME 8 to 10 hours

HANDVO BATTER

1 cup (200 g) rice, such as basmati, Sona Masoori, or jasmine

½ cup (110 g) toor dal/split pigeon peas

¼ cup (50 g) chilka urad dal/ unpeeled black gram

¼ cup (50 g) chilka moong dal/ green split moong dal

¼ cup (50 g) chana dal/peeled and split chickpeas

½ cup (115 g) plain yogurt

HANDVO CAKE

½ cup oil, such as peanut, sunflower, olive, or avocado

2 cups shredded vegetables (such as zucchini, cabbage, carrot, and/or Indian bottle gourd, shredded on the medium holes of a box grater)

1 tablespoon sugar

2 teaspoons fine sea salt

1 teaspoon ground turmeric

½ teaspoon Kashmiri red chili powder

2 tablespoons minced fresh ginger

2 tablespoons minced garlic

2 Thai green chiles, minced, or to taste

1 teaspoon baking soda

1 teaspoon Eno fruit salt

2 teaspoons lemon juice

2 teaspoons distilled white vinegar

TADKA

¼ cup (60 ml) oil, such as peanut, sunflower, olive, or avocado

¼ teaspoon hing/asafoetida powder

2 teaspoons cumin seeds

2 teaspoons black mustard seeds

2 teaspoons white sesame seeds

½ teaspoon Kashmiri red chili powder

Make the handvo batter: Rinse the rice and all the dals in a fine-mesh sieve under cold running water until the water runs clear, about a minute. Transfer to a medium bowl, add water to cover by 2 inches (5 cm), and soak for 6 to 8 hours. Reserve ¾ cup (180 ml) of the soaking water as you drain the rice and dals.

Transfer the rice and dals along with reserved soaking water to a high-powered blender and grind to a thick coarse batter. Transfer to a bowl. Add the yogurt to the batter and mix vigorously with your clean hand or a spoon in a circular motion for a minute to incorporate some air into the batter. The batter should be thick but of pouring consistency, similar to a cake batter. Cover the bowl with a lid and place in a draft-free area of your kitchen to ferment for 8 to 10 hours (see Fermenting Batters, page 193). The fermentation creates a mild sweet-and-sour aroma with small bubbles and some rise in the batter.

Special handvo flour is available in Indian grocery stores. If you want to skip the soaking and grinding, use 2 cups (380 g) handvo flour plus 1½ cups (360 ml) water and proceed with fermentation and baking as directed in the recipe.

Instead of baking one big batch of handvo in a pan, you can cook the batter as a thick pancake in a skillet on the stovetop. Heat the oil in the pan and sprinkle black mustard seeds, cumin seeds, and sesame seeds on the bottom before pouring in 1 cup (240 ml) batter. Cook over medium heat for 3 to 4 minutes and flip to cook for another 3 to 4 minutes on the other side. The handvo pancake should have a crispy golden-brown top and be soft and spongy in the center.

Make the handvo cake: Preheat the oven to 350°F (180°C). Generously grease a 10- or 12-inch (25 or 30 cm) cast-iron skillet or a 9-by-13-inch (23-by-33 cm) baking pan with ¼ cup (60 ml) of the oil. Smear the oil on the sides and have a thin layer of oil on the bottom of the pan.

Add the shredded vegetables, sugar, salt, turmeric, and Kashmiri powder to the fermented batter and mix well.

In a small saucepan, heat the remaining ¼ cup (60 ml) oil over medium heat. Add the ginger, garlic, and green chiles and sauté for a few seconds. Pour this warm oil/spice mixture into the batter and mix well.

Add the baking soda and fruit salt to the batter. Pour the lemon juice and vinegar on top and it will start foaming. Mix vigorously in one circular motion for 30 to 40 seconds. The mixture will expand in volume. Pour the batter into the greased pan and prepare the final tempering.

Make the tadka: In the same small saucepan, heat the oil over medium heat. Add the asafoetida, cumin seeds, and mustard seeds and let the seeds sizzle in hot oil for 30 to 40 seconds. Stir in the sesame seeds and Kashmiri powder, then pour this tempering evenly over the batter.

Bake the handvo for 30 minutes. Increase the oven temperature to 400°F (200°C) and bake until a thick golden-brown crust forms on the top and a toothpick inserted into the center comes out clean, about 15 minutes.

Let the handvo cool in the pan for 5 minutes and then cut into squares or wedges. Serve warm.

AYURVEDA NOTES

- **VATA** Use more zucchini and/or bottle gourd in the grated vegetable mixture. Reduce or omit Thai green chile.
- **PITTA** Reduce or skip the green chile. Choose sunflower, olive, or avocado oil for the tadka. Use lime instead of lemon juice.
- **KAPHA** Choose sunflower oil for the tadka.

Fermenting Batters

- During cold winter months, an ideal location to ferment batter is in an oven with the oven light turned on for 30 minutes. This introduces enough warmth without turning on the actual oven to create a suitable warm environment for fermentation to occur. If the oven is too hot, it will cause the batter to overheat and prevent fermentation.

- In the summer months, leaving the batter on the countertop might work just fine—unless your kitchen is air-conditioned or in an area of the home that lacks adequate light and warmth, in which case use the oven-light method.

CHAKKARA PONGAL

SWEET RICE-AND-DAL PORRIDGE WITH JAGGERY AND SPICES

Served during the harvest festival of Pongal and traditionally sweetened with jaggery, *chakkara pongal* combines dal and rice. It works just as nicely with nutty coconut sugar instead of jaggery, and adding a cup of thick coconut milk toward the end brings a richer texture and taste. One year, inspired by the burnt sugar topping of crème brûlée, I prepared individual portions of chakkara pongal in small ramekins to serve at my Friendsgiving dinner, caramelizing the tops in the toaster oven with a sprinkle of sugar, which made for a fun presentation.

PERFECT PAIRING Serve with a meal of coconut rice and paasi paruppu (page 51) or alongside Kala Chana Sundal (page 91).

SERVES 6

SOAK TIME 30 minutes to 1 hour

- ½ cup (100 g) any short- to medium-grain rice, such as Sona Masoori, Surti Kolam, or jasmine
- ½ cup (100 g) dhuli moong dal/ yellow split moong dal
- 4 cups (960 ml) water
- ¾ cup (180 g) tightly packed grated jaggery or jaggery powder
- 1 cup (240 ml) canned coconut milk (optional)
- 1 teaspoon ground cardamom
- 4 cloves, coarsely ground
- ¼ teaspoon freshly grated nutmeg
- ¼ cup (60 g) ghee
- ½ cup (40 g) unsweetened coconut flakes
- ¼ cup (37 g) cashews
- ¼ cup (40 g) golden raisins

TIPS

The chakkara pongal will thicken once it is cooled. Adjust the consistency by adding ½ to 1 cup (120 to 240 ml) hot water as needed.

To cook the soaked rice and dal in an electric pressure cooker, pressure-cook on high for 5 minutes. Let the pressure release naturally before opening the lid.

Use coconut oil instead of ghee to make the dish vegan.

Use coconut sugar or brown sugar in place of jaggery. Reduce the amount of sweetener as per individual preference.

Heat a large skillet over low heat and dry-roast the rice and dal, stirring for a couple of minutes until they become aromatic but not browned. Remove from the pan and set aside to cool to room temperature.

Rinse the rice and dal in a fine-mesh sieve under cold running water until the water runs clear, about a minute. Transfer to a medium bowl, add water to cover by 2 inches (5 cm), and soak for 30 minutes to 1 hour. Drain.

Transfer the rice and dal to a 3-quart (3 L) pot. Add 3 cups (720 ml) of the water, partially cover, and cook over medium heat until the rice/dal porridge is soft and mushy, 25 to 30 minutes.

In a 2-quart (2 L) saucepan, combine the jaggery and remaining 1 cup (240 ml) water and heat over medium heat until all the jaggery is melted. Transfer the syrup to the pot of cooked rice and dal. Add the coconut milk (if using), cardamom, cloves, and nutmeg. Mix well and simmer over low heat for 5 minutes.

Meanwhile, in the same saucepan heat the ghee over medium heat. Add the coconut flakes, cashews, and raisins and fry over low heat until the raisins plump up and the nuts turn golden brown, 3 to 4 minutes.

Pour the hot ghee, cashews, raisins, and coconut over the sweet porridge. Mix well and simmer over low heat for an additional 5 minutes before serving.

AYURVEDA NOTES

- **VATA** Especially nourishing and grounding for vata.
- **PITTA** Opt for coconut milk and reduce ground cloves slightly.
- **KAPHA** Enjoy this heavy, sweet dish in moderation as it shares many qualities with kapha.

MASALA DAL VADA

MIXED DAL FRITTERS

Dal vada (lentil fritters), a popular afternoon snack in South India, can be made with only chana dal or combined with other dals. These vadas shaped as flattened discs are crispy and crunchy and make for a perfect after-school or after-sport snack. Note, if the dals are soaked for more than a couple of hours, the vadas may be a little softer rather than crunchy. I replace cilantro with fresh moringa (drumstick pods) or fenugreek leaves when in season.

PERFECT PAIRING Serve with Nariyal ki Chutney (page 216) and a cup of Masala Chai (page 238).

SERVES 6

SOAK TIME 1½ hours to 2 hours

Rinse the dals in a fine-mesh sieve under cold running water until the water runs clear, about a minute. Transfer to a medium bowl, add water to cover by 2 inches (5 cm), and soak for 1½ to 2 hours. Drain.

Transfer the soaked dals to a blender and grind to a coarse paste. Transfer the paste to a bowl and add the onion, cilantro, green chiles, ginger, curry leaves, rice flour, salt, and turmeric. Mix well and let the mixture rest for 15 to 20 minutes.

Meanwhile, pour 3 inches (7.5 cm) of oil into a 6-quart (6 L) heavy-bottomed pan and heat to 350°F (177°C). Maintain the heat between 350° and 375°F (177° and 190°C) for optimal frying. To check if the oil is hot enough, drop a small ball of batter into the oil. If it rises almost instantly without turning brown, it's ready. If it gets too brown, the oil is too hot, so reduce the heat to low.

Scoop out about ¼ cup (60 ml) of the dal mixture and shape it into a ball. Place the ball on a greased parchment paper and flatten to a disc shape. You should be able to make about 12 discs from the mixture.

Line a plate with paper towels and have it near the stove. Working in batches of 4 or 5 vadas, carefully lift one of the discs and slide it into the hot oil with extreme caution. Do not overcrowd the pan as it will drop the temperature of the oil and the vadas won't cook properly. Cook the vadas for 2 minutes and then flip them over with a slotted spoon or spider and cook until the vadas are golden brown on both sides, another 2 minutes. Remove with a slotted spoon and transfer to the paper towels to drain.

Serve warm.

1 cup (200 g) chana dal/peeled and split chickpeas

¼ cup (50 g) chilka moong dal/green split moong dal

¼ cup (50 g) dhuli urad dal/peeled split black gram

1 medium red onion, finely chopped

¼ cup (15 g) finely chopped cilantro (leaves and tender stems)

2 to 3 Thai green chiles, finely chopped

1-inch (2.5 cm) piece fresh ginger, peeled and finely chopped

8 to 10 fresh curry leaves, roughly torn

2 tablespoons rice flour

1 teaspoon fine sea salt

½ teaspoon ground turmeric

Neutral oil, such as peanut, sunflower, or vegetable oil, for deep-frying

---

AYURVEDA NOTES

- **VATA** Reduce the Thai green chiles if they cause dryness or indigestion.
- **PITTA** Cut back or omit the green chiles. Use sunflower or vegetable oil for frying. Pitta, being naturally oily, can be sensitive to fried foods, so enjoy this dish in moderation.
- **KAPHA** Enjoy in moderation as fried foods are heavy for kapha. Use sunflower oil for frying.

RAM LADDOO WAFFLE CHAAT

SAVORY DAL WAFFLES WITH RADISH SALAD AND CHUTNEYS

I first discovered *ram laddoo* at a roadside food stall on the streets of New Delhi. I was surprised to discover savory *pakodis* (petite deep-fried balls of dal batter) dressed with a generous drizzle of green chutney and topped with daikon radish salad, as I associate the term *laddoo* with sweet treats. The sensory satisfaction from the dance of different tastes and textures is forever etched in my memory. Because my kids love waffles, I adapted the North Indian ram laddoo *chaat* into crispy waffles, delivering the perfect crunch.

PERFECT PAIRING Serve with Saunf ka Sharbat (page 235) in summertime or Kanji (page 232) in the winter.

SERVES 6

SOAK TIME 3 to 4 hours

WAFFLES

½ cup (100 g) dhuli moong dal/ yellow split moong dal

¼ cup (50 g) chana dal/peeled and split chickpeas

¼ cup (50 g) dhuli urad dal/peeled split black gram

1 Thai green chile

1-inch (2.5 cm) piece fresh ginger, peeled and roughly chopped

¼ cup (60 ml) water

¼ cup (15 g) finely chopped radish greens (optional)

½ teaspoon cumin seeds

½ teaspoon Kashmiri red chili powder

¼ teaspoon ground turmeric

1 teaspoon fine sea salt

½ teaspoon baking soda

Neutral oil

RADISH SALAD

1 cup (115 g) grated daikon radish

¼ cup (30 g) grated carrots

2 tablespoons finely chopped radish greens (optional)

2 tablespoons finely chopped cilantro (leaves and tender stems)

1 Thai green chile, finely chopped

1 teaspoon lime juice

½ teaspoon fine sea salt

¼ teaspoon chaat masala

¼ teaspoon Kashmiri red chili powder

GARNISH

½ cup Hari Chutney (page 214)

1 tablespoon chaat masala

Rinse the dals in a fine-mesh sieve under cold running water until the water runs clear, about a minute. Transfer to a medium bowl, add water to cover by 2 inches (5 cm), and soak for 3 to 4 hours. Drain.

Meanwhile, make the radish salad: In a bowl, combine the daikon, carrots, radish greens (if using), cilantro, chile, lime juice, salt, chaat masala, and Kashmiri powder. Refrigerate until ready to assemble.

Make the waffle batter: Transfer the soaked dals to a blender. Add the green chile and ginger and grind with about ¼ cup (60 ml) water to a smooth batter. Transfer the batter to a bowl. Add the radish greens (if using), cumin, Kashmiri powder, turmeric, salt, and baking soda. Add additional water if needed. Whisk the batter well for a minute to make it light and fluffy. It should have a pouring consistency like waffle mix.

Preheat a waffle iron according to the manufacturer's instructions (or to 400°F/200°C). Grease the waffle iron evenly with oil. Drop large spoonfuls of batter onto the greased waffle iron until most of the wells are covered. Close the lid and cook until crispy golden brown, 3 to 5 minutes. Repeat with the rest of the batter.

To assemble, place one waffle in a shallow bowl. Top with a large spoonful of chilled radish salad. Drizzle a generous amount of hari chutney over the top. Sprinkle some chaat masala and serve immediately.

AYURVEDA NOTES

- **VATA** Reduce the Thai green chile in the radish salad. Balance its cold, raw qualities with ample chutney and lime juice.
- **PITTA** Enjoy laddoos in moderation due to their pungent taste. Reduce or skip Thai green chile and Kashmiri powder.
- **KAPHA** The pungency of daikon radish, combined with cleansing greens and digestive spices, balances kapha.

MASALA DOSA

SAVORY FERMENTED RICE-AND-LENTIL CREPES WITH SPICED POTATO MASH

The pride of South India, dosas have gained worldwide popularity over the years. The precise proportion of rice and peeled urad dal holds the key to this savory crepe, and every household has its own special nuances for each step, from soaking and grinding to fermentation. When rice and lentils are combined, they form a complete protein—containing all the essential amino acids, especially important for individuals on a vegetarian diet.

Soaking softens the rice and plumps the dal, making it easier to grind, and urad dal also begins fermentation almost immediately—a thin film of bacteria will form after soaking for just a few hours. Adding a small amount of fenugreek seeds to the soaking dal also assists in the fermentation process, and the soaking water is then used for grinding to help with the fermentation of the batter. Dal needs to be ground to a smooth, fluffy texture and the rice to a fine sandpaper texture. When the batter ferments, the beneficial bacteria convert the carbohydrates and sugars into lactic acid, giving dosas their characteristic sour tang while unlocking a treasure trove of prebiotics and probiotics, making them easier to digest and an ideal choice for those with sensitive stomachs or digestive issues.

Different types of rice can be used for the dosa batter, but the two favorites in my home are the traditional idli rice and Sona Masoori, varieties easily found now in many large grocery stores. I have also made dosa batter with equal success with basmati rice. Versatile dosas, much like tortillas, can be paired with chutney for breakfast, sautéed vegetables for lunch, or served with warm lentil stew or curry for dinner. They can be enjoyed plain or filled with spiced potato mash, as here. Use your imagination and experiment with creative fillings for dosas, both sweet and savory!

PERFECT PAIRING
Dosas are traditionally served with Nariyal ki Chutney (page 216) and Tiffin Sambhar (page 120).

MAKES about sixteen 8-inch (20 cm) dosas

SOAK TIME 8 hours or overnight

FERMENTATION TIME 8 to 10 hours

Rinse the rice in a bowl under cold tap water a couple of times. Add enough water to cover the rice by 3 to 4 inches (7.5 to 10 cm) and set aside to soak on the kitchen counter for 8 hours or overnight. Reserve 1 cup (240 ml) of the soaking water as you drain the rice.

In another bowl, combine the dals and the fenugreek seeds. Rinse under cold tap water a couple of times. Add enough water to cover the dals and fenugreek by 3 to 4 inches (7.5 to 10 cm) and set aside to soak on the kitchen counter for 8 hours or overnight. Reserve ¾ cup (180 ml) of the soaking water as you drain the dals.

About 30 minutes before making the batter, soak the poha in about 1 cup (240 ml) of water and set aside. The poha should absorb most of the water it was soaked in.

Transfer the soaked dals, fenugreek seeds, and the reserved soaking water to a high-powered blender. Start at low to medium speed and grind the batter to a smooth consistency, 3 to 4 minutes. Give breaks in between to scrape down the batter and to keep the blender and batter from heating up. Scrape the batter into a large bowl.

- 2 cups (420 g) rice, such as idli rice or Sona Masoori
- ½ cup (100 g) dhuli urad dal/peeled split black gram
- 1 tablespoon (15 g) chana dal/ peeled and split chickpeas
- 1 tablespoon (15 g) toor dal/split pigeon peas
- ½ teaspoon fenugreek seeds
- ½ cup (60 g) poha/flattened rice flakes (see Tips)
- 1 teaspoon fine sea salt
- Oil or ghee, for cooking
- Spiced Potato Mash (recipe follows), for serving

Continued—

Transfer the soaked rice, its reserved soaking water, and the poha to the same blender. Grind to a smooth but superfine grainy paste starting at low speed and working your way to medium speed, taking breaks in between to scrape the batter down the sides. If you feel the rice batter between your fingers, it should have a fine, grainy, sandpaper-like feel to it. Add it to the bowl with the dal batter.

Using your clean hand or a spoon, mix the batter vigorously for a minute to incorporate some air into it. The consistency should be similar to pancake batter. Cover the bowl with a plate or lid and set it aside in a draft-free area in your kitchen (see Fermenting Batters, page 193) for 12 to 24 hours, depending on the temperature, or until the batter appears to have doubled in volume. The batter should have small bubbles and a slight sweet-and-sour aroma. This fermented batter can be used to make dosas right away or can be refrigerated for up to 1 week. If the batter has been refrigerated, allow it to come to room temperature before making the dosas.

When ready to cook, stir the salt into the dosa batter and mix well. If the batter is thick, add up to ¼ cup (60 ml) water if needed and mix to achieve a pouring consistency (as for pancake batter).

Preheat a large cast-iron skillet over medium-high heat until the pan is nice and hot. Once hot, brush 1 teaspoon oil or ghee on the pan to season it.

Using a ladle with a wide curved bottom, pour ¼ to ½ cup (60 to 120 ml) batter (depending on the size of your pan or how thick you want the dosa) into the center of the hot pan. Using a circular motion, moving from the center to the outer edge, spread the batter to form a crepe. Drizzle about ½ teaspoon or more of oil or ghee on top of the dosa and also along its edges. Reduce the heat to medium-low, cover, and cook until the dosa is crispy on the bottom, 1 to 1½ minutes. (The lid holds in the moisture and keeps the dosa soft on top.)

Use a thin metal spatula or flat turner to carefully scrape along the edges, release the dosa from the pan, and transfer to a plate. Add a spoonful of spiced potato mash, fold the dosa in half, and serve immediately. A dosa without the potato stuffing is called plain dosa and with the potato stuffing is referred to as masala dosa.

TIPS

If you can't find poha, add another ½ cup (100 g) rice to the soaking rice.

To flip or not to flip your dosa: The choice is yours! An ideal dosa in my kitchen is one that is spread thin, soft and spongy on top, and golden brown on the bottom. If the dosa is spread thick, I flip it so it gets cooked evenly on both sides.

Some other suggestions for dosa fillings include chopped spinach and cheese, rice, beans and cheese, tossed salads, or sweet fillings like chocolate-hazelnut spread with fresh berries.

Cook the dosa batter in a waffle maker to create dosa waffles.

AYURVEDA NOTES

In general, fermented foods help spark the digestive fire, but each dosha should balance its sour taste with appropriate side dishes and toppings.

- **VATA** The sour taste of dosa increases salivation and kindles digestive fire. Fenugreek seeds balance the airy quality of ferments and prevent bloating.
- **PITTA** Excess sour taste can increase pitta. Enjoy in moderation with cooling side dishes like coconut chutney.
- **KAPHA** Excess sour taste increases kapha. Enjoy in moderation with warming side dishes like sambhar.

SPICED POTATO MASH

A traditional filling for a classic dosa is a spiced potato mash of boiled potatoes cooked with spices. This filling is what makes a dosa become a masala dosa. You can also serve this as a side dish.

SERVES 6

1¾ pounds (800 g) russet potatoes
  (3 to 4 medium)
2 tablespoons oil, such as sesame, peanut,
  or sunflower
⅛ teaspoon hing/asafoetida powder
1 teaspoon black mustard seeds
2 Thai green chiles, halved lengthwise
8 to 10 fresh curry leaves (optional)
1½ cups (150 g) thinly sliced red onions
1 teaspoon ground turmeric
1 teaspoon fine sea salt
Juice of 1 lemon
¼ cup (15 g) finely chopped cilantro
  (leaves and tender stems)

Bring a large pot of water to a boil. Add the whole unpeeled potatoes and cook until fork-tender, 15 to 20 minutes.

Drain the potatoes and, when cool enough to handle, peel and cut them into about 1-inch (2.5 cm) cubes. Set aside.

In a large skillet, heat the oil over medium heat. Add the asafoetida and mustard seeds and let them sizzle for a few seconds. Reduce the heat to medium-low, add the green chiles and curry leaves, and fry for a few seconds. Be careful as the moisture in the chiles and curry leaves will splutter in the oil. Add the onions and sauté until translucent and about to get brown, 3 to 4 minutes.

Add the potatoes, turmeric, and salt. Sprinkle with a couple of tablespoons of water and mix well. Cover and cook over medium heat for a couple of minutes. Uncover and mix again. Gently smash the potatoes with the back of a spatula as desired.

Remove from the heat and stir in the lemon juice and cilantro.

AYURVEDA NOTES

- **VATA** Cut back on or omit the Thai green chile. Add crushed black pepper, which aids in the digestion of potato.
- **PITTA** Use sunflower oil. Reduce or omit the Thai green chile. Use lime juice instead of lemon. Substitute red potato for the russet if desired.
- **KAPHA** Use sunflower oil.

DAL KA PITHA

STEAMED RICE FLOUR DUMPLINGS WITH SAVORY CHANA DAL FILLING

Dal pitha is a traditional rice flour dumpling from the state of Bihar, in eastern India, popularly enjoyed as a breakfast dish but also as a snack, appetizer, or a side dish. Pithas are stuffed with sweet or savory fillings, and *bihari dal pithas* are steamed dumplings made with rice flour and filled with a spiced dal mixture, with hari chutney on the side. They are associated with special occasions, including harvest festivals, such as Nabanna (meaning "new rice"), or Makar Sankranti, or prepared during Govardhan pooja (a special Hindu festivity) as part of Annakut (grand mountain of food) offering, a day after Diwali, to celebrate the child form of Lord Krishna.

Dal pithas can be shaped in different ways, but the half-moon shape is the classic way. The edges can be sealed with a decorative pleating or the filling can be left partially exposed (similar to a bao sandwich) before they are steamed and served warm.

PERFECT PAIRING
Serve with chutneys such as Hari Chutney (page 214) and Thecha (page 218) on the side.

MAKES 8 to 10 dumplings

SOAK TIME 3 to 4 hours

PITHA FILLING
½ cup (90 g) chana dal/peeled and split chickpeas
1 Thai green chile
2 garlic cloves, peeled but whole
1-inch (2.5 cm) piece fresh ginger, roughly chopped
¼ teaspoon black peppercorns
1 tablespoon neutral oil
½ teaspoon cumin seeds
¼ teaspoon ajwain/carom seeds
1 teaspoon fine sea salt
¼ cup (15 g) finely chopped cilantro (leaves and tender stems)

DUMPLING DOUGH
1 cup (240 ml) water
½ teaspoon fine sea salt
½ teaspoon cumin seeds
½ cup (90 g) rice flour

ASSEMBLY
Banana leaf or neutral oil, for the steamer

Make the pitha filling: Rinse the dal in a fine-mesh sieve under cold running water until the water runs clear, about a minute. Transfer to a bowl, add water to cover by 2 inches (5 cm), and soak for 3 to 4 hours. Drain.

In a small blender (or using an immersion blender), combine the soaked dal, green chile, garlic, ginger, and peppercorns. Grind to a coarse paste without any water.

In a small skillet, heat the oil over medium heat. Add the cumin seeds and carom seeds and sizzle for 10 seconds. Add the dal mixture and salt and cook the mixture until the dal is a dark-golden color and has a soft crumbly texture, 5 to 7 minutes. Remove from the heat and mix in the cilantro. Set the filling aside.

Make the dumpling dough: In a small saucepan, bring the water to a boil and add salt and cumin seeds once it starts to boil. Remove from the heat and add the rice flour. Mix well until it becomes a shaggy dough. Cover the pan to let the dough steam for about 5 minutes. Transfer to a shallow bowl and allow to cool slightly. Dip your fingers in water and then knead the rice flour mixture for a couple of minutes to a smooth dough. Cover with a wet cloth to rest for 5 minutes.

Continued—

To assemble: Divide the dough into 8 or 10 equal portions, depending on the desired size of pithas, and roll into balls. Cover to keep them from drying out. Take one ball and press it between the palms of your hands and shape to form about a 4-inch (10 cm) round. Scoop out a tablespoon of pitha filling and place it in the center of the flattened dough. Carefully fold the dough to form a half-moon shape and pinch the edges to seal. You can make pleats along the edge using your forefinger and thumb. The other option, which is my preferred method, is simply folding the rice dough layer in a half-moon shape with the filling exposed along the edge.

Set up a steamer (a metal tiered steamer, a bamboo steamer and wok, or simply a pan with a steamer insert) and fill it with enough water to simmer for 10 minutes without drying out but not so deep that it touches the steamer basket. Line the steamer with either a banana leaf precut to size or perforated parchment paper liners. If using a metal steamer plate or insert, simply brush with oil. Bring the water in the steamer to a boil.

Arrange the dal pithas about 1 inch (2.5 cm) apart in the steamer basket. Cover and steam over medium heat until a knife inserted into the center comes out clean, 10 to 12 minutes.

Serve warm.

TIPS

Pan-fry any leftover pithas in a little oil and garnish with spices for another version of this traditional dish.

Try the pitha filling mixture with yellow split moong dal.

AYURVEDA NOTES

- **VATA** Steaming adds moisture to the dry chana mixture, balancing vata. Use peanut oil.
- **PITTA** Reduce the Thai green chile. Use sunflower, grapeseed, or olive oil.
- **KAPHA** Use sunflower oil for making the filling.

PANCHMEL DAL

FIVE-LENTIL STEW

Panch means "five" and *mel* means "mixed" or "coming together." The five varieties of dal used in this signature dish from the western state of Rajasthan include chana dal (split chickpeas), chilka moong dal (green split moong dal), masoor dal (split red lentils), chilka urad dal (split black gram), and toor dal (split pigeon peas), each lending layers of flavor and texture to this hearty one-pot dish that is ideal for quick weeknight meals. My version includes any extra vegetables I might have in my refrigerator, making it an ideal weekly "fridge-clean-out stew."

PERFECT PAIRING Serve as a complete meal by itself or over steamed basmati rice.

SERVES 6

SOAK TIME 15 to 30 minutes

LENTILS

¼ cup (50 g) chana dal/peeled and split chickpeas

¼ cup (50 g) chilka moong dal/green split moong dal

¼ cup (50 g) masoor dal/split red lentils

¼ cup (50 g) chilka urad dal/split black gram

¼ cup (50 g) toor dal/split pigeon peas

4 cups (960 ml) water

1 teaspoon fine sea salt

1 teaspoon ground turmeric

1 tablespoon (15 g) ghee

STEW

¼ cup (60 g) ghee

⅛ teaspoon hing/asafoetida powder

1 bay leaf

2 to 3 dried Kashmiri red chiles

1 teaspoon cumin seeds

2 whole cloves

2 black peppercorns

1-inch (2.5 cm) piece fresh ginger, minced

3 to 4 garlic cloves, minced

1 medium red onion, thinly sliced

2 medium tomatoes, finely chopped

1 teaspoon deggi mirch chili powder

½ teaspoon fine sea salt

2 cups (150 g) finely chopped leafy greens (optional), such as spinach, kale, chard, carrot greens, and/or radish greens

1½ cups (150 g) chopped seasonal veggies (optional), such as carrots, squash (yellow or butternut), turnips, and/or zucchini

½ cup (30 g) chopped cilantro

Lemon wedges, for squeezing

Cook the lentils: Rinse all the dals together in a fine-mesh sieve under cold running water until the water runs clear, about a minute. Transfer to a bowl, add water to cover by 2 inches (5 cm), and soak for 15 to 30 minutes. Drain.

In a medium pot or Dutch oven, combine the soaked dal, water, salt, turmeric, and ghee. Partially cover and cook over medium heat until the dal is soft and mushy when pressed between your fingers, 30 to 40 minutes. Skim off any foam that forms on the surface, and uncover the pot every 10 minutes to stir the dal so that it doesn't stick to the bottom of the pan. Add more water as necessary; the consistency of the cooked dal should be thick and not very soupy. Once cooked, simmer on low.

Continued—

Make the stew: In a large skillet, heat the ghee over medium heat. Add the asafoetida, bay leaf, dried chiles, and cumin seeds and sizzle the spices for a few seconds. Coarsely smash the cloves and black peppercorns with a mortar and pestle. Add them to the pan and sauté for a few seconds. Add the ginger, garlic, and onion and sauté until translucent and just starting to brown, 4 to 5 minutes.

Add the tomatoes, deggi mirch, and salt and sauté until the ghee starts to separate from the mixture, 2 to 3 minutes. If adding any seasonal greens and/or vegetables, add them now and cook for an additional 2 to 3 minutes.

Transfer this tempered spice mixture to the pot of cooked dal and mix well. Season with more salt to taste and simmer the dal for 5 to 10 minutes.

Serve garnished with cilantro and with lemon wedges on the side for squeezing.

TIPS

To cook the soaked dals in a pressure cooker, pressure-cook on high for 7 minutes. Let the pressure release naturally before opening the lid.

For a vegan version, use oil of choice instead of ghee.

AYURVEDA NOTES

- **VATA** Reduce the Kashmiri and deggi mirch powder if pungency causes dryness.
- **PITTA** Reduce or omit the Kashmiri and deggi mirch powder. Use white onion instead of red. Use avocado, grapeseed, or sunflower oils if not using ghee. Favor cooling greens like chard and kale over spinach. Avoid turnips, favoring squash, carrots, and zucchini for the chopped vegetables.
- **KAPHA** Reduce the ghee/oil slightly and use plenty of greens and chopped vegetables in this dish.

DHANSAK WITH GOR AMLI NU KACHUMBER

CLASSIC PARSI DAL AND SPICED VEGETABLE CURRY

Mumbai, a city with a rich kaleidoscope of culture and religions, is also home to the largest population of a dwindling Parsi community. Descendants of Persian Zoroastrians, a small group of Parsis emigrated to India in the seventh century CE to escape religious persecution in Iran, settling in the coastal town of Sanjan in present-day Gujarat, on India's west coast. It's said that when the Parsis arrived, the local leader, Jadi Rana, displayed a vessel full of milk to the refugees, a visual illustration of an area already densely populated with no room for more. The head Parsi priest poured a spoonful of sugar into the milk, symbolizing the way in which his community would sweeten without overpowering or destabilizing the local society. My children and I once spent a perfect day touring Mumbai with my dearest Parsi friend, who shared the city through the lens of her rich Parsi lineage, iconic Parsi restaurants and bakeries, familial ties to some heritage buildings, and how this minority community has woven themselves into India's civic tapestry.

Parsi food is influenced by Persian, French, Portuguese, British, Hindu, and especially Gujarati cuisine, a symbiotic relationship developed over the centuries as they adapted to new ways of cooking and eating. Arguably the most famous of all Parsi dishes is *dhansak*, a flavorful stew made with lentils (*dhan*), spices, and vegetables (*shaak*), with or without meat.

There are countless ways to make dhansak, a dish dear to every Parsi family, and I am glad for my recipe to be developed and blessed with the help of my dear Parsi friend from Mumbai over many WhatsApp text exchanges, video calls, and phone calls. The recipe was also tested on three different continents, between her in Mumbai, her daughter who lives in the UK, and me in my Texas kitchen in the United States. The one takeaway for me in developing this recipe was the importance of perfecting the balance of *tikhu-khatu-mithu* (spicy-sour-sweet), the holy trinity of Parsi cuisine. This dhansak combines the synchronized dance of spices with the sweetness of jaggery and a perky dash of sour from tamarind.

PERFECT PAIRING
Serve with *gor amli nu kachumber*, a briny sweet-and-sour chopped salad, and caramelized onion rice (*bhuga chawar*, page 163).

SERVES 6

SOAK TIME 15 to 30 minutes

½ cup (100 g) toor dal/split pigeon peas

½ cup (90 g) masoor dal/split red lentils

¼ cup (50 g) chana dal/peeled and split chickpeas

¼ cup (50 g) dhuli moong dal/yellow split moong dal

1 small fairytale eggplant or any small variety, diced

1 cup (100 g) diced peeled butternut squash

1 medium chayote or yellow squash, diced

1 cup (80 g) finely chopped fresh fenugreek leaves, or ¼ cup (10 g) kasuri methi/dried fenugreek leaves

1 teaspoon fine sea salt

1 teaspoon ground turmeric

4 cups (960 ml) water

SPICE PASTE

2-inch (5 cm) cinnamon stick

6 green cardamom pods

3 whole cloves

10 black peppercorns

2 tablespoons cumin seeds

1 tablespoon coriander seeds

4 dried Kashmiri red chiles

1-inch (2.5 cm) piece fresh ginger, peeled and roughly chopped

10 garlic cloves, peeled but whole

1 cup (80 g) roughly chopped cilantro (leaves and tender stems)

DRY SPICE MIX

3 green cardamom pods

3 whole cloves

2 star anise

1 tablespoon cumin seeds

5 black peppercorns

2 dried Kashmiri red chiles

2 tablespoons kasuri methi/dried fenugreek leaves

TADKA

¼ cup (60 g) ghee or oil, such as peanut, sunflower, avocado, or grapeseed

1 medium red onion, pureed

2 medium tomatoes, pureed

1 teaspoon fine sea salt

2 tablespoons tamarind concentrate

½ cup (106 g) grated jaggery or powdered jaggery

FOR SERVING

2 tablespoons finely chopped cilantro (leaves and tender stems)

2 tablespoons finely chopped mint (leaves and tender stems)

Gor Amli Nu Kachumber Salad (recipe follows)

Bhuga Chawar (page 163)

Rinse all the dals together in a fine-mesh sieve under cold running water. Transfer to a bowl, add water to cover by 2 inches (5 cm), and soak for 15 to 30 minutes. Drain.

In a 4-quart (4 L) pot, combine the soaked dals, eggplant, butternut, chayote, fenugreek leaves, salt, turmeric, and water. Bring to a boil over high heat. Reduce the heat to medium, partially cover, and cook until the dals and vegetables are soft and mushy, 25 to 30 minutes.

With an immersion blender, puree to a smooth consistency. (Alternatively, transfer to a stand blender and puree with the steam vent in the lid open.) Set the dal/vegetable puree aside.

Meanwhile, make the spice paste: In a small dry skillet over low heat, lightly toast the cinnamon stick, cardamom pods, cloves, peppercorns, cumin seeds, coriander seeds, and dried chiles until the spices release their aroma, 3 to 4 minutes. Transfer to a blender, add the fresh ginger, garlic cloves, and cilantro, and grind to a paste. Set the paste aside.

Make the dry spice mix: In the same skillet over low heat, lightly toast the cardamom pods, cloves, star anise, cumin seeds, black peppercorns, and dried chiles until the spices release their aroma, 3 to 4 minutes. Let the spices cool down to room temperature. Transfer to a spice grinder and add the dried fenugreek leaves. Grind to a fine powder and set aside.

Continued—

Make the tadka: In a 4-quart (4 L) pot, heat the ghee over medium heat. Add the pureed onions and cook until golden brown, 10 to 12 minutes. Stir regularly for even cooking.

Add the pureed tomatoes and salt and cook for 3 to 4 minutes. Add the wet spice paste and cook with the onions and tomatoes until well combined and the ghee starts to separate to the edges of the cooked mixture, 3 to 4 minutes. Stir in the tamarind concentrate and all or half of the dry spice mix according to your preferred level of spiciness. Add the dal/vegetable puree and jaggery to the pot and simmer over low heat for 5 to 10 minutes.

Season with salt to taste. Just before serving, garnish the pot of dhansak with chopped cilantro and mint leaves. Serve alongside caramelized onion rice (bhuga chawar) and Gor Amli Nu Kachumber Salad.

AYURVEDA NOTES

- **VATA** While the balanced sweet-and-sour flavors in this dish are balancing for vata, be mindful of the pungency and nightshades in this dish and adjust accordingly.
- **PITTA** Favor sunflower, avocado, or grapeseed oil. Reduce the red chiles. Use a white onion instead of red.
- **KAPHA** Favor sunflower or grapeseed oil.

GOR AMLI NU KACHUMBER SALAD

A briny combination of cilantro, cucumber, red onions, green chiles, and tamarind incorporates the tikhu-khatu-mithu (spicy-sour-sweet) of Parsi cuisine.

PERFECT PAIRING Serve alongside Dhansak (page 208) and Bhuga Chawar (page 163).

SERVES 6

1 large red onion, thinly sliced
1 large tomato, seeded and diced
½ English cucumber, diced
½ cup (25 g) tightly packed finely chopped cilantro (leaves and tender stems)
2 tablespoons tamarind concentrate (see Tip)
1 or 2 Thai green chiles, finely chopped
1 to 2 tablespoons grated jaggery or jaggery powder
1-inch (2.5 cm) piece fresh ginger, finely chopped
½ teaspoon fine sea salt

In a bowl, combine the onion, tomato, cucumber, cilantro, tamarind, green chiles, jaggery, ginger, and salt. Adjust the tamarind and sugar until you are satisfied with the balance of flavors.

TIP
Instead of tamarind concentrate, you can dissolve ½ cup (114 g) seedless tamarind pulp in ¼ cup (60 ml) water, or use apple cider vinegar.

AYURVEDA NOTES

- **VATA** Reduce or omit the Thai green chiles.
- **PITTA** Reduce or omit the Thai green chiles. Use white onion instead of red.
- **KAPHA** Substitute apple cider vinegar for the tamarind.

CHUTNEY + ACHAAR

Indians have a universal love for their condiments, and no meal is complete without some form of chutney or pickle (*achaar*). Achaars and chutneys offer a true glimpse into a family's palate, their lineage, and their distinct cooking traditions. The next time you sit down to have a meal in an Indian home, pay extra attention to the jars of achaar and chutney on the table, the keepers of family traditions and stories.

An achaar can instantly transport one home. I still remember carrying a small jar of my mom's *nimbu ka achaar* (lemon pickle) when I first came to the US more than two decades ago, the spice kick keeping me warm during many lonely meals while I was finishing grad school. Even now, the most treasured gifts I bring back from India are the homemade chutneys and achaar lovingly packaged by friends and family.

Just like *chaat*, the word *chutney* is derived from the Hindi word *chatna*, which means "to lick." Fresh chutneys, prepared from raw ingredients—usually a combination of herbs and spices—like cilantro-mint chutney (page 214) or coconut chutney with cilantro (page 216), are fast to prepare with just a quick blend of ingredients. On the other hand, cooked chutneys like Imli Khajur ki Chutney (page 215) are a bit laborious but can be stored for a few months in the refrigerator. From an Ayurvedic perspective, chutneys and achaars incorporate all six tastes into a single bite: sweet, sour, salty, bitter, pungent, and astringent. A tablespoon or so goes a long way to add flavor and a little sparkle to any meal while supporting overall digestion.

Achaars are a potent dose of flavor, and although they take just a square inch of space in most Indian meals, the meal feels incomplete without them. Achaars are prepared using a variety of fruits, like tart green mango, lemons, and sometimes even vegetables like carrots, cauliflower, and onions; summer is a popular season to whip up big batches to be carefully packaged to last for the whole year. Almost every Indian home has its own heirloom achaar recipes that hold special memories, the oils and spices providing a distinct culinary identity of the region—for example, mustard oil, fenugreek, and nigella seeds in northern parts of India and *gingelly* (sesame) oil and fresh curry leaves in the southern states. The spices help produce healthy bacteria through fermentation and create probiotics, aiding digestion and improving gut health.

If rice is the body of the meal and dal is the heart, then chutneys and achaar form its soul. It completes the meal with shadrasa—the six Ayurvedic tastes that create balance. At any given time, my pantry and refrigerator are stocked with a dozen chutneys and achaars to add a delicious flair to any meal. A spoonful of Gajar ka Achaar (page 221) can easily elevate a simple bowl of Dheeli Khichdi (page 188), while a combination of Hari Chutney (page 214) and Imli Khajur ki Chutney (page 215) adds the perfect drama to Mumbai Bhelpuri (page 179), and a drizzle of Thecha (page 218) over steaming Khichu (page 167) adds extra heat.

Indians truly have an unconditional love for their condiments, making chutneys and achaar out of fruits, vegetables, nuts and seeds, pulses, herbs, spices, and even veggie stalks and peels. The chutneys and achaar recipes I have chosen for this chapter complement the dal and chawal dishes in this cookbook. In addition, I encourage you to make an extra batch to give as gifts during the holidays.

HARI CHUTNEY

CILANTRO, MINT, AND GREEN APPLE CHUTNEY

Almost every Indian home has its own version of a classic *hari*, or green chutney, using cilantro or mint leaves or a combination. I have tried many versions of this classic chutney, but the one that is a staple in my home includes a Granny Smith apple, which adds a perfect mild tartness and touch of sweetness. To keep this chutney vibrant, add 3 to 4 ice cubes to the blender. This prevents the herbs from heating up and turning a dull green.

This chutney looks and tastes best when served fresh. Since it is a fresh chutney, it has a short shelf life. If you have any extra, you can store it in the refrigerator and use it within a few days.

PERFECT PAIRING From drizzling over chaat and serving with appetizers like pakoras or Kothimbir Wadi (page 101) to an accompaniment to Besan ka Chila (page 89) or Dal ka Pitha (page 202), this chutney complements a variety of savory dishes.

MAKES about 1 cup (240 ml)

---

2 cups (150 g) chopped cilantro
   (leaves and tender stems)
1 cup (60 g) chopped mint
1 medium Granny Smith apple,
   cored and cubed
1-inch (2.5 cm) piece fresh ginger,
   peeled and chopped
2 Thai green chiles, or 1 serrano
   chile
2 tablespoons lemon or lime juice
1 teaspoon ground cumin
1 teaspoon fine sea salt
3 to 4 ice cubes

In a blender, combine the cilantro, mint, apple, ginger, green chiles, lemon juice, ground cumin, salt, and ice cubes. Blend the ingredients into a puree. Season to taste with salt. Use immediately or transfer to an airtight container and store in the refrigerator for up to 3 to 4 days.

AYURVEDA NOTES

With a sweet, pungent, astringent taste and cooling effect, cilantro is balancing and strengthens digestion.
   - **VATA** Use lemon rather than lime in this recipe as lemon is warming and aids digestion, balancing the cooling ingredients like mint and cilantro.
   - **PITTA** Reduce the fresh ginger to half. Reduce or omit the green chiles. Use lime for cooling properties.
   - **KAPHA** The astringency of apple, combined with spices and ginger, is favorable for kapha. Reduce the salt amount.

IMLI KHAJUR KI CHUTNEY

TAMARIND DATE CHUTNEY

I simply can't imagine any *chaat* dish without a generous drizzle of imli khajur ki chutney. This chutney is rightfully glorified as the classic sweet-and-sour chutney of India. The tropical sourness from the tamarind combined with the rich sweetness of dates slow-cooked with spices results in a rich sauce that can be easily tucked away in the refrigerator for up to 1 month. Hari Chutney (page 214) and this chutney are best buddies, and having these two jars on hand gives me the power to create a chaat party in a matter of minutes.

PERFECT PAIRING
This is the ideal condiment for chaat and appetizers.

MAKES about 3 cups (720 ml)

TIP
If using dried tamarind pulp in this recipe, pick through the fruit to discard any tough fibers.

In a medium pot, combine the tamarind, dates, jaggery, and water and bring to a boil. Cook over medium heat until the dates and tamarind are softened and mushy, about 10 minutes.

Let cool. Transfer to a blender and process to a smooth puree. Return the puree to the pot, add the cumin, black salt, ginger, and Kashmiri powder and cook over medium-low heat until it is thick and coats the back of a spoon, 15 to 20 minutes.

Taste and adjust the black salt to taste. Cool and store in an airtight container for up to 1 month in the refrigerator.

- 2 ounces (55 g) seedless tamarind pulp (see Tip), or 2 tablespoons tamarind concentrate
- 1 cup (150 g) chopped pitted dates
- ½ cup (100 g) jaggery powder or brown sugar
- 2½ cups (600 ml) water
- 1 teaspoon ground cumin
- 1 teaspoon kala namak/Indian black salt
- ½ teaspoon ground ginger
- ½ teaspoon Kashmiri red chili powder

AYURVEDA NOTES

- **VATA** The sweet, sour, and salty flavors of chutney are balancing for vata.
- **PITTA** The sour taste of tamarind and heating qualities of Kashmiri powder and ground ginger may aggravate pitta and should be reduced.
- **KAPHA** Increase the pungency of this recipe by increasing the Kashmiri powder and ginger.

NARIYAL KI CHUTNEY

COCONUT CHUTNEY WITH CHANA AND CILANTRO

Coconut chutney is one of South India's signature condiments, especially in coastal regions where coconuts are abundant, and is an essential accompaniment to idlis and dosas. I love to add roasted chana to my coconut chutney recipe for a bit of protein and nuttiness while cilantro balances the coconut's heaviness. The sizzling tadka (tempered spices) poured over the coconut chutney just before serving enlivens this condiment, making for a dressy presentation.

PERFECT PAIRING Serve with Masala Dosa (page 199), Masala Dal Vada (page 195), and Medu Vada (page 137).

MAKES 1 cup

---

1 cup (85 g) shredded coconut (fresh, thawed frozen, or dried)

1 cup (60 g) roughly chopped cilantro (leaves and tender stems)

1 cup (240 ml) water

½ cup (113 g) chana dalia/split roasted chickpeas

1½ teaspoons tamarind concentrate (see Tip)

1-inch (2.5 cm) piece fresh ginger, peeled and chopped

1 dried Guntur Sanam or Kashmiri red chile

1 Thai green chile (optional)

1 teaspoon fine sea salt

TADKA

1 tablespoon sesame oil

⅛ teaspoon hing/asafoetida powder

1 teaspoon black mustard seeds

1 tablespoon dhuli urad dal/peeled split black gram

1 tablespoon chana dal/peeled and split chickpeas

6 to 7 fresh curry leaves

In a blender, combine the coconut, cilantro, water, roasted chickpeas, tamarind, ginger, dried chile, green chile (if using), and salt and process to a coarse paste on a low speed to avoid separation of natural oils from the coconut. Transfer the chutney to a bowl. Season with salt to taste.

Make the tadka: In a small pan, heat the oil over medium heat. Add the asafoetida and mustard seeds and let sizzle for a few seconds. Add the urad dal and chana dal and fry for a minute until golden brown. Add the curry leaves carefully to the oil (it will splutter), stir, and pour the tempered spices over the chutney.

Serve at room temperature. Store any leftover chutney in an airtight container and refrigerate for up to 3 days. The chutney will thicken in the refrigerator but will return to regular consistency at room temperature.

TIP
You could use seedless tamarind pulp here; you will need a small key-lime-size ball. Pull out the fibers before using.

AYURVEDA NOTES

Coconut is nourishing and cooling and provides healthy fats, but can be heavy if consumed in excess. The addition of cilantro, tamarind, roasted chickpeas, and spices provides all six Ayurvedic tastes in every spoonful. Feel free to adjust the ingredients to balance for specific doshas.

- **VATA** Use half the amount of dried red chile and Thai green chile to prevent excess dryness. The tadka balances vata dosha.
- **PITTA** Cooling coconut and cilantro are balancing for pitta. Omit or reduce both the chiles and tamarind due to their heating quality.
- **KAPHA** Consume in moderation, as coconut is heavy and oily and sour tamarind may increase kapha. Chiles stimulate digestive fire and balance heaviness.

SHENGA TIL CHUTNEY

ROASTED PEANUT AND SESAME SEED CHUTNEY

When I have only 10 minutes to spare and need a quick, delicious, and nutritious chutney on the table, I make my version of *shenga* (peanuts) *til* (sesame seeds) chutney. A few pantry staples blitzed to a puree with a quick tadka on top and I have a perfect accompaniment to idlis, dosas, vadas, and more. I love my peanut chutney—the same way my American-born Indian kids love their peanut butter—and have often generously spread this chutney over a slice of sourdough toast, much to their amusement. This also makes a surprisingly delicious dip with crudités and crackers, in my opinion, and I have added it to my charcuterie boards for a delightful fusion of flavors.

PERFECT PAIRING
Great with idlis, dosas, and vadas.

MAKES 1½ cups (360 ml)

TIP
You could use seedless tamarind pulp here; you will need a small key-lime-size ball. Pull out the fibers before using.

In a blender, combine the peanuts, water, sesame seeds, tamarind, dried chile, ginger, curry leaves (if using), salt, and sugar and grind to a smooth paste. Transfer the chutney to a bowl. It should be thick in consistency but flowing. Add 2 to 3 tablespoons (30 to 45 ml) additional water as needed. Season with salt to taste.

Make the tadka: In a small pan, heat the oil over medium heat. Add the asafoetida followed by the mustard seeds and fry until the seeds start to sputter, 30 to 40 seconds. Add the curry leaves and fry for 10 to 15 seconds. Add the Kashmiri powder and immediately pour the hot tempering over the peanut chutney.

Serve at room temperature. Store any leftover chutney in an airtight container and refrigerate for 5 to 7 days. The peanut chutney will thicken in the refrigerator but will return to regular consistency at room temperature.

¾ cup (100 g) unsalted roasted peanuts
½ cup (120 ml) water
2 tablespoons white sesame seeds
1½ teaspoons tamarind concentrate (see Tip)
1 dried red chile, such as Byadagi or Guntur
1-inch (2.5 cm) piece fresh ginger, peeled and roughly chopped
10 to 12 fresh curry leaves (optional)
1 teaspoon fine sea salt
1 teaspoon sugar
TADKA
1 tablespoon sesame oil
⅛ teaspoon hing/asafoetida powder
1 teaspoon black mustard seeds
6 to 7 fresh curry leaves
¼ teaspoon Kashmiri red chili powder

AYURVEDA NOTES

- **VATA** Reduce or omit the red chile.
- **PITTA** Consume in moderation. Reduce or omit the red chile because peanuts, sesame oil, and the sour taste of tamarind are heating.
- **KAPHA** Increase the red chile slightly to balance the heaviness of peanuts and oil.

THECHA

SPICY CHILE GARLIC CHUTNEY

Thecha comes from the Marathi word *thechanya*, which means "to grind." A dear friend from Maharashtra always had a jar close by, ready to sprinkle the fiery rustic chutney over any meal. While there are many regional variations, the two main ingredients are chiles, either green or red, and generous amounts of garlic. The addition of roasted peanuts is an ode to my friend's traditional stone-ground thecha. I find taking the extra time to grind the ingredients with a stone mortar and pestle elevates the taste to the next level, but you can also use a food processor.

PERFECT PAIRING A jar of thecha comes in handy to sprinkle over dals or serve with *bhajjis* (page 98) or any appetizers. When thinned out with water, it becomes a lovely garlic chutney for *chaat*, and the addition of some oil to thecha makes it a delightful drizzle over warm *khichu* (page 167).

MAKES 1 pint (480 ml)

---

2 tablespoons peanut oil, plus more as needed

1 cup (142 g) raw peanuts, peeled

3½ ounces (100 g) garlic cloves (12 to 15), peeled

6 to 8 dried Kashmiri red chiles or any variety of red chiles based on heat preference

2 teaspoons lemon juice

1 teaspoon fine sea salt

In a skillet, heat the oil over medium-low heat. Add the peanuts and sauté for 2 to 3 minutes until they begin to brown slightly. Add the garlic cloves and sauté along with the peanuts for an additional 2 minutes. Add the dried chiles and sauté for another minute.

Remove from the heat, add the lemon juice and salt, and mix well. Transfer the contents to a mortar and hand pound the ingredients to a coarse texture. (Alternatively, use a food processor to pulse the ingredients to a coarse texture.) If you find the thecha is a bit dry while grinding, add an additional tablespoon of peanut oil.

Store in an airtight container in the refrigerator for up to 2 weeks.

AYURVEDA NOTES

Peanuts, garlic, and spices in thecha can be grounding, especially in the cooler months, aiding the digestive fire when consumed in moderation.

- **VATA** Adjust the red chiles based on heat tolerance.
- **PITTA** Use lime instead of lemon juice.
- **KAPHA** Pungency benefits kapha, but be mindful of peanuts' heaviness.

GUNPOWDER PODI

FIERY DAL AND SEED DRY CHUTNEY POWDER

The official name of gunpowder podi is *milagai podi,* or chile powder, and it's the abundance of dried red chiles that gave gunpowder podi its name. This podi is extremely popular in South India, and I gladly exchanged my *parathas* for my South Indian Tamil friends' soft spongy *idlis* coated with gunpowder podi and sesame oil paste at school lunches. A spoonful of podi can lift any dish to new heights. Traditionally it is mixed with rice and a dollop of ghee, or with an equal amount of toasted sesame oil, to use as a condiment with dosas or vadas. Kashmiri chiles are milder in heat, while Byadagi chiles pack a fiery punch, so choose your red chile wisely.

MAKES about 1 pint (500 g)

TIP
Sprinkle podi over soup or grilled cheese sandwiches, or mix with plain yogurt to create a dip.

In a skillet over low heat, dry-roast each dal separately to a light golden brown for 2 to 3 minutes and transfer to a bowl. Dry-roast the rice over low heat until warm and just beginning to change color, 2 to 3 minutes. Transfer to the bowl with the dals. Dry-roast the sesame seeds over low heat to a light brown, about 2 minutes. Add it to the dal and rice mixture.

Add the oil to the pan and toast the chiles over low heat for a couple of minutes. Add the curry leaves, if using, and toast until they become crispy. Be careful not to burn any of the ingredients. Transfer the chiles and curry leaves to the bowl with the dals. Set the bowl aside to cool.

Once the ingredients are completely cool, stir in the salt and transfer the mixture to a spice grinder. Process to a coarse powder and store in an airtight container. It will keep on your kitchen countertop or in a pantry for 2 to 3 weeks. Store in a refrigerator for a longer shelf life of up to 6 weeks.

½ cup (100 g) chana dal/peeled and split chickpeas
½ cup (100 g) dhuli urad dal/peeled split black gram
¼ cup (50 g) rice, such as basmati, Sona Masoori, or jasmine
¼ cup (50 g) white sesame seeds
1 teaspoon peanut or sesame oil
10 to 12 dried red chiles, such as Byadagi or Kashmiri
10 to 12 curry leaves (optional)
1 tablespoon fine sea salt

AYURVEDA NOTES

Roasting the lentils, seeds, and spices before grinding them into a powder elevates the flavor and aroma while easing digestion.
- **VATA** Add ½ teaspoon asafoetida.
- **PITTA** Reduce the red chiles. Use sunflower oil.
- **KAPHA** Skip the sesame seeds.

JAVAS CHUTNEY

FLAXSEED AND SPICE DRY CHUTNEY MIX

Every regional Indian cuisine has its own dry chutney recipes prepared with a combination of spices, seeds, nuts, and often some dried dals. This chutney is an essential daily condiment in many homes in my home state of Maharashtra. The nutritional value of *javas* (flaxseeds) is well documented in evidence-based medical literature, and most nutrition experts recommend consuming ground over whole flaxseeds for ease of digestion. They are a good source of many nutrients, including protein, fiber, omega-3 fatty acids, thiamine, and copper, and regular consumption is linked to many health benefits. Use this blend to spice up plain steamed rice, mix with extra-virgin olive oil for a tasty dip, or simply sprinkle over meals and salads.

MAKES about 1 pint (500 g)

½ cup (70 g) javas/flaxseeds
½ cup (40 g) tightly packed fresh curry leaves
¼ cup (35 g) white sesame seeds
¼ cup (20 g) unsweetened shredded coconut (fresh or thawed frozen)
4 to 8 dried Kashmiri red chiles
6 garlic cloves, peeled but whole
1½ teaspoons coriander seeds
1½ teaspoons cumin seeds
1 teaspoon fine sea salt

In a large skillet, dry-toast the flaxseeds for 3 to 5 minutes over medium-low heat, stirring constantly, until lightly toasted. Add the curry leaves, sesame seeds, coconut, chiles, garlic, coriander, cumin, and salt and roast over medium-low heat for an additional 3 to 5 minutes, until the coconut and spices are lightly toasted and the garlic starts to turn golden brown.

Let the ingredients cool to room temperature. Grind this mixture in a high-powered blender or coffee grinder to a coarse powder. Transfer the javas chutney to an airtight container. It will keep on your kitchen countertop or in a pantry for up to 10 days. Store in the refrigerator for a longer shelf life of up to 6 weeks.

AYURVEDA NOTES

- **VATA** Reduce the Kashmiri red chiles to avoid dryness from pungency.
- **PITTA** Reduce or omit the Kashmiri red chiles. Reduce the garlic cloves by half.
- **KAPHA** Enjoy in moderation due to heaviness of sesame seeds and coconut.

GAJAR KA ACHAAR

QUICK CARROT PICKLE

This tangy and crunchy carrot *achaar* (pickle) is quick to prepare and is a staple in many North Indian homes during cool weather. While some achaars can take days, weeks, or months to mature, this achaar can be enjoyed immediately. The flavors begin to develop in just 2 to 3 days as the fermentation process kicks in, when the carrots begin to soften, the flavor intensifies, and the probiotic quality is enhanced. The flavors will continue to develop in the refrigerator, and the use of mustard oil imparts a warm, sharp, wasabi-like flavor to balance the natural sweetness of carrots.

PERFECT PAIRING Any hearty dal such as Dal Makhani (page 134), Amritsari Pindi Chole (page 84), or Kolhapuri Akkha Masoor (page 77) with a side of Gajar ka Achaar is an ideal combination, especially during cooler months of the year.

MAKES 1 pint (500 g)

TIPS
You can customize this pickle and combine daikon radish along with carrot.

Based on your spice heat tolerance, you can reduce or increase the number of green chiles or omit completely.

In a mortar, coarsely grind the mustard seeds. Transfer to a small bowl. Repeat the process for the coriander seeds and fennel seeds. Combine these together in a small bowl.

In a skillet, heat the oil over medium heat. Add the asafoetida and allow it to sizzle. Add the mustard seed/coriander/fennel mixture and cook for 30 seconds until spices start to get fragrant. Add the nigella seeds, turmeric, and chile flakes (if using) and sauté for another 20 to 30 seconds. Stir in the garlic chives and cook for a minute. Add the carrots, fresh chiles, and salt and mix well. Remove from the heat. Add the lemon juice and zest and mix the pickle well.

Allow to cool completely before transferring to a clean 1-pint (500 g) glass jar. Keep it on the countertop for a day and then refrigerate it for up to 4 weeks. This achaar can be enjoyed fresh, and with each passing day the slow fermentation from the mustard seeds deepens the flavor and softens the carrots.

- 1 tablespoon black mustard seeds
- 1 tablespoon coriander seeds
- 2 teaspoons fennel seeds
- ½ cup (120 ml) mustard oil
- ⅛ teaspoon hing/asafoetida powder
- 1 teaspoon nigella seeds
- 1 teaspoon ground turmeric
- 1 teaspoon red chile flakes (optional)
- ¼ cup (10 g) finely chopped fresh garlic chives
- 4 medium carrots, peeled and cut into 3-inch (7.5 cm) matchsticks
- 1 jalapeño, 1 serrano, or 2 to 3 Thai green chiles (seeded if desired), thinly sliced lengthwise
- 2 teaspoons fine sea salt
- ¼ cup (60 ml) lemon juice
- 1½ teaspoons grated lemon zest

AYURVEDA NOTES

Carrots are a great example of how tastes and qualities can change depending on preparation. Raw carrots are hard, rough, heavy, astringent tasting, and heating—aggravating to both vata and pitta. Cooking brings out the naturally sweet taste of carrots and changes their qualities to light and soft, making them more digestible to vata and pitta. Kapha can enjoy carrots either raw or cooked.

- **VATA** The fermentation process of this achaar and spices benefits vata.
- **PITTA** Reduce or omit the chile flakes and substitute lime juice and zest for lemon.
- **KAPHA** Combine carrots with daikon radish for added pungency. Reduce the sea salt.

HALDI ADRAK MIRCH KA ACHAAR

FRESH TURMERIC AND GINGER PICKLE

The use of turmeric in Indian cooking is both second nature and intentional. While ground turmeric is used in everyday cooking, this pickle is a classic example of how fresh turmeric root finds its special place on the kitchen table. My mom always had a jar of *kachi haldi* (fresh turmeric) pickle so we could add a small spoonful of the crunchy peppery pieces of turmeric along with spicy lemon-juice brine to our meal—the surest way to wake up our taste buds and include the potent healing benefits of turmeric.

MAKES about 1 pint (500 g)

---

6 ounces (170 g) fresh turmeric

4 ounces (115 g) fresh ginger

4 ounces (115 g) Thai green chiles, cut into ½-inch (1.3 cm) lengths (about ½ cup)

Grated zest of 2 lemons

½ cup (120 ml) lemon juice

2 teaspoons fine sea salt

Rinse the turmeric and ginger roots and pat dry. Peel the turmeric and ginger and slice into thin rounds. Add to a clean, dry 1-pint (500 ml) glass jar. Add the chiles, lemon zest, lemon juice, and salt and mix with a clean, dry spoon.

Cover and set on the kitchen counter. Open the jar the next day and mix well. Even though the achaar is ready to be enjoyed the minute it is prepared, the flavors can be quite pungent. After a day or so, the lemon-juice flavor mellows while also softening the texture of the turmeric and ginger.

After 2 days, transfer the jar to the refrigerator. This raw pickle will keep for 2 to 3 weeks refrigerated.

TIPS

Combine equal amounts of regular orange turmeric root with another variety called aamba haldi *(mango turmeric), which is a cream color after peeling the brown skin and can be easily found in Indian grocery stores.*

Swap Thai green chiles for serranos or jalapeños.

AYURVEDA NOTES

- **VATA** Choose a milder variety of chile pepper, such as banana peppers.
- **PITTA** Reduce or omit the green chiles. Substitute lime juice for the lemon juice.
- **KAPHA** Add some black peppercorns to the jar.

KHATTA MEETHA NIMBU KA ACHAAR

SWEET, TANGY, AND SPICED LEMON PICKLE

Nearly every Indian home has some form of *nimbu* (lemon) *achaar* (pickle) tucked away in the pantry or refrigerator. Lemon pickle, when prepared and stored correctly, has no expiration date—it simply gets better with age, like a bottle of good wine. I have jars of my mom's lemon pickle that are more than ten years old that taste heavenly and are filled with amazing digestive medicinal properties. The art of achaar making is a special tradition that is passed down in families, and every home has its own unique nuances of preparation and specific proportions of spices; every jar is a keeper of tradition, an heirloom recipe, a delicious medicine, holding family stories just waiting to be explored. This *khatta* (sour) *meetha* (sweet) nimbu achaar is one that my mom prepares during her annual visits with us. You can make this achaar even if you don't have all the spices listed, just by using the ones you can find or have available. The achaar will be equally special and tasty, and the lemons will soften as they age; the combination of lemons and spices is a perfect remedy for stomachache, nausea, and overall digestion. I like to make it in a large glass jar to slowly age over time, then portion a small amount into a smaller jar for everyday use so I don't disturb the main achaar jar in the cupboard.

MAKES About 1 quart (900 g)

PERFECT PAIRING Serve with any and all meals.

Prepare the lemons: Wash and wipe the lemons completely dry with a kitchen towel. Cut in half from top to bottom through the stem end. Take half of the lemon and cut it into 4 quarters. Repeat the same for the other half and remainder of lemons. Transfer the cut lemons to a clean, dry quart-size jar. Add the sea salt and black salt and mix well with a clean spoon. Cover the jar with the lid but not very tightly and place the jar in a sunny spot next to a window, in a sunroom, or on a patio for about a week. Gently shake the jar every day and you will notice by the end of the week the skin of the lemons will soften a bit and lighten in color. Over the 7 days, the salt will help release the juices.

Make the dry spice mix: In a medium skillet, dry-roast the pippali (if using), cloves, green cardamom pods, black cardamom pods, cumin seeds, black peppercorns, and carom seeds over medium-low heat, about 5 minutes. Cool completely to room temperature.

Transfer the toasted spices to a spice or coffee grinder, add the ground ginger and asafoetida, and grind to a fine powder. Set the powdered spice blend aside until ready to finish the pickle.

Finish the pickle: After a week, open the jar of lemons and add the powdered spice blend, cane sugar, jaggery, fresh ginger, and Kashmiri powder and mix well with a clean dry spoon. Close the lid and keep the jar once again in a sunny spot or on the patio for 10 to 15 days with daily mixing and gentle shaking of the jar.

Continued—

LEMONS
1 pound 5 ounces (600 g) whole organic lemons (6 to 8), preferably thin-skinned varieties, such as Lisbon or Meyer

2 tablespoons (36 g) fine sea salt

2 tablespoons (36 g) kala namak/ Indian black salt

DRY SPICE MIX
10 pippali/Indian long pepper (optional)

15 whole cloves

5 green cardamom pods

5 black cardamom pods

1 tablespoon cumin seeds

2 teaspoons black peppercorns

2 teaspoons ajwain/carom seeds

2 teaspoons ground ginger

1 teaspoon hing/asafoetida powder

PICKLE
¾ cup (150 g) cane sugar

¾ cup (150 g) grated jaggery or jaggery powder

½ cup (120 g) thinly sliced peeled fresh ginger

2 teaspoons Kashmiri red chili powder

The achaar is ready once it darkens a bit with a thick syrup. Portion out a small amount into a separate container for everyday use and store the main jar in a dark, draft-free area of your home. The achaar will continue to soften and get darker over time. If you are worried about spoilage, you can refrigerate the achaar, but it won't age the same way as it will at room temperature.

This achaar is quite potent in flavor, and a normal serving of a tablespoon is enjoyed with meals.

TIP
Choose bright, blemish-free, firm lemons, but ones that have a slight give when pressed, not rock hard—similar to choosing avocados. In addition to choosing thin-skinned varieties, such as Lisbon or Meyer, I also always use organic lemons.

AYURVEDA NOTES

A small amount of nimbu ka achaar with meals is a tridoshic digestive, though pitta should use in moderation due to its pungency.

DIGESTIVE DRINKS

Jal, or water, is sacred in Hindu culture, one of the *panchama-habhutas*, or "five great elements," of our universe. The way we drink water and other liquids has a great impact on digestion and overall health, and Ayurveda teaches us that how we drink our water can impact our digestive health.

While ice and water often seem inseparable in American culture, that's not the case in India. And I have never seen my mom take a sip of water during her meals in all my life; she waits for 15 to 20 minutes after her meal before filling a cup with room-temperature water to slowly sip. But I distinctly remember the first time I asked for a cup of water after arriving in the United States. It was at a gas station during a quick stop on my way to the university campus in Cleveland where I was doing my graduate studies. I watched, puzzled, as the guy behind the counter filled a 32-ounce cup, the largest I'd ever seen, with tiny ice cubes and a splash of water. He was puzzled, in turn, by my confusion, because, in his mind, he had given me water, but to me it was just a large cup of ice. I politely asked him for plain water, no ice. He shrugged, dumped out the ice, and handed me back a cup of water.

One of the first things I learned from my Ayurveda teacher, Dr. Vasant Lad, is that "ice is not nice," because cold is shocking to the system and dampens the digestive energy—like pouring water over fire. Water is best taken at room temperature and, while Ayurveda also recommends having small sips of warm water or a digestive drink if needed with a meal to aid in digestion, the quantity should be no more than a cup. Many spices and herbs have a carminative or an anti-bloat effect, and, when added to drinks, help stimulate *agni*, or digestive fire. The spiced drinks in this section aim to support digestion before, during, or after a meal that contains legumes and rice.

CUMIN CORIANDER FENNEL TEA (CCF TEA)

DIGESTIVE SPICED TEA

This is a classic Ayurvedic drink popularly referred to as CCF tea. You can enjoy this drink every day, especially during lunchtime, either a few minutes before a meal, with a meal, or an hour after a meal. Sipping a cup of this tea on a daily basis offers great support to overall digestion as the spices help eliminate gas, burping, and bloating after a meal.

SERVES 2

½ teaspoon cumin seeds
½ teaspoon coriander seeds
½ teaspoon fennel seeds
2 cups (480 ml) boiling water

In a small saucepan or teapot, steep the spices in the boiling water for about 10 minutes.

Strain the seeds if desired or enjoy chewing the spices while sipping on the tea.

AYURVEDA NOTES

CCF tea is tridoshic, meaning it is suitable for all three body constitutional types—vata, pitta, and kapha.

PUDINA JALJEERA

TANGY CUMIN MINT DIGESTIVE DRINK

Jal means "water" and *jeera* means "cumin." Cumin and its deep connection to support digestion has been known in Ayurveda for centuries. *Jaljeera* is my go-to drink during the hot summer months or at the slightest feeling of indigestion after a heavy meal; the fresh *pudina* (mint), along with cilantro, is particularly refreshing in the warm weather to help release excess heat from the body. The secret to a zesty glass of jaljeera lies in the dried spice mix, which can be prepared ahead of time, ready whenever you have a craving for this refreshing drink.

SERVES 6

TIPS

Swap water for sparkling water or club soda and garnish with mint and sliced limes to make a fun summer mocktail.

For another jaljeera mocktail, add 1 cup (240 ml) mango juice when blending herbs and spices to make a mango pudina jaljeera.

Make the jaljeera spice mix: Heat a small skillet, dry-roast the cumin seeds and black peppercorns over medium heat for 3 to 4 minutes, until the aroma of the spices is released. Remove from the heat and let cool.

In a spice grinder, combine the toasted spices, mango powder, black salt, and ginger and grind everything to a fine powder.

Make the pudina jaljeera: In a blender, combine the jaljeera spice mix, cilantro, mint, fresh ginger, lime juice, and ice cubes and puree until smooth.

Transfer the pudina jaljeera to a pitcher and add the water. Serve at room temperature garnished with mint and lime wheels.

JALJEERA SPICE MIX

2 teaspoons cumin seeds
¼ teaspoon black peppercorns
2 teaspoons amchur/dried mango powder
1½ teaspoons kala namak/Indian black salt
¼ teaspoon ground ginger

PUDINA JALJEERA

½ cup (30 g) cilantro
½ cup (30 g) mint
½-inch (1.3 cm) piece fresh ginger, peeled and roughly chopped
3 tablespoons (45 ml) lime juice
6 ice cubes
6 cups (1.4 L) room-temperature filtered water
Mint leaves, for garnish
Thinly sliced lime, for garnish

AYURVEDA NOTES

The heating quality of the jaljeera spice mix in this recipe is well balanced by the cooling nature of the cilantro, mint, and lime. Pitta and kapha may adjust accordingly—pitta to lessen the heating spices and kapha to increase them.

SHIKANJI

INDIAN-SPICED HYDRATING DRINK

Given the heat of India's tropical climate, it is no surprise that many Indian beverages are refreshing thirst quenchers—but one doesn't need to wait for humid hot weather to enjoy *shikanji*. Limes have a cooling effect, while the ground toasted cumin aids digestion, and Indian black salt is rich in natural minerals, making it excellent for replenishing electrolytes in the heat of summer.

SERVES 2

1 teaspoon cumin seeds
3 cups (720 ml) room-temperature filtered water
2 tablespoons lime juice
1 tablespoon raw turbinado sugar or cane sugar
1 tablespoon chopped mint
½ teaspoon kala namak/Indian black salt

In a small skillet, dry-roast the cumin seeds over medium heat for a couple of minutes or until the cumin releases its aroma and darkens in color. Remove from the heat and crush into a coarse powder with a mortar and pestle.

In a pitcher, combine the cumin powder, water, lime juice, sugar, mint, and black salt and enjoy at room temperature.

TIP
Swap water with sparkling water or ginger-flavored soda for a refreshing mocktail.

AYURVEDA NOTES

Kapha should enjoy this drink in moderation and increase the amount of cumin seeds.

PANAKAM

SPICED JAGGERY THIRST QUENCHER

This traditional drink is served in many South Indian temples as an offering
to the deities and later distributed among the devotees, especially during
the spring festival of Ram Navami, celebrating the birth of Lord Rama. My
first taste of *panakam* was at a South Indian friend's wedding as it is a popular
welcome drink first served to the bridegroom and later to all the guests.
The subtle flavor of saffron, the aromatic freshness of cardamom, the tang
of lime, and the sharpness of ginger complement the earthy sweetness of
jaggery, reviving the appetite and bolstering the immune system.

SERVES 4

In a bowl, combine the water and jaggery and set
aside while you prepare the spices.

Crush the cardamom pods and black peppercorns
with a mortar and pestle to a fine powder and
add to the jaggery water along with the lime
juice, ginger juice, saffron strands, and nutmeg.
Stir well until there are no lumps.

Strain and serve at room temperature (or chilled,
if preferred, during warm weather).

4 cups (960 ml) room-temperature
  filtered water
½ cup (56 g) grated or powdered
  jaggery
3 green cardamom pods
1 teaspoon black peppercorns
2 tablespoons lime juice
1 tablespoon ginger juice (extracted
  from grated fresh ginger)
8 to 10 strands of saffron
⅛ teaspoon freshly grated nutmeg

AYURVEDA NOTES

*This drink is tridoshic, meaning it is suitable for all three body con-
stitutional types—vata, pitta, and kapha.*

KANJI

FERMENTED BEET, CARROT, AND SPICES

Kanji is a salty-sour fermented drink traditionally prepared in the late winter/early spring, and quite popular in North Indian homes such as mine. Growing up, I knew it was time for kanji when Mom would bring home black or dark-purple carrots from the market (though a combination of beets and regular carrots work as well). The ground mustard seeds activate the aerobic fermentation, and, along with wild yeasts present on the surface of carrot and beets, help build the kanji's flavor. It's packed with gut-friendly probiotics and antioxidants, and ferment enthusiasts will appreciate its unique flavor—I am surprised how much my kids enjoy this drink and request it every year.

SERVES
10 to 12

---

10 ounces (280 g) carrots (5 to 6 medium)
1 medium beet
1 tablespoon black mustard seeds
1 tablespoon kala namak/Indian black salt or fine sea salt
1 teaspoon Kashmiri red chili powder
10 cups (2.4 L) room-temperature filtered water

Rinse and peel the carrots and beet. Cut them into spears, about 2 inches (5 cm) long and about ½ inch (1.3 cm) thick.

Grind the mustard seeds with a mortar and pestle or in a spice grinder to a coarse powder.

Transfer the beet, carrot, ground mustard seeds, salt, and Kashmiri powder to a clean wide-mouth ceramic or glass jar (see Tips) and add the water. Stir with a clean spoon.

Cover the opening of the jar with cheesecloth and secure around the rim with a rubber band or twine. Let the jar sit in a sunny spot to begin fermenting, 48 to 72 hours. Stir the kanji with a wooden spoon once a day.

As the fermentation process begins, the kanji will develop a deep color and a sour taste. That's how you know it is ready. To stop further fermentation, store kanji, covered, in the refrigerator, where it will last for a couple of weeks.

Enjoy a glass of kanji at room temperature or chilled.

TIPS
It is important to prepare this drink in a glass or ceramic container rather than plastic or metal jars, which can spoil the drink and disrupt the fermentation process.

Serve strained carrots and beets along with kanji or add to salads or as a side with meals.

Mix kanji with sparkling water in a 1:1 ratio and a squirt of lemon juice for an amazing bubbly probiotic drink.

AYURVEDA NOTES

This probiotic drink is suitable for all doshas in cooler months, with an ideal serving of 8 to 12 ounces a day before or after a meal to aid digestion.
- **VATA** The blend of beets, mustard seeds, and salt supports vata, but adjust spice level for individual tolerance as excessive pungency can exacerbate vata dryness.
- **PITTA** While beets are beneficial for the liver, limit consumption due to their heating nature.
- **KAPHA** Enjoy the benefits of carrots, beets, mustard seeds, and Kashmiri powder, but moderate salt intake.

SAUNF KA SHARBAT

FENNEL COOLER

Most Indian restaurants have a bowl of candied fennel seeds for guests to have a spoonful on their way out. The aromatic *saunf* (fennel seeds) are sweet in *rasa* (taste), relieve hyperactivity, and cool the digestive system. For this cooling drink, best served a few minutes after a meal, fennel seeds are combined with *mishri*, or *khadi sakhar*, a crystallized and unrefined form of sugar easily found in Indian grocery stores. You can substitute raw or turbinado sugar in its place.

Make a big batch of powdered ingredients and store in an airtight container for several months.

SERVES 2

In a small skillet, lightly toast the fennel seeds over medium heat for a couple of minutes, until the aroma is released. Remove from the pan and let cool.

Add the cooled fennel seeds to a mortar and add the rock sugar, cardamom pods, and black salt and crush to a fine powder.

Make the sharbat: In a pitcher, combine the powder, lime juice, mint, and water. Mix well and serve immediately.

POWDER
1 tablespoon fennel seeds
2 tablespoons mishri/crystallized rock sugar
2 green cardamom pods
½ teaspoon kala namak/Indian black salt

SHARBAT
1 tablespoon lime juice
1 tablespoon chopped mint
2½ cups (600 ml) room-temperature filtered water, or lightly chilled

---

AYURVEDA NOTES

This drink is tridoshic but especially balancing for pitta and kapha.
- **VATA** Substitute lemon for lime.
- **PITTA** Fennel and lime are both cooling and balancing for pitta.
- **KAPHA** Enhance with a pinch of black pepper to alleviate congestion and stimulate sluggish digestion.

Sharbat

In many Indian homes, chilled *sharbat* is offered as a welcome drink, especially during the hot summer months. It is often called the world's first soft drink. My kids love trying a variety of sharbats at the homes of family and friends during summer trips to India, and there are also many commercial brands on the market.

Sharbat, from the Persian word *shariba*, meaning "to drink," is usually made by combining fruit concentrates or extracts from flowers or herbs with sugar and water, which is then cooked down to a concentrated, shelf-stable syrup. A couple of tablespoons of the concentrated syrup is diluted in a glass of water before serving. You can also prepare fresh sharbat by combining fresh extracts of fruit, flowers, spices, and herbs along with sugar and water.

SATTU KA SHARBAT

ROASTED CHICKPEA FLOUR SUMMER COOLER

During the scorching summers in the North Indian state of Uttar Pradesh, *sattu* is enjoyed as a traditional cooling beverage that helps protect against heat stroke and support overall digestion. Referred to as the poor man's protein drink, sattu is prepared using sattu flour, which is ground-up dry-roasted brown chickpeas, and can be sweet or savory. Sattu is a powerhouse of nutrients, rich in minerals, protein, and fiber, and has a low glycemic index. Sattu flour is easily available in Indian grocery stores or you can grind dry-roasted brown chickpeas to a fine powder at home. I love combining salt and spices with a hint of sugar for a refreshing sweet-and-salty version. You can also skip the sugar completely for a salty savory version that is equally delicious.

SERVES 4

In a pitcher, stir together the flour, sugar, chaat masala, cumin, black salt, and mint leaves. Add the lime juice and water and mix well. Serve and enjoy!

½ cup (60 g) sattu flour

2 tablespoons raw sugar or turbinado sugar

1 teaspoon chaat masala

1 teaspoon ground toasted cumin

1 teaspoon kala namak/Indian black salt

½ teaspoon dried mint leaves

¼ cup (60 ml) lime juice

4 cups (960 ml) room-temperature filtered water, or lightly chilled

---

AYURVEDA NOTES

Roasting pacifies vata and kapha and helps to predigest dals and beans.

- **VATA** The sweet, sour, and salty flavors in this drink balance vata.
- **PITTA** The combination of sattu, lime, and mint is cooling for pitta.
- **KAPHA** Increase the amount of chaat masala and cumin seeds to balance the sweet, sour, and salty ingredients.

MASALA CHAI

INDIAN-SPICED TEA

Chai—an aromatic concoction prepared by boiling water, black tea, milk, and spices—is a delicious ritual that has been enjoyed in every Indian household for many centuries. Every Indian home has its own chai recipe with unique proportions and ingredients.

SERVES 2

A cup of chai is more than a warm beverage—it also has many health benefits. The combination of spices in a masala (meaning "spiced") chai is rich in antioxidants and can help improve digestion, and the spices can be changed with the seasons. My favorite spices for everyday tea include ginger and cardamom. Feel free to adjust the amount of milk from as little as ⅓ cup (80 ml) to ⅔ cup (160 ml), based on preference, and the same goes for the amount of loose black tea.

---

1 green cardamom pod
½-inch (1.3 cm) piece cinnamon stick
1 whole clove
2 black peppercorns
½-inch (1.3 cm) piece fresh ginger, peeled and sliced
2 cups (480 ml) water
2 teaspoons loose black tea, preferably Darjeeling or Assam
2 teaspoons cane sugar
⅔ cup (160 ml) whole milk or nondairy milk

Gently grind the cardamom, cinnamon stick, clove, peppercorns, and fresh ginger with a mortar and pestle.

In a saucepan, bring the water to a boil. Add the ground spices and boil with the water for a good 1 minute.

Add the loose black tea and sugar and boil for another 1 to 2 minutes. Add the milk and allow all the ingredients to come to a rolling boil. Strain the chai through a fine-mesh tea strainer and divide between two cups. Serve hot.

TIPS

Darjeeling or Assam tea varieties from India are my personal favorites. Other options include Earl Grey and English breakfast. During winter, add tulsi (holy basil) leaves or use a tea variety with tulsi added to it.

If you would like to use honey as a sweetener, stir it into your cup just before drinking. Never add it when the chai is cooking to avoid exposure to direct heat. Brown sugar or maple syrup are other sweetener options.

AYURVEDA NOTES

Although chai contains black tea, the addition of milk, sugar, and spices, especially cardamom, neutralizes the stimulating effects of caffeine. Change the spices according to the season or your dosha to create your own custom cup of chai.

- **VATA** Chai is overall calming for vata. If you are sensitive to black tea, choose a decaf black tea or opt for rooibos tea.
- **PITTA** Reduce the ginger and peppercorns or skip them. Try fennel and dried rose petals in your chai for a calming effect.
- **KAPHA** All spices are excellent for kapha. If digestion is weak, opt for a lighter milk alternative, such as almond or oat milk.

INDEX

W

V

ANDEVI

DED ASAFOETIDA

& Marketed in India by:

OOD PVT. LTD.

e & Factory :
Area, MIDC, Mahape,
Maharashtra, (India)
+91-22-27781161,
s @gmail.com
ence from)

GWALA & SONS

devi, Mumbai-400007.

ructions:
Asafoetida can be
while cooking
and most vegetables.

VA

COMPO

BATCH

PKG.DT

EXP.DT

V.N.THAKKA

788, The

Mumbai

®

For Export Only (Not for Sale in India)

469020

RESOURCES

SUPPLIES

Build your Dal Chawal pantry one jar at a time. You can easily order online but buy and support local when you can. Don't hesitate to walk into your local Indian grocery store to explore the aisles and stock up on spices, grains, and dals. Start small both in the number and size of items.

burlapandbarrel.com   single-origin spice supplier

diasporaco.com   single-origin spice supplier specializing in Indian spices

indiabazaardfw.com   my go-to south-Asian grocery store chain in North Texas

pureindianfoods.com   organic Indian and Asian grocery products

KITCHENWARE

Here are some trusted brands for my kitchen essentials that support me in my daily dal chawal cooking.

instantpot.com   electric pressure cookers

cuisinart.com   food chopper especially for quick onion, ginger, and garlic chopping

nutribullet.com   small blender for spice pastes, quick purees, and chutneys

vitaclaychef.com   electric clay rice and slow cooker

vitamix.com   high-speed blender

zishta.com   traditional Indian cookware

REFERENCES AND FURTHER READING

To support your curiosity about Ayurveda, plant proteins, pulses, and vegetarian diets in general, here are some resources I lean on often.

Ayurveda: The Science of Self-Healing by Vasant Lad

Prakriti: Your Ayurvedic Constitution by Robert Svoboda

Textbook of Ayurveda Vol 1: Fundamental Principles by Vasant Lad

Position of the American Dietetic Association: Vegetarian Diets - Journal of the American Dietetic Association. 2009, July; Vol. 109, Issue 7, p 1266–1282.

Protein and amino acid requirements in human nutrition. Report of a joint FAO/WHO/UNU expert consultation. World Health Organ Tech Rep Ser. 2007;(935):1-265, back cover. PMID: 18330140.

pulses.org

beansishow.com

For more Ayurvedic insights, guided Indian grocery store tours, and vegetarian Indian resources, visit **bespiced.com/book** to get access to interactive cooking, spice guides, and continued support in your dal chawal journey.

ACKNOWLEDGMENTS

This book will always be a reminder to me that dreams (*sapna*) do come true if we show up, don't give up, get back up, and most importantly, fearlessly believe in our dreams. I was named Sapna by my dad and he would always remind me that I was his dream come true and to never be afraid to dream big, work even harder, and leave the rest to the universe to create its magic. My papa, Arjun Punjabi—this book is a tribute to you!

I vividly remember signing the contract for this cookbook at a time when my personal life was undergoing a catastrophic yet radical transformation. As I was shedding the old version of myself, the universe was preparing its ground for me to welcome new beginnings. Slowly, I found I was surrounded by strong, loving women—many of whom I have yet to meet in person but who believe in me, my work, and my vision for this book. These women became part of a sisterhood that helped bring this cookbook to life.

To my mom, Sarojini—Thank you for being my rock as I endured the storms. Thank you for traveling from Mumbai to be by my side testing and retesting every single recipe, for our marathon week of cooking for the book's photo shoot, and for making sure the kids and I were well-fed as I spent countless hours on my manuscript. Your hands on the cover will serve as an eternal blessing and gift to my cookbook. Thank you, mama!

My literary agent and my guardian angel, Sally Ekus. It's an honor to know you and a privilege to have you in my life. Thank you for believing in my proposal and pitching me to publishing companies I could only dream of. I love that your dreams for my book are bigger than mine. Thank you for our friendship and for being in my corner always!

Thank you to my editor and publisher at Hardie Grant, Jenny Wapner. I formed an instant connection with you from our first virtual meeting and knew I found my publishing home because of you. I had laid out a few requests (actually they were non-negotiable in my mind) as my book was being pitched: the book to be called '*Dal Chawal*' and not given a modern translation to appeal to Western audiences. I also wanted the recipe titles to remain as traditional Indian names, without any changes to make it easy for readers unfamiliar with Indian cuisine. Lastly, I insisted the chapters be based on ingredients, not menu categories, as is common in most cookbooks. Jenny, you embraced these requests as key differentiators and strengths for my book. You celebrated my authentic self and voice as I tested your patience. You gave me space and time to get a hold of my life first before turning in my manuscript even though it caused you stress by pushing your deadlines. Your unwavering support for me, your genuine excitement for this book, and having my back from day one means the world to me.

Jenny, you also gathered an impeccable team to rally behind *Dal Chawal*. Thank you to my Hardie Grant family of exceptional creatives. Carolyn Insley, Natalie Lundgren, thank you for being my extra set of eyes throughout the different transformations of this book. Erin Cusick for your proofreading diligence. Nitya Jain for photography, Kristina Wolter for your prop styling skills, and for assisting me as I prepped, cooked, and styled my food during the recipe photoshoot. Thank you, Blair Richardson, the book design is how I envisioned it—vibrant, bold yet timeless. The marketing wizards, Maddy Kalmowitz and Liz Correll—thank you for your creative strategies to make *Dal Chawal* reach audiences far and wide.

Kristen Hartke, I am so glad that our random Instagram connection grew into a professional relationship to now a long-lasting friendship. From recipe testing, and copyediting, to simply lifting my spirits when I needed a pep talk, thank you for showing up for me with love and compassion.

Thank you to my Ayurvedic sister and friend, Uma Jolicoeur, for being an extra set of eyes reviewing, researching, and copyediting as needed with the Ayurvedic content integrated throughout this cookbook.

My heartfelt gratitude to India Bazaar of Dallas, for generously providing all Indian groceries for this cookbook.

A huge thank-you to all my recipe testers: Kathy Draves, Amy Hofland, Jennifer Skidmore, Gowri Sharma, Hemali Majithia Premji, Neha Patel, Laura Marquard, Soudary Kittivong-Greenbaum, Rashna Cooper, Natasha Cooper, Karen Cassady, and LK Blackard, for helping out with all the recipe testing and giving me your constructive feedback.

To my beSPICED community, thank you for always supporting me over the years, both in person and online—through my cooking classes, wellness workshops, and as loyal customers of my heirloom spice blends and products at the farmers market. You've encouraged me to write this cookbook over the years, and for that, I thank you from the bottom of my heart!

Lastly, the two most important people, without whom this cookbook would not exist—my children, Aditya (sunshine) and Mihika (morning dew). Being your mom is without a doubt the most fulfilling role of my life. Thank you for being my eager taste testers, giving me your unfiltered feedback, and being excellent hand models. Aditya, thank you for being my sounding board, my copyeditor, my brainstorming buddy, and stepping in even to be a photographer. Seeing your name as one of the photographers for *Dal Chawal* makes this book extra special. Mihika, my strong-willed girl who is unafraid to share her opinions in any room, you were the spark I needed on the days my flame was barely flickering. You became my accountability coach throughout this cookbook journey and reminded me why this book is important to share with the world. I'll always remember how you reminded me that this book is, first and foremost, for both you and your brother, and your future families. You insisted that every recipe be approved by the two of you, as it would one day be shared with my future grandchildren—ha!

To my readers, you make this cookbook come alive. Welcome to my *Dal Chawal* family!

Namaste,

Sapna

Hardie Grant
PUBLISHING

Hardie Grant North America
2912 Telegraph Ave
Berkeley, CA 94705
hardiegrant.com

Published in the United States by Hardie Grant North
America, an imprint of Hardie Grant Publishing Pty Ltd.

Library of Congress Cataloging-in-Publication Data is
available upon request.

ISBN 9781958417232
ISBN 9781958417362 (eBook)
Printed in China
Design by Blair Richardson, MiniSuper Studio
Food styling by Kristina Wolter
First Edition

MIX
Paper | Supporting
responsible forestry
FSC
www.fsc.org   FSC® C020056